Ring-tailed cat   *Mallette Dean*

SIERRA NORTH

100 Back-Country Trips in the High Sierra

Thomas Winnett, Jason Winnett, and Lyn Haber

 WILDERNESS PRESS • BERKELEY

First printing May 1967
Second printing July 1967
Third printing July 1969
SECOND EDITION May 1971
Second printing April 1972
Third printing September 1974
THIRD EDITION January 1976
Second printing February 1978
FOURTH EDITION May 1982
Second printing July 1983
FIFTH EDITION June 1985
Revised second printing May 1987
Third printing November 1988
SIXTH EDITION May 1991

Photos by the authors except as noted
Drawings by Lucille Winnett
Design by Thomas Winnett

Library of Congress card number 91-18112
ISBN 0-89997-120-2
Manufactured in the United States of America

Published by Wilderness Press
2440 Bancroft Way, Berkeley CA 94704
(415) 843-8080 Write for free catalog

Library of Congress Cataloging-in-Publication Data

Winnett, Thomas.

    Sierra North : 100 back-country trips in the High Sierra / by Thomas
Winnett, Jason Winnett, and Lyn Haber. —6th ed.

        p. cm.

    Includes bibliographical references and index.

    ISBN 0-89997-120-2

1. Backpacking—Sierra Nevada (Calif. and Nev.)—Guide-books. 2. Hik-
ing—Sierra Nevada (Calif. and Nev.)—Guide-books. 3. Sierra Nevada
(Calif. and Nev.)—Description and travel—Guide-books.
I. Winnett, Jason. II. Haber, Lyn. III. Title.
GV199.42.S55W56 1991
917.94'4—dc20   91-18112
                                            CIP

Hiking in the backcountry entails unavoidable risk that every hiker assumes and must be aware of and respect. The fact that a trail is described in this book is not a representation that it will be safe for you. Trails vary greatly in difficulty and in the degree of conditioning and agility one needs to enjoy them safely. On some hikes routes may have changed or conditions may have deteriorated since the descriptions were written. Also trail conditions can change even from day to day, owing to weather and other factors. A trail that is safe on a dry day or for a highly conditioned, agile, properly equipped hiker may be completely unsafe for someone else or unsafe under adverse weather conditions.

You can minimize your risks on the trail by being knowledgeable, prepared and alert. There is not space in this book for a general treatise on safety in the mountains, but there are a number of good books and public courses on the subject and you should take advantage of them to increase your knowledge. Just as important, you should always be aware of your own limitations and of conditions existing when and where you are hiking. If conditions are dangerous, or if you are not prepared to deal with them safely, choose a different hike! It's better to have wasted a drive than to be the subject of a mountain rescue.

These warnings are not intended to scare you off the trails. Millions of people have safe and enjoyable hikes every year. However, one element of the beauty, freedom and excitement of the wilderness is the presence of risks that do not confront us at home. When you hike you assume those risks. They can be met safely, but only if you exercise your own independent judgment and common sense.

Contents

Introduction 1
The Care and Enjoyment of the Mountains 5
Safety and Well Being........................... 8
Maps and Profiles.............................. 13
Wilderness Permits 15
The Trailheads................................. 18

Carson Pass

1 Silver Lake to Scout Carson Lake 25
2 Silver Lake to Summit City Canyon 27
3 Silver Lake to Mokelumne River 29
4 Silver Lake to Long Lake 32
5 Silver Lake to Camp Irene 35
6 Silver Lake to the Mokelumne River............ 37
7 Carson Pass to Showers Lake.................. 39
8 Carson Pass to Echo Summit 41

Ebbetts Pass

9 Mosquito Lake to Bull Run Lake............... 45
10 Wolf Creek Meadows to Soda Springs........... 48
11 Wolf Creek Meadows to Wolf Creek............. 54
12 Wolf Creek Meadows to Sonora Pass 57
13 Wolf Creek Meadows to Poison Lake 62
14 Rodriguez Flat to Lower Fish Valley............ 64
15 Rodriguez Flat to Ebbetts Pass 68
16 Rodriguez Flat to Lake Alpine 72

Sonora Pass

17 Kennedy Meadow to Summit Creek 78
18 Kennedy Meadow to Emigrant Meadow......... 80
19 Kennedy Meadow to Emigrant Lake............ 82
20 Kennedy Meadow to Emigrant Lake............ 84
21 Kennedy Meadow to Cow Meadow Lake........ 85
22 Kennedy Meadow to Hetch Hetchy............. 88
23 Gianelli Cabin to Y Meadow Lake 93
24 Gianelli Cabin to Wire Lkes................... 95
25 Crabtree Camp to Deer Lake 97
26 Gianellli Cabin to Crabtree Camp 100
27 Gianelli Cabin to Kennedy Meadow 102

28 Kennedy Meadow to Gianelli Cabin 104
29 Leavitt Meadow to Fremont Lake 106
30 Leavitt Meadow to Cinko Lake 110
31 Leavitt Meadow to Dorothy Lake 113
32 Leavitt Meadow to Tower Lake 116

Yosemite

33 Leavitt Meadow to Buckeye Creek 119
34 Twin Lakes to Peeler Lake 124
35 Twin Lakes to Crown Lake 127
36 Twin Lakes to Upper Piute Creek 129
37 Twin Lakes to Buckeye Creek 131
38 Twin Lakes to Kerrick Meadow 133
39 Twin Lakes to Hetch Hetchy 135
40 Twin Lakes to Benson Lake 140
41 Twin Lakes to Smedberg Lake 142
42 Green Creek to East Lake 146
43 Green Creek to Tuolumne Meadows 148
44 Green Creek to Virginia Lakes 153
45 Hetch Hetchy to Rancheria Creek 155
46 Hetch Hetchy to Tiltill Valley 157
47 Saddlebag Lake to McCabe Lakes 159
48 Saddlebag Lake to Tuolumne Meadows 162
49 Saddlebag Lake to Twin Lakes 164
50 Tuolumne Meadows to Young Lakes 167
51 Horse Meadow to Gibbs Lake 170
52 Tenaya Lake to Sunrise Camp 172
53 Tioga Road to Lower Cathedral Lake 174
54 Tioga Road to Sunrise Camp 176
55 Tioga Road to Merced Lake 178
56 Tioga Road to Tenaya Lake 182
57 Tioga Road to Yosemite Valley 184
58 Tenaya Lake to Yosemite Valley 186
59 Tuolumne Meadows to Nelson Lake 188
60 Tuolumne Meadows to Lyell Canyon 190
61 Tuolumne Meadows to Vogelsang 192
62 Tuolumne Meadows to Emeric Lake 194
63 Tuolumne Meadows to Lyell Fork 197
64 Tuolumne Meadows to Triple Peak Fork 200
65 Tuolumne Meadows to Agnew Meadows 203
66 Yosemite Valley to Merced Lake 205

67 Bridalveil Creek to Royal Arch Lake 208
68 Bridalveil Creek to Glacier Point............. 211
69 Bridalveil Creek to Yosemite Valley........... 214
70 Bridalveil Creek to Royal Arch Lake 216
71 Glacier Point to Merced Lake 218
72 Glacier Point to Rutherford Lake 220
73 Glacier Point to Granite Creek............... 224

Devils Postpile

74 Silver Lake to 1000 Island Lake 227
75 Agnew Meadows to Shadow Creek 231
76 Agnew Meadows to Garnet Lake............. 233
77 Agnew Meadows to 1000 Island Lake 236
78 Agnew Meadows to 1000 Island Lake 238
79 Agnew Meadows to Ediza Lake.............. 240
80 Agnew Meadows to Devils Postpile 241
81 Agnew Meadows to Devils Postpile 244

South of Yosemite

82 Chiquito Creek to Chain Lakes 247
83 Chiquito Creek to Rutherford Lake 249
84 Chiquito Creek to Bridalveil Creek 252
85 Granite Creek Road to Rutherford Lake....... 254
86 Granite Creek Road to Isberg Lakes.......... 257
87 Lake Edison to Graveyard Meadows 260
88 Lake Edison to Graveyard Lakes 262
89 Rock Creek to Gem Lakes 264
90 Rock Creek to Ruby Lake.................... 266
91 McGee Creek to Steelhead Lake 268
92 McGee Creek to McGee Lake 270
93 McGee Creek to Lake Edison 271
94 Rock Creek to Lake Edison 275
95 McGee Creek to Rock Creek 278
96 Mammoth Lakes to Purple Lake 281
97 Mammoth Lakes to Lake Edison.............. 283
98 Mammoth Lakes to Lake Edison.............. 286
99 Mammoth Lakes to Deer Lakes............... 288
100 Mammoth Lakes to Iva Bell Hot Springs 290
Recommended Reading 293
Trip Cross-Reference Table................... 295
Index....................................... 298

Introduction

This Book's Purpose

The Sierra Nevada is the longest and most extensively trailed mountain range in the United States. With its complex valley-ridge makeup, its lofty eastern escarpment, and its mild weather, it is a backpacker's paradise unequaled in intrinsic beauty and scenic grandeur. Much of the finest scenery and best fishing lie in the back country, accessible only by trail. There has been, therefore, a growing trend toward wilderness trips, and with the trend has come a demand for reliable back-country trip suggestions. This book is a selective effort to meet that demand.

Galen Clark, Yosemite's beloved "Old Man of the Valley," was once asked how he "got about" the park. Clark scratched his beard, and then replied, "Slowly!" And that is the philosophy the authors have adopted in this book. Hiking descriptions, with the exception of a few "Moderate" ratings and an occasional "Strenuous" trip, are based on a leisurely pace, in order that the hiker can absorb more of the sights, smells and "feel" of the country he has come to see. Pace may not be everything, but Old Man Clark lived to a ripe old age of 96 and it behooves us to follow in his footsteps.

This Book's Terms

Sierra North encompasses the region from the volcanic battlements of Carson Pass to the aspen-lined banks of Mono Creek, where the companion volume, *Sierra South*, takes over. The individual trips were selected on the basis of (1) scenic attraction, (2) wilderness character (remoteness, primitive condition) and (3) recreational potential (fishing, swimming, etc.) After walking the trip, the author decided how long it should take if done at a leisurely pace, how long at a moderate pace, and how long at a strenuous pace. In deciding, he or she considered not only distance but also elevation change, heat exposure, terrain, availability of water, appropriate campsites and finally, his or her subjective feeling about the trip. For each trip, then, we suggest how many days you should take to do it at the pace (*Leisurely, Moderate* or *Strenuous*) you prefer. Some trips simply don't lend themselves to a leisurely pace—maybe not even a moderate pace—and some are never strenuous unless you do the whole thing in one day. Such trips have a blank in the number-of-days spot for the corresponding pace at the beginning of the trip.

The last decision about pace was the decision of which pace to use in describing the trip, day by day. Since this book is written for the average backpacker, we chose to describe most trips on either a leisurely or a moderate basis, depending on where the best overnight camping places were along the route.

Subjective considerations also carry over to the evaluation of campsites. Campsites are labeled *poor, fair, good* or *excellent.* The criteria for assigning these labels were amount of use, immediate surroundings, general scenery, presence of vandalization, availability of water, kind of ground cover and recreational potential—angling, side trips, swimming, etc.

Angling, for many, is a prime consideration when planning a trip. The recommendations in this book are based on (1) on-site samplings and feeding evaluations, (2) word of mouth, (3) *Sierra Trout*, by Dean Cutter, (4) literature of the California Department of Fish and Game, and (5) interviews with commercial packers. When a conflict arose between paper research and trail sampling, the later was given precedence. Like the campsites, fishing was labeled *poor, fair, good* or *excellent.* It should be noted that these labels refer only to the size, quantity, and general catchability of the fish, not the fishes' inclination to take the hook at any moment. Experienced anglers know that the size of their catch relates not only to quantity, type and general size of the fishery, which are given, but also to water temperature, feed, angling skill, and that indefinable something known as "fisherman's luck." Generally speaking, the old "early and late" adage holds: fishing is better early and late in the day, and early and late in the season.

Deciding when in the year is the best time for a particular trip is a difficult task because of yearly variations. Low early-season temperatures and mountain shadows often keep some of the higher passes closed until well into August. Early snows have been known to whiten alpine country in late July and August. Some of the trips described here are low-country ones, offered specifically for the itchy hiker who, stiff from a winter's inactivity, is searching for a "warm-up" excursion. These trips are labeled *early season*, a period that extends roughly from late May to early July. *Mid season* is here considered to be from early July to the end of August, and *late season* from then to early October.

Stream crossings vary greatly depending on snow-melt conditions. Often, the same small creek you saw in September will be a raging torrent the next June. We have indicated the problems of fording some creeks as "wet in early season," meaning that in times of high water you will probably have to wade, perhaps in water over your waist, but that the crossing is fairly easy and not dangerous. If a ford is described as "difficult in early season" fording that creek may be difficult because it is hard to walk through deep or fast water, and getting caught in the current would be dangerous. Whether you attempt such a crossing depends on the presence or absence of logs or other bridges and of downstream rapids, your ability and equipment, and your judgment.

Most of the trails described here are well maintained (the exceptions are noted), and are properly signed. If the trail becomes indistinct, look for *blazes* (peeled bark at eye level on trees) or *ducks* (two or more rocks piled one atop the other). Two other significant trail conditions have also been described in the text: (1) degree of openness (type and degree of forest cover, if any, or else "meadow," "brush" or whatever); and (2) underfooting (talus, scree, pumice, sand, "duff"—deep humus ground cover of rotting vegetation—or other material).

Three other terms used in the descriptive text warrant definition. *Packer campsite* is used to indicate a semipermanent camp (usually constructed by packers for the "comfort of their clients") characterized by a nailed-plank table and/or a large, stand-up rock fireplace. *Improved campsite* is a U.S. Forest Service designation for a place where a simple toilet has been installed. A *use trail* is an unmaintained, unofficial trail that is more or less easy to follow because it is well worn by use.

The text contains occasional references to points, peaks and other landmarks. These places will be found on the appropriate topographic maps cited at the beginning of the trip. ("Point 9426" in the text would refer to a point designated simply "9426" on the map itself.)

In recent years the Forest Service and the Park Service have had a policy of letting fires in the backcountry burn so long as they were not a threat to people or structures. One result has been some pretty poor looking scenery on some trips in this book. However, most of the fire-damaged areas have begun to recover soon enough that the authors have chosen not to delete the affected trips from the book.

Lyell Fork of the Tuolumne River near Tuolumne Lodge

The Care and Enjoyment of the Mountains

The mountains are in danger, particularly the High Sierra. About a million people camp in the Sierra wilderness each year. Backpacking is something everybody knows about and almost everybody is going to want to try. With California's population edging toward 30 million, the wilderness is threatened with destruction, particularly the High Sierra.

Litter is not the problem! Increasingly, wilderness campsites, even when free of litter, have that "beat out" look of overcrowded roadside campgrounds. The fragile high country sod is being ground down under the pressure of too many feet. Lovely trees and snags are being stripped, scarred, and removed altogether for firewood. Dust, charcoal, blackened stones and dirty fireplaces are accumulating. These conditions are spreading rapidly, and in a few years *every* High Sierra lakeshore and streamside may be severely damaged.

The national park service and the forest service are faced with the necessity for reservation systems, designated campgrounds, restrictions on fire building, increased ranger patrols, and rationing of wilderness recreation. Not only the terrain but the wilderness experience is being eroded. Soon conditions may be little different from those we wanted to leave behind at the roadhead.

The solution to the problem depends on each of us. We must change our habits so as to have as little effect on the terrain as possible. We must try to leave no traces of our passing. This was the rule in the wilderness when Indians and trappers traveled through other people's territory. It is still a good rule today. It does take a little trouble. In an earlier day that extra trouble was the price of saving one's scalp or load of beaver pelts. Today it is the price of saving the wilderness. A few basic principles of wilderness preservation—particularly aimed at High Sierra conditions but applicable elsewhere too— are offered below.

Learn to go light. This is largely a matter of acquiring wilderness skills, of learning to be at home in the wilderness rather than in an elaborate camp. The *free spirits* of the mountains are those experts who appear to go anywhere under any conditions with neither encumbrances nor effort but always with complete enjoyment. John Muir, traveling along the crest of the Sierra in the 1870s with little more than his overcoat and pockets full of biscuits, was the archetype.

Modern lightweight equipment and food are a convenience and a joy. The ever-practical Muir would have taken them had they been available in his day. But a lot of the stuff that goes into the mountains is burdensome, harmful to the wilderness, or just plain annoying to other people seeking peace and solitude. Anything that is obtrusive or that can be used to modify the terrain should be left at the roadhead: gigantic tents, gas lanterns, radios, saws, hatchets, firearms (except in the hunting season), etc.

Pick "hard" campsites, sandy places that can stand the use. The fragile sod of meadows, lakeshores and streamsides is rapidly disappearing from the High Sierra. It simply cannot take the wear and tear of campers. Its development depends on very special conditions. Once destroyed, it does not ordinarily grow back.

Be easy with the trees! In the timberline country wood is being burned up faster than it is being produced. The big campfires of the past must give way to small fires or to no fires at all. Wood is a precious resource; use it sparingly. Where it is scarce use a gas stove, not a saw or hatchet. Trees, both live and dead, are part of the scenery. They should never be *cut*. The exquisite golden trunks left standing after lightning strikes should be left completely alone. Sadly, in some popular areas they have already been destroyed for firewood, and you would never know they *were* there.

In established, regularly used campsites a single, small, substantial fireplace should serve for both cooking and warming. If kept scrupulously clean it should last for many years. Unfortunately, fireplaces (and campsites) tend to become increasingly dirty and to multiply. There are now, by actual survey, a hundred times as many fireplaces as are needed in the High Sierra. The countless dirty fireplaces should be eradicated. Many campsites situated at the edge of the water should be entirely restored to nature and not used again. It is a noble service to use and clean up established campsites where they are present, and to restore them to nature where called for.

Elsewhere build a small fireplace, if one is legal, and always eradicate it and restore your campsite to a natural condition before you leave. This is facilitated if you build with restoration in mind: two to four medium-sized stones along the sides of a shallow trench in a sandy place. When camp is broken the stones are returned to their places. The coals are thoroughly burned down and pulverized under a heavy foot until nothing is left but powder. The trench is filled with clean sand. *Fires should never be built against cliffs or large boulders.*

Protect the water from soap and other pollution.

Scatter organic garbage in dry, out-of-the-way places. It disappears most quickly when dry and exposed to the air. Talus slopes and dry brush are the best hiding places. Garbage should never be burned in the fireplace. Orange peels are an exception. They seem to be destructible only in a hot fire.

Thoroughly cold and pulverized charcoal may be broadcast away from camp in a fireproof site. Charcoal is part of the natural scene.

Pack cans and foil back to the roadhead. Smelly or oily cans and foil can be cleaned easily in a hot fire but please do remove them. The accumulation of garbage, cans, and charcoal around fireplaces is the principal reason campsites are abandoned and new, redundant fireplaces and campsites are created.

Latrines. By and large, the giardia in Sierran waters comes from improper disposal of human wastes. Keeping giardia and other infectious organisms out of the water supply requires proper burial, 6–8 inches deep, at least 50 yards away from lakes, streams, dry watercourses and campsites. Be sure to completely bury or burn your toilet paper.

8

Safety and Well Being

Hiking in the high country is far safer than driving to the mountains, and a few precautions can shield you from most of the discomforts and dangers that could threaten you.

Health Hazards.

1. **Altitude Sickness.** If you normally live at sea level and come to the Sierra to hike, it may take your body several days to acclimate. Starved of your accustomed oxygen, for a few days you may experience shortness of breath with even minimal activity, severe headaches, or nausea. The best solution is to spend time at altitude before you begin your hike, and to plan a very easy first day.

2. **Giardia.** Giardia is not new to the Sierra but it has recently become a widespread problem. This protozoan (*Giardia lamblia*) can cause acute gastrointestinal distress, as anyone who has had it can tell you. The illness is treatable, but prevention is best. There is giardia in the water in most of the popular areas, and the Park Service and Forest Service recommend that you treat all water to be sure, as giardia can be anywhere. Among the methods used to treat water (for giardia) are commercial tablets, filters and boiling. It is hard to say which method is the most effective. In popular areas, we use a filter for water that is not boiled for 5 minutes, as in cooking. We have never contracted giardia. Some hikers say they never treat their water and have never contracted giardia. It is likely that most people can ingest some giardia without any problem, and some people are probably immune to giardia. But anyone can be a carrier, whether they have symptoms or not. It takes 2–3 weeks for symptoms to appear after exposure.

3. **Hypothermia.** Hypothermia refers to subnormal body temperature. More hikers die from hypothermia than from any other single cause: it represents the greatest threat to your survival in the wilderness. Caused by exposure to cold, often

intensified by wet, wind and weariness, the first symptoms of hypothermia are uncontrollable shivering and imperfect motor coordination. These are rapidly followed by loss of judgment, so that you yourself cannot make the decisions to protect your own life. To prevent hypothermia, stay warm: carry wind-and-rain-protective clothing, and put it on as soon as you feel chilly. Stay dry: carry or wear wool or a suitable synthetic (not cotton) against your skin; bring raingear even for a short hike on an apparently sunny day. If weather conditions threaten and you are inadequately prepared, flee or hunker down. Protect yourself so you remain as warm and dry as possible.

Treat shivering at once—remember, hypothermia acts quickly and destroys judgment. Get the victim out of the wind and wet, replace all wet clothes with dry ones, put him or her in a sleeping bag and give him or her warm drinks. If the shivering is severe and accompanied by other symptoms, strip him or her and yourself (and a third party if possible), and warm him or her with your own bodies, tightly wrapped in a dry sleeping bag.

4. **Lightning.** Although the odds of being struck are very small, almost everyone who goes to the mountains thinks about it.

An afternoon thunderstorm may come upon you rather quickly, but not so fast that you can't get to a better place if you are exposed. Most people know that a mountain peak is a no-no. So is a mountain ridge. So is an open field. So is a boat on a lake. And so are a small cave and an overhang.

Then where should you be if the thunderstorm is upon you? The safest place is an opening or a clump of small trees in a forest. But one is not always handy. If you are above treeline, and can get next to any pinnacle, do so, taking a position no farther from the pinnacle than its height. Lacking any pinnacles, position yourself atop a small boulder that is detached from bedrock. If caught in an open area, get to the lowest place that is not wet.

Wherever you position yourself, the best body stance is one that minimizes the area your body covers. You should drop to your knees and put your hands on your knees. This is because the more area your body covers, the more chance that ground currents will pass through it.

Most people believe that metal as such attracts lightning,

but the actual danger from your packframe, tent poles, etc. is due to *induced* currents. In any event, get all your metal away from you as fast as you can.

And what if lightning strikes you anyway? There isn't much you can do except pray that someone in your party is adept at CPR—or at least adept at artificial respiration if your breathing has stopped but not your heart. It may take hours for a victim to resume breathing on his own. If it's your companions who are victims, attend first to those who are not moving. Those who are rolling about or moaning are at least breathing. Finally, a victim who lives should be evacuated to a hospital, because other problems often develop in lightning victims.

Wildlife Hazards

1. **Rattlesnakes**. They occur at lower elevations (they are rarely seen above 7000 feet) in a range of habitats, but most commonly near riverbeds and streams. Their bite is rarely fatal to an adult. If you plan a trip below 6000 feet along a watercourse, you may want to carry a snake-bite kit. If you hear a snake rattle, stand still long enough to determine where it is, then leave in the opposite direction.

2. **Marmots**. They live from about 6,000 to 11,500 feet. Because they are curious and always hungry, and like to sun themselves on rocks in full view, you are likely to see them. Marmots enjoy many foods you do, including cereal and candy (especially chocolate). They may eat through a pack or tent when other entry is difficult. Marmots cannot climb trees or ropes, so you can protect your food by hanging it.

3. **Bears**. Since backpackers' food is attractive to bears, and all too often easily available, the animals have developed a habit of seeking it and eating it. They patrol popular campsites nightly. As the bears have become more knowledgeable and persistent, backpackers have escalated their food-protecting methods. From merely putting it in one's pack by one's bed at night, and chasing away any bear that came, backcountry travelers switched to hanging the food over a branch of a tree. But bears can climb trees, and they can gnaw or scratch through the nylon line that you tie around a tree trunk. When they sever the line, the food hanging from the other end of the line of course falls to the ground.

To avoid food loss due to line severance, you can learn the *counterbalance* method of "bearbagging." First, tie a small stone to the end of a 30-foot length of nylon line (⅛" or so in diameter) as a weight to hurl up and over a likely branch. The branch should be at least 16 feet up, and long enough that the line can rest securely at a point at least 6 feet from the tree trunk. When you have the line over the branch, tie a rock that weighs about the same as the food bag to one end of the line. (Instead of a rock, you could tie a bag containing half the food, if you have two appropriate bags.) Now pull the rock up to the branch that the line passes over. Then tie your food bag to the other end of the line, as high as you can conveniently reach, and stuff any extra line into the mouth of the food bag. Now push up on the food bag with just enough force—you hope—that the system will come to rest with the rock and the bag equally high. If they aren't equally high, take a long enough stick, preferably forked, and push up the lower of the two until they are even. If you can reach them standing on tiptoes, they are too low. Try again. Next morning, push up either rock or bag until one descends enough that you can reach it. As a high-tech version of a tree limb, rangers have installed cables up high between two trees at popular campsites in Yosemite. In addition, steel food-storage boxes have been placed at some campsites in the Sierra.

REMEMBER: If a bear does get your food, he will then consider it his, and he will fight any attempts you make to retrieve it. Don't try! Remember also never to leave your food unprotected even for a short while during the daytime.

4. **Mosquitoes**. If you have no protection against mosquitoes, they can ruin your trip. However, protection is easy. Any insect repellent containing *N, N diethylmeta-toluamide* will keep them off. Don't buy one without it. Clothing is also a bar to mosquitoes—a good reason for wearing long pants and long-sleeved shirts. If you are a favorite target for mosquitoes (they have their preferences) you might take a head net—a hat with netting suspended all around the brim and a snug neckband. Planning your trip to avoid the height of the mosquito season is also a good preventive.

Terrain Hazards

1. **Snow bridges and snow cornices**. Stay off them.

2. **Stream crossings**. In early season, when the snow is melting, crossing a river can be the most dangerous part of a backpack trip. Later, ordinary caution will see you across

safely. If a river is running high, you should cross it only if 1) the alternatives to crossing are more dangerous than crossing, 2) you have found a suitable place to ford, and 3) you use a rope.

As for #1, obviously it's better to turn back than to risk accident. As for #2, it may take considerable looking around to find a suitable place to ford. If you can find a viewpoint high above the river, you can better check out the river's width, speed and turbulence, any obstructions in it, and the nature of its bottom.

Whichever method you use to cross a stream, you should:
• If the water is at all high, wait till morning to cross, when the level will be at its daily low.
• Unfasten the hip belt of your pack, in case you have to jettison it.
• Keep your boots on. They will protect your feet from injury and give your feet more secure placement.
• Never face downstream. The water pushing against the back of your knees could cause them to buckle.
• Move one foot only when the other is firmly placed.
• Never allow your legs to cross; keep them apart.
• Use a stick as a support on the upstream side.

Maps and Profiles

Today's Sierra traveler is confronted by a bewildering array of maps, and it doesn't take much experience to learn that no single map fulfills all needs. There are topographic maps, base maps (U.S. Forest Service), shaded relief maps (National Park Service), artistically drawn representational maps (California Department of Fish and Game), aerial-photograph maps, geologic maps, three-dimensional relief maps, soil-vegetation maps, etc. Each map has different information to impart, and the outdoorsman contemplating a backcountry trip is wise to utilize several of these māps in his planning.

For trip-planning purposes, the reader will find a plan map in the back of this book. Trails and trailheads used in the trip descriptions are shown on this map in red, the access roads in black, water in blue, and the topographic map grid in orange.

The profile of each trip in this book gives a quick picture of the ups and downs. All profiles are drawn with the same *ratio* of horizontal miles to feet of elevation except 44 and 87. The vertical scale in all is exaggerated.

On the trail most backpackers prefer to use a topographic (*topo*) map, because it affords a good deal of accurate information about terrain and forest cover. Topo maps come in a variety of sizes and scales, but the best, because it covers the whole Sierra in one useful scale, is the U.S. Geological Survey's 15' Topographic Quadrangle series. The 15' series scale is approximately $1'' = 1$ mile; the contour interval (elevation difference between contour lines) is 80 feet in the Sierra; and the area covered by each map is about 14×17 miles. They show most of the maintained trails (exceptions are noted in the text of this book), the elevations, the relief, the watercourses, the forest cover and the works of man. Learning to read these maps takes a little practice, but the savings in shoe leather and frayed tempers make it a worthy undertaking. For the reader's convenience, the appropriate 15' topo maps for each are cited in the text.

By far the best topo maps—for the quadrangles for which they are available—are the 15' quadrangle maps published by Wilderness Press. These maps are based on the USGS versions, but were completely updated in the late 1970s and early 1980s after thorough fieldwork. Trails are much easier to see on these maps because they are shown as solid black lines. And each map has an index grid and an index for locating all the features on it. In the area of *Sierra North*, Wilderness Press 15' maps are available for these quadrangles: Hetch Hetchy, Tuolumne Meadows, Yosemite, Merced Peak and Devils Postpile. In addition, Wilderness Press has published an updated topographic map of Yosemite National Park and Vicinity. This map alone shows more than half of the trails described in *Sierra North*. In the tabular matter at the start of each trip in the book, the topo maps needed for the trip are listed. If a map's name is in **boldface**, that quadrangle is available in the Wilderness Press series, and it is the best one available.

Another useful map series is the USDA Forest Service topographic series for each individual wilderness area. This series is almost identical in scale to the USGS 15' series (1:62,500) but conveniently covers the entire Wilderness Area on one map. This series is also more nearly up to date.

All pertinent maps and books are available in person or by phone from The Map Center, 2440 Bancroft Way, Berkeley, CA 94704, (415) 841-6277, and The Map Center, 63 Washington Street, Santa Clara, CA 95050, (408) 296-6277. US Geological Survey topographic maps and US Forest Service maps are available locally at most Yosemite and National Forest ranger stations and other wilderness-permit sources.

Additional Map Sources:

USGS offices: Room 504, 555 Battery Street, San Francisco, CA 94111, (415) 705-1010; 345 Middlefield Road, Menlo Park, CA 94025, (415) 329-4390; Room 7638 Federal Bldg., 300 N. Los Angeles St., Los Angeles, CA 90012, (213) 894-2850.

USDA Forest Service, Pacific Southwest Region, 630 Sansome St., Room 533A, San Francisco, CA 94111, (415) 705-2874.

Wilderness Permits

Anyone traveling overnight into designated National Park or National Forest (except Toiyabe) Wilderness is asked to carry a wilderness permit from the administering agency. Knowing the number and distribution of backcountry users helps the agencies make better decisions and get more tax money for wilderness areas.

In the national forests, permits are available both by reservation and on a first-come, first-served basis at ranger district offices. Permits are required only from May 25 to September 15, when most trailheads have a daily quota. Reservations are taken by mail after March 1, and cost $3 per person. If you reserve a permit by mail or phone, you can pick it up in person 24 hours per day. But to get a permit without a reservation, you must go during business hours, generally 8–5, six or seven days a week, during the summer. During the summer, some areas have seasonal stations that dispense permits, maps and information such as the station at Carson Pass. Call ahead for details. The following is a list of permit locations by wilderness area, highway, or National Forest or Park.

Echo Summit (Highway 50, Echo Summit): From the west, Information Center, 3070 Camino Heights Drive, Camino, CA 95709, (916) 644-6048, just off Highway 50 east of Placerville. From the east, Lake Tahoe Basin Management Unit, Box 8465, South Lake Tahoe, CA 95731, (916) 573-2600, or 870 Emerald Bay Rd., Suite 1, South Lake Tahoe, CA 96150.

Mokelumne Wilderness (Highway 88, Carson Pass): Amador Ranger Station, 26820 Silver Drive, Pioneer, CA 95666, (209) 295-4251, 3 miles east of Pioneer on Highway 88. Plasses Resort at Silver Lake and Carson Pass Station are open in summer only, first-come, first-served.

Carson-Iceberg Wilderness (Highway 4, Ebbetts Pass): The trailheads on the east side—Wolf Creek and Rodriquez Flat—are in Toiyabe National Forest and have sign-in at the trailhead. On the west side: Calaveras Ranger Station, on Highway 4, Box 500, Hathaway Pines, CA 95232, (209-795-1381, and Alpine Ranger Station, on Highway 4 between Bear Valley and Lake Alpine—summer only (209) 753-2811).

Emigrant Wilderness (Highway 108, Sonora Pass): Summit Ranger Station, Star Rt. Box 1295, Sonora, CA 95370. (209) 965-3434, at the Pinecrest Y, 30 miles east of Sonora, 1.5 miles beyond the turnoff to Gianelli Cabin. Kennedy Meadows Resort and Brightman Flat Fire Station are summer only.

Ansel Adams Wilderness: From the west (Sierra National Forest): if you are going over Chiquito Pass you can go to Oakhurst Ranger Station, on Highway 41 just east of Oakhurst. For other trailheads on the west side: Minarets Ranger Station in North Fork, CA 93646, (209) 877-2218, and Clover Meadow Ranger Station, between the Fernandez Trailhead and the Granite Creek Trailhead (summer only). On the east side (Inyo National Forest) one can go to Mono Lake Ranger Station (also known as Lee Vining Ranger Station), Box 10, Lee Vining, CA 94541, (619) 647-6527, 1 mile west from Highway 395 on Highway 120, near Lee Vining. If you're going through Mammoth Lakes, you can go to Mammoth Ranger Station, Box 148, Mammoth Lakes, CA 93456, (619) 934-2505, on Highway 203 just east of town. If you are near Devils Postpile National Monument, you can go to the Devils Postpile Ranger Station (summer only).

John Muir Wilderness: From the east (Inyo National Forest) one can go to White Mountain Ranger Station, 798 N. Main (Highway 395), Bishop, CA 93514, (619) 873-4207. Nearer to the trailheads is Rock Creek Entrance Station, less than 1 mile up the Rock Creek Road from Tom's Place on Highway 395, (619) 935-4253 (summer only). From the west (Sierra National Forest) one can go to Pineridge Ranger Station, Box 300, Shaver Lake, CA 93664, (209) 841-3311, just before the town of Shaver Lake on Highway 168. Closer to Lake Edison is the High Sierra Ranger Station, on the road between Kaiser summit and the turnoff to Lake Edison (summer only).

Yosemite: In Yosemite permits are available on a first-come-first-served basis the day before your departure into the backcountry. In Tuolumne Meadows you can get your permit from a booth in the parking lot near the west end of the Tuolumne Lodge spur road. The Park Service realizes that many Yosemite hikers are weekend visitors, so from late June through Labor Day weekend they keep the booth open on Friday nights and open it early (sometimes 6 a.m.) on Saturday mornings. In Yosemite, you can also get a permit in person at the Big Oak Flat entrance station on Highway 120, in Yosemite Valley and at Wawona—and at the Mather Ranger Station on the road to Hetch Hetchy from April through October.

In addition, permits for Yosemite summer trips may be obtained by mail *between Feb. 1 and May 31* by writing: Wilderness Permits, Box 577, Yosemite National Park, CA 95389. After May 31 you must appear in person. Groups of 15 or more are requested to make mail reservations for any trip between Memorial Day and October 1.

If your trip extends through more than one national forest, or through both a national forest and a national park, obtain your permit from the forest or park where your trip starts.

A wilderness permit is issued for a single trip during a specified period of time. A separate permit is necessary for each trip. A campfire permit is required for campfires anywhere in a national forest.

Capacities have been established for high-use areas in the region covered by this book, including all the backcountry of Yosemite. If the capacity of the area where you want to go has been filled, you must select another overnight destination. A number of other rules exist for backcountry use, many of which are simply codifications of the principles in the chapter "The Care and Enjoyment of the Mountains." One rule that is all too often broken is that summer camping is prohibited within 100 feet of a trail, flowing stream or other body of water unless otherwise designated. *Except:* Camping is permitted within 100 feet of a stream, trail, or body of water provided a well-established campsite exists there or terrain permits no other options. But camping is never permitted within 25 feet of a stream, trail or body of water. Copies of all these special regulations are available from the government agencies that issue wilderness permits.

When writing for a permit, please state 1) where and when you will enter and leave the wilderness, 2) your entire route, and where you will stop each night, 3) how many people in your party, 4) how many head of stock you are taking, if any, and 5) your mode of travel: hiking, skiing or riding horses.

The Trailheads

Here are the descriptions for driving to all the trailheads used in trips in this book. At the beginning of each trip is a trailhead number, keyed to the numbers here. Shuttle trips have two trailheads, so the beginning trailhead number is given first in the trip, and the ending trailhead number is given second.

1. **Horse Canyon Trailhead**. Go 0.8 mile north on State Highway 88 from Silver Lake to Oyster Creek Roadside Rest, where there is plenty of parking, and walk 100 yards farther up the highway to the signed trailhead. There is room for a very few cars right by the trailhead.

2. **Plasse's Resort**. Go east on State Highway 88 to the last downhill stretch before arriving at the shore of Silver Lake and turn right on a road signed PLASSE ROAD. At the bottom of the hill, turn right and drive past the resort's main buildings to an informal parking area where there are many signs of use by horses and horse trailers. East across the stream here is your trailhead.

3. **Echo Summit**. Go ⅓ mile south from Echo Summit (on U.S. 50) to the end of a graded summer-home-tract road.

4. **Carson Pass**. Go 0.9 mile west of Carson Pass on State Highway 88 or 3 miles east of the west end of the Caples Lake dam to a small parking area with a sign OLD MEISS TRAILHEAD.

5. **Upper Wolf Creek Meadows**. About 2½ miles south on State Highway 4 from State Highway 89, turn left and go south-east up Wolf Creek Road 3⅓ miles to a fork left, where you could descend northeast to the north end of Wolf Creek Meadows. Continue straight ahead—south—1½ miles beyond the fork to road's end at Wolf Creek Meadows Undeveloped Camping Area. The Wolf Creek Trail heads south up a creekside jeep road.

6. **Wolf Creek Meadows**. Follow Wolf Creek Road 3⅓ miles to a fork left and descend northeast on it to the north end

of Wolf Creek Meadows. In ⅔ mile from the fork, the road reaches a stock corral and a spur road heading southeast. Park here. This spur climbs ¼ mile to two adjacent trailheads. The two trailheads serve the High Trail and the East Carson River Trail.

7. **Ebbetts Pass**. This is the highest point on State Highway 4. The Pacific Crest Trail crosses State Highway 4 only 0.1 mile northeast of the pass, and in another 0.3 mile a short spur road veers right up to a PCT parking lot. A short spur trail up to the PCT leaves from the lot's south end.

8. **Heiser Lake Trailhead**. From the east end of Lake Alpine go 6 miles northeast up State Highway 4 to the west end of Mosquito Lake, beside which is the signed trailhead.

9. **Bull Run Lake Trailhead**. From the east end of Lake Alpine go 4 miles northeast up State Highway 4 to a spur road branching right signed STANISLAUS MDW BULL RUN TRAIL. Follow this road ½ mile to its end, or just 0.35 mile if you don't have 4-wheel drive.

10. **Lake Alpine**. At the east end of Lake Alpine on State Highway 4 turn right ⅓ mile to the Silver Valley Overnight Campground. At the campground entrance is the trailhead for the Highland Creek Trail.

11. **Rodriguez Flat**. From the State Highway 4/89 junction with U.S. 395, go 5½ miles south on U.S. 395 to Coleville, then another 2¼ miles to a road west, signed both LOST CANNON CREEK ROAD and MILL CANYON ROAD. Alternatively, from the State Highway 108/U.S. 395 junction, drive 13 miles north to Walker, then another 2½ miles to Lost Cannon Creek Road. This dirt road west quickly becomes the Golden Gate Road. Go up it 6¼ miles; following LITTLE ANTELOPE PACK STATION signs. From the mountain crest junction at broad, open Rodriguez Flat, drive ½ mile south to road's end at signed Trail 1020.

12. **Kennedy Meadow**. Go 1 mile up an oiled road from State Highway 108, 27 miles east of the Pinecrest Y. You can let passengers out at the resort, and park there for a fee or drive ½ mile back to a public parking area.

13. **Gianelli Cabin**. From the junction of State Routes 108 and 120, go 33.5 miles northeast on 108 to tiny Cold Springs, and 1.2 miles beyond turn right on signed Crabtree Road. Follow this paved road 6.8 miles to a junction just before a

pack station. Go straight ahead onto dirt road and drive 2.65 miles to a junction. Turn left and go 4 miles to road's end.

14. **Crabtree Camp**. Proceed as above to the last-named junction, and go right 0.7 mile to the trailhead parking lot beside Bell Creek.

15. **Sonora Pass**. This is the highest point of State Highway 108, 67 miles northeast of Sonora and 15 miles west of the U.S. 395 junction.

16. **O'Shaughnessy Dam (Hetch Hetchy Reservoir)**. Go east on State Highway 120 4 miles beyond Buck Meadows and turn left at a signed junction.Go 6 miles to another signed junction, turn right and go 6½ miles to Camp Mather and then 9½ more miles to the roadend.

17. **Leavitt Meadow**. Go 8 miles east from Sonora Pass on State Highway 108, or 7 miles west from U.S. 395 on the same highway to the Leavitt Meadow Campground backpackers parking area.

18. **Buckeye Roadend**. Go 7 miles west from Bridgeport on the Twin Lakes road and turn north for 4 dirt-road miles at the junction signed **Buckeye Campground**. Just beyond Buckeye Creek, turn left and go 1.1 miles, passing through a Forest Service Campground, to the end of the road. Alternatively, leave U.S. 395 3.8 miles north of Bridgeport and drive 6.0 miles to the same roadend.

19. **Twin Lakes**. Drive to the end of the paved 13½-mile road marked *Twin Lakes* that branches west from U.S. 395 in downtown Bridgeport. For $5 you can park in a hot, exposed backpacker parking area at the campground entrance in Mono Village, or you can park free if you can find space before entering the village. About 40 yards inside the campground entrance kiosk is a sign BARNEY LAKE TRAIL. From it, follow orange rectangles nailed to trees to another sign BARNEY LAKE TRAIL at the top of the campground. This village is eroded, hot, dusty and crowded!

20. **Green Creek Roadend**. Take the dusty dirt road (Road 142) which leaves U.S. 395 4.3 miles south of Bridgeport and 21 miles north of Lee Vining. Go 9½ miles west to the roadend. (After 3½ miles, don't take Road 20, which leads to the Virginia Lakes Road.)

21. **Virginia Lakes Trailhead**. From Conway Summit on U.S. 395 go 6 miles on paved Virginia Lakes Road, then ½ mile

on dirt road to the campground on the right.

22. **Saddlebag Lake**. Go 2 miles up a gravel road that branches northwest from State Highway 120 2 miles north of the Tioga Pass entrance to Yosemite.

23. **Glen Aulin Trailhead**. From State Highway 120 in Tuolumne Meadows, just east of the bridge over the Tuolumne River, turn west on a dirt road and go 0.3 mile to a parking area near the stables. On crowded days you may have to park immediately off the highway at the Dog Lake trailhead parking lot.

24. **Gibbs Lake Trailhead**. Go 1.3 miles south from the junction of U.S. 395 and State Highway 120 just south of Lee Vining, turn right on the road signed *Horse Meadow,* and go 2.1 miles up it.

25. **Tuolumne Meadows Campground**. Turn south off State Highway 120 in Tuolumne Meadows east of the store and drive up the road nearest the river.

26. **Tuolumne Lodge**. Following State Highway 120 in Tuolumne Meadows, drive ½ mile east from the bridge over the Tuolumne River, turn right on a paved road, and go ¾ mile to the roadend parking lot to let your passengers out. You must park at one of the two backpackers' parking lots along this road.

27. **Tioga Road Trailhead**. Go 0.5 mile west of the Visitors Center in Tuolumne Meadows, or 0.5 mile east of the west end of the meadows.

28. **Tenaya Lake**. Park in the lot at the west end of Tenaya Lake on State Highway 120 in Yosemite, where signs indicate the Walk-in Campground.

29. **Happy Isles**. Take the Yosemite Valley shuttle bus to Happy Isles, or park at Camp Curry and hike along a trail 1 mile southeast to Happy Isles.

30. **Glacier Point**. Drive 9.3 miles up State Highway 41 from Yosemite Valley, turn left, and drive 15.5 more miles to a parking lot at road's end.

31. **Bridalveil Creek**. Drive 9.3 miles up State Highway 41 from Yosemite Valley, turn left, drive 7.6 more miles to the Bridalveil Campground road, branching right, and follow this road through the campground to the southeast end of it.

32. **Chiquito Creek Trailhead**. From the north shore of Bass Lake, drive northeast 20 miles up Beasore Road 434 (which becomes Road 5S07) to Globe Rock. There, turn left

and drive 2.4 miles up Road 5S04 to a signed trailhead atop a small, flat ridge area.

33. Granite Creek Campground. From the north shore of Bass Lake, drive northeast 20 miles up Beasore Road 434 (which becomes Road 5S07) to Globe Rock, then continue 9.8 miles along your road to the Minarets road, which goes south 52 paved miles to the town of North Fork. Still on Road 5S07, you reach the Clover Meadow Ranger Station in 1.7 miles, then continue past it for 0.5 mile to Road 4S57. Branch right on this road and follow it 1.0 mile to a hikers' parking area in Granite Creek Campground. Road 4S57 may be undrivable as late as early July.

34. Fernandez Trailhead. From the north shore of Bass Lake follow Beasore Road 434 (which becomes Road 5S07) 20 miles east to Globe Rock. Continue on 5S07—the main road—for 8.0 miles, past Bowler Group Camp. Then, 100 yards beyond Ethelfreda Creek, veer left onto Road 5S05 toward the Fernandez Trailhead. This road climbs steadily for 2.3 miles to a turn-around loop at the trailhead.

35. Rush Creek. The June Lake Loop intersects U.S. 395 about 4 miles south of Route 120 on the outskirts of Lee Vining and at June Lake Junction, about 6 miles farther south. Follow the June Lake Loop to the northeast end of Silver Lake (7.3 miles from June Lake Junction). The trailhead is on the west side of the road between the Frontier Pack Station and a mobile-home park.

36. Agnew Meadows. Go 9 miles west from U.S. 395 through Mammoth Lakes and over Minaret Summit. Turn right 2.7 miles from Minaret Summit and go ¼ mile to a parking area. There is an overflow parking area just beyond it. You may have to park just before Minaret Summit and take a shuttlebus.

37. Devils Postpile. Go 9 miles west from U.S. 395 through Mammoth Lakes and over Minaret Summit. Turn right 6.7 miles from Minaret Summit to go 0.35 mile to a parking area at the spur road's end. You may have to park just before Minaret Summit and take a shuttlebus.

38. Reds Meadow. Go 9 miles west from U.S. 395 through Mammoth Lakes and to Minaret Summit, then 8.5 more miles to road's end at the resort.

39. Lake George. Go west from U.S. 395 4 miles to

Mammoth Lakes. At the upper end of town go straight on the Lake Mary Road. Reaching the basin of lakes, follow the signs to Lake George and its parking area.

40. **Coldwater Campground**. Go west from U.S. 395 4 miles to Mammoth Lakes, and at the top of town take the Lake Mary Road. Follow it 3.5 miles to the northeast shore of Lake Mary, turn left on a road signed for Coldwater Campground, go ½ mile, and turn left into the campground. Go 1 mile to the trailhead at campground's end.

41. **Vermilion Campground**. Go east from Clovis (near Fresno) 81 miles on State Highway 168 to the Florence Lake/Lake Edison junction, then 8 miles north on a mostly paved road to Vermilion Campground.

42. **Mosquito Flat**. Go 25 miles north from Bishop or 15 miles south from the Mammoth Lakes turnoff on U.S. 395 and then 11 miles on paved road to road's end in Mosquito Flat beside Rock Creek.

43. **McGee Creek Roadend**. Go 32 miles north of Bishop or 8 miles south of the Mammoth Lakes turnoff to a dirt road that leads west 4.0 miles to a roadend parking area.

Crown Point over Barney Lake

Carson Pass

The Carson Pass area flanks the first trans-Sierra highway south of Lake Tahoe. As a recreational area, it boasts many lakes off the highway and a few beside the highway. The scenery is superb, mixing as it does volcanic rocks with granitic ones. You'll want a camera to catch the volcanic battlements north of Silver Lake rising above the granite bosses of the lake basin.

Some of the best flower displays in the entire Sierra grow alongside the trails in this part of *Sierra North*, such as the trails to Scout Carson Lake and Showers Lake.

Highway 88, designated a scenic highway, is the main gateway to the 105,165-acre Mokelumne Wilderness, enlarged in 1964 from 50,450 acres, when a number of new wilderness areas were created in California and many existing ones were enlarged.

To acclimate your body to the 8000-foot-plus altitudes, you could spend the night before hiking at Sorensen's, Kit Carson Lodge, Caples Lake Resort or Kay's Silver Lake Resort—all near the pass and the trailheads. And there are plenty of campgrounds nearby.

Silver Lake to Scout Carson Lake **1**

Distance	11 miles
Type	Round trip
Best season	Mid
Topo maps	Silver Lake

Grade (hiking days/recommended layover days)
    Leisurely 2/1
    Moderate 2/0
    Strenuous ---

Trailhead 1

HIGHLIGHTS The mountains around Silver Lake are a startling amalgam of light-gray granite and dark-brown lava, the granite being gently rounded, but the lava arrayed in tiers of jagged cliffs. This trip follows a boundary between the two types of terrain, ascending gently southeast under the soaring lava cliffs of Thunder Peak and Thimble Peak to a lovely, small lake near timberline.

DESCRIPTION

1st Hiking Day (**Silver Lake** to **Scout Carson Lake**, 5.5 miles): From the aspen grove at the trailhead just north of Oyster Creek Roadside Rest, the duff-colored trail ascends gently, sometimes moderately, through a red-fir forest. In early season, open patches in the forest are carpeted with lupine, and showy red columbines grow here and there. Eroded blocks of lava beside the trail have taken on grotesque and fascinating shapes which your imagination can identify as what it will. Even more compelling are the dark lava cliffs on the northern skyline, the crenelated battlements of a 3-mile-long igneous castle.

About 2 miles up from the trailhead an unsigned trail comes in on the right beside a large boulder; this is one route up from the Boy Scout Camp below. A more-used path from the camp, the trail shown on the topo map, meets our route ½ mile farther up, on an open hillside, and 70 yards beyond this junction is the first water you will cross in midsummer. From this cooling pause, we break out onto an open slope dotted with red fir and great numbers of yellow-flowered mule ears, mixed with bits of blue lupine. Then the blazed trail re-enters red-fir forest, and just how brittle the wood of the conifer species is, is shown by the tremendous amount of broken wood littering the forest floor—seemingly enough for a thousand campfires.

Leaving the forest, our rocky trail climbs across an open hillside dotted with many large granite boulders, a large assortment of wildflowers and a few lodgepole pines, red firs and Sierra junipers. As we come into earshot of a plunging stream, we turn steeply uphill and in 100 yards reach and jump-ford this creek. The walk up the far bank is enhanced by the gurgling sounds and by the brilliant chutes and cascades of this unnamed stream, which drains the bowl between Thunder Peak (not named on the topo map) and Thimble Peak.

About 300 yards later the trail veers away from the stream to make an unrelenting steep ascent, then levels off just before it tops out on a granite ridge. Here again the hillside is very open, and we now have excellent views of Silver Lake and the mountains surrounding it. Then a short, strolling descent brings the hiker to an all-year stream with flanking flower gardens, a good place to stop for lunch. The many mountain birds around here will eat any crumbs you leave.

Beyond the stream our trail contours an open hillside where the flower display in season is among the best for miles around. Using one of the guides listed in the Recommended Reading chapter, the budding botanist will recognize woolly sunflower, Indian paintbrush, sulfur flower, scarlet gilia, pennyroyal, mule ears, corn lily and sagebrush, among others. Soon our route passes the hard-to-find trail to Kirkwood Meadow and Caples Lake, and ½ mile farther, in a sandy flat, meets the signed lateral trail to Scout Carson Lake. From this junction an unmaintained trail leads south for a good ¼ mile to this small, grass-and-heather-fringed lake with good campsites.

2nd Hiking Day: Retrace your steps, 5.5 miles.

Silver Lake to Summit City Canyon   **2**

Distance	20 miles
Type	Round trip
Best season	Mid
Topo maps	Silver Lake

Grade (hiking days/recommended layover days)
   Leisurely 4/1
   Moderate 3/0
   Strenuous 2/0
Trailhead 1

HIGHLIGHTS The first leg of this trip is a long traverse of very flowery open hillsides with fine views of the Silver Lake basin and its surrounding volcanic battlements. Then the trail enters a new stream valley and winds down through solitude-filled Horse Canyon to a variety of campsites along beautiful Summit City Creek.

DESCRIPTION (Leisurely trip)

1st Hiking Day: Follow Trip 1 to **Scout Carson Lake**, 5.5 miles.

2nd Hiking Day (**Scout Carson Lake** to **Summit City Canyon**, 4.5 miles): First we retrace the long ¼ mile of use trail to the Horse Canyon Trail and turn right (east) on it. Our sometimes muddy trail ascends moderately through a thinning tree cover almost to timberline, passing through upland meadows rife with flower color in early season. Approaching Squaw Ridge, we cross a set of little-used jeep tracks and in 100 yards arrive at an unnamed pass which is the border of Mokelumne Wilderness, a region of 105,165 acres where only foot travel is permitted and trails are generally kept up to a standard sufficient for walkers but not horses or mules.

The descent into steep Horse Canyon proceeds on a great

number of switchbacks that zigzag down among tall, elegant silver pine trees past plentiful patches of daisies, groundsel, phlox, brodiaea, paintbrush and whorled penstemon, among other blossoms. At a natural overlook spot less than a mile down, the far-gazing hiker can see deep into Summit City Canyon and the Mokelumne River Canyon. Farther south, standing above the south canyon rim, are some peaks beyond Kennedy Meadow, including Cooper Peak, Granite Dome and Three Chimneys.

Shortly after, our descending trail passes a trail that leads back to Squaw Ridge. After a few more switchbacks, the trail grade abates to moderate, and then almost to level, as it winds through a delightful meadowy area with lots of grass growing underneath a moderate cover of lodgepole pines, and flower swatches flanking bubbling little streams. This would be a fine camping area for lovers of seclusion. It was not always so secluded. Horse Canyon was part of the route of one emigrant trail, and eye bolts can still be found in some trees, where they were used to rope the wagons up or down.

After a mile of this meadowy forest, our trail crosses the Horse Canyon stream to its east side and leaves the main draw of the canyon, passing east over a ridge. A new section of well-graded trail reconstructed in 1990 provides an easy descent toward the canyon floor and allows the descender to lift his eyes to enjoy the surrounding greenery and flowers, and to look down to the bottom of Summit City Canyon, far below. Gentle switchbacks lead the last ½ mile down to the Tahoe-Yosemite Trail beside Summit City Creek. Fair-to-good campsites lie near the junction. Fishing is fair-to-good for rainbow (to 10") in Summit City Creek.

3rd and 4th Hiking Days: Retrace your steps, 10 miles.

Silver Lake to the Mokelumne River **3**

Distance 29 miles
Type Round trip
Best season Mid
Topo maps Silver Lake
Grade (hiking days/recommended layover days)
   Leisurely 6/1
   Moderate 5/1
   Strenuous 4/0
Trailhead 1

HIGHLIGHTS The largest wilderness river in the northern
                Sierra is the goal of this trip. Virgin forests here
shade the cool, green river, brown trout often rise to the fly, and
except at trail crossings solitude is plentiful.

DESCRIPTION (Leisurely trip)

1st and 2nd Hiking Days: Follow Trip 2 to **Summit City
Canyon**, 10 miles.

3rd Hiking Day (**Summit City Canyon** to the **Mokelumne River**, 4.5 miles): Some readers have complained that
previous editions didn't mention the rattlesnakes in Summit
City Canyon and along the Mokelumne River. Now they are
mentioned. But we have yet to see one there.

Several hundred yards below the Horse Canyon Trail junction, our route, following the Tahoe-Yosemite Trail, easily
crosses the Horse Canyon stream and then winds down Summit
City Creek to cross Telephone Gulch. The main canyon narrows, but not so much as to force our path right next to the
creek, and we follow a sandy duff tread across flats dotted with

many lodgepole pines and aspens. The commonest flower here, as it has been since before we reached the floor of Summit City Canyon, is the pink-cupped sidalcea. The second commonest has been squaw root, also called yampa, with hundreds of little white flowers making up flattish flowerheads. Finally the regular trail ends just beyond a charming if now illegal campsite right beside the creek.

From here to the Mokelumne River, the essentially cross-country route is variously marked, and sometimes more clear, sometimes less, but at worst you will be delayed in your passage; you can't get lost. You should cross Summit City Creek about 200 yards downstream from the illegal campsite, at a point where deep, narrow channels in the bedrock can contain all the stream flow except in early season, and immediately scramble up the east slope before veering south to parallel the stream. You will go behind a knoll about 30 feet high with a small Jeffrey pine on it, and then proceed parallel to the creek but separated from it by a series of rock prominences. From time to time ducks give some guidance.

About ½ mile from the main stream crossing, we dip down beside a very small stream and parallel it for ½ mile, then cross it and contour high on a red-fir-shaded hillside, looking down on a green, aspen-dotted flat where Summit City Creek meanders south. After a little bushwhacking through willow thickets, we descend on open granite to an almost flat area near the stream, then on a fallen log cross a tributary that runs till late summer. After penetrating more brush, we again descend on open granite, this time to a large, sandy-bottomed pool below a spectacular cataract on Summit City Creek. This pool makes a fine lunch spot.

From the pool we pick up the ducked route again and make two half-loops away from the creek and back to it. In some places there are competing ducks, but they all lead in the correct general direction. About ¼ mile from the pool we get a good look down into the river canyon, and see that it is not too far below us now. After the second half-loop returns to the creek momentarily, our route veers east, tops a small ridge, and descends steeply south for ¼ mile to a crossing of Summit City Creek. A fallen tree that does not quite reach the north bank may still be here, and would help one across the creek during high water. About 100 yards beyond the crossing, a faint trail forks left and we follow it 300 yards to an unsigned junction in a sandy flat. Turning right here, we reach, in 300 more yards, a sign indicating *Cedar Camp Trail.* A few yards farther is the beautiful, clear Mokelumne River.

If you miss these faint trails, you can of course just follow Summit City Creek down to its confluence with the river. There are good campsites near the confluence. Fishing in the river for brown and rainbow trout (to 14″), is good—better if you go upstream, because that's tough walking.

4th, 5th, and 6th Hiking Days: Retrace your steps, 14.5 miles.

Mokelumne River near Summit City Creek

4   Silver Lake to Long Lake

Distance   13 miles
Type   Round trip
Best season   Mid
Topo maps   Silver Lake
Grade (hiking days/recommended layover days)
    Leisurely 2/0
    Moderate ---
    Strenuous ---
Trailhead   2

DESCRIPTION (Leisurely trip)

From Highway 88 at Tragedy Springs, a 4WD vehicle with high clearance can be driven on the Mud Lake Road past Allen's Ranch, to the trailhead on Squaw Ridge just south of Plasse's old trading-post site. Driving to the trailhead at the Mokelumne Wilderness Boundary will shorten the hike by over 3 miles each way.

1st Hiking Day (**Silver Lake** to **Long Lake**, 6.5 miles): Near the informal parking area at Plasse's Resort, a dirt road fords a small unnamed stream and heads south past Stockton Municipal Camp on the right. Our wide, dusty trail leaves the road as we continue southbound in a moderate forest of small lodgepole pines east of the creek. Soon the trail begins to rise gradually, and then more steeply, under a welcome forest canopy of red fir and lodgepole pine. It passes several long, grassy meadows flanking the unnamed stream, fine spots for a breather stop or an early lunch. In 1½ miles our route passes a junction with a trail to Hidden Lake and then reaches the steep south wall of the basin we have been ascending. Here the path proceeds by way of long switchbacks up a mountain-hemlock-shaded volcanic slope. Views from the ridgetop include Silver Lake and Hidden Lake in the northern foreground, the Crystal Range and the Jacks Peak-Dicks Peak range farther north in

Desolation Wilderness, and in the south, the meadow that we will walk through south of Allen's ranch, and the top of buff-brown Mokelumne Peak.

About 75 yards downhill from this saddle we meet a dirt road. (The northbound hiker could identify the place to leave the dirt road by noting that beyond Allen's ranch a two-track rough road veers right from the main dirt road at a pile of several hundred tan volcanic rocks.) Our route eastward on the dusty dirt road descends gently past the entrance to Allen's ranch and crosses the headwaters of Bear River—at this point not even a trickle in late summer. Shortly beyond, we ford running water in the lee of hundreds of brilliant yellow mimulus flowers and reach a sort of parking area for 4WD vehicles. Just beyond, we veer right on a trail as the jeep road ascends left-ward, and traverse gently up in the shade of pine and hemlock to Squaw Ridge.

The junction on the ridge is in the middle of a forest of signs, identifying the Squaw Ridge Trail going northeast and south-west, the site of Plasse's Trading Post of Gold Rush days, and our Cedar Camp Trail, numbered 17E27. Here also we enter the 105,165 acre Mokelumne Wilderness. About 130 yards down our trail from this sign, a jeep road continues toward Pardoe Lake. In another 110 yards, at the bottom of the hill and across the road from a blazed lodgepole tree, is Horsethief Springs, where amid more yellow mimulus a pipe delivers the best drinking water on this entire trip, a fine place for lunch. Continuing on the two-track road, our route soon arrives at the former border of Mokelumne Wilderness, which was enlarged in 1984 by Congressional action from 50,165 acres to 105,165 acres, to be held forever in trust for those who prefer their out-doors unmechanized.

In the wilderness our route for the next mile is almost level, slightly down, past several large meadows awash in corn lilies, groundsel and lupine in midseason. After a short descent on open hillside, the trail leads down through cool forest with a very green understory. Then it levels again in a moderate forest cover of pine and fir and passes the trail to Black Rock Lake. The next descent, over open granite slabs that look south to the plateau around our destination and to Mokelumne Peak, passes a signed trail to Cole Creek Lakes. The sign is nailed to a lodge-pole pine near its base, and is easily missed. These lakes are a

fine alternative campsite for this trip. The largest lake is ½ mile
south on the lateral trail, and swimming and fishing for rainbow and brook trout are excellent.

Continuing on the Cedar Camp Trail, we wind among
boulders shaded by silver and lodgepole pine and descend
rockily to cross the dwindling outlet of a small lakelet which is
the southernmost of the Cole Creek Lakes. A use trail up its
east side leads to the main lake, mentioned above.

Now in red-fir forest, our path switchbacks down for a mile
of decreasing gradient, recrossing the dwindling outlet, to the
signed turnoff to Long Lake. Here we turn east and wind levelly
beside snowmelt ponds for a short ½ mile to the west end of
warm, reedy, tree-bound Long Lake. Fishing for brook trout (to
14″) is fair, with a midsummer slowdown, and swimming from
the granite slabs at the east end is first-rate. At night, you may
be entertained by the excited calls of convening coyotes. On
my first visit here, before I knew any were around, I let out a
yip-yip, and was astounded that two real ones answered.

2nd Hiking Day: Retrace your steps, 6.5 miles.

Brook trout from Long Lake

Silver Lake to Camp Irene

5

Distance	25 miles
Type	Round trip
Best season	Mid
Topo maps	Silver Lake

Grade (hiking days/recommended layover days)

> *Leisurely* 5/1
> *Moderate* 4/0
> *Strenuous* 3/0

Trailhead 2

HIGHLIGHTS The hiker taking this trip will stop overnight at two highly contrasting places. Long Lake is at 8000 feet elevation, in the cool belt, and the green water is still, with no visible inflow or outflow after early season. In contrast, the Mokelumne River is a good-sized, clear-flowing river at an elevation of only 5000 feet, where middays can be very hot.

DESCRIPTION (Moderate trip)

1st Hiking Day: Follow Trip 4 to **Long Lake**, 6.5 miles.

2nd Hiking Day (**Long Lake** to **Camp Irene**, 6 miles): After retracing the short lateral trail to Long Lake, this day's route turns left (south) on the Cedar Camp Trail and rises gradually through a dense forest of fir and pine. Many rivulets lace this slope into midseason, and their courses are fertile growing grounds for lavender shooting stars and other meadow flowers. As the grade levels off, the trail swings eastward and soon arrives at green, sloping Munson Meadow, where in late season you will find the first flowing water since Horsethief Springs. For northbound hikers, it is the first water since the beginning of the long, unshaded climb up the manzanita-lined sandy trail from the "oasis" in the Mokelumne River canyon.

From Munson Meadow the trail wanders southeast over a forested plateau for a mile before it starts to descend in earnest into the river canyon. At first, the trail is rocky and dusty, shaded by a sparse forest cover of red firs. Then it steepens and becomes completely exposed to the sun as it leads down a series of long switchback legs on very sandy underfooting. Views across the canyon are quite expansive, and time passes quickly—for the descending traveler. Coming back is a very different story.

Nearly 2 miles from the start of the switchbacks, the trail, still steep, enters much more hospitable territory where all-year water allows alders, willows, aspens and a great panoply of wildflowers to flourish. About 100 yards below the first of these wet "oasis" areas is a flat spot where one could camp if he were up-bound and exhausted. The trail continues to descend, moderately to steeply, but it is well shaded much of the time, and it often crosses unmapped streams that flow all year. At these streams the thirsty hiker can pleasure his mouth with the sweet water (purify it) and pleasure his eyes with the multicolors of orange tiger lily, pink columbine, yellow groundsel and white milfoil flowers, and the rich green of bracken ferns. After about four stream crossings—depending on the season—it is a steep 200-yard descent on a rocky-dusty trail to the junction of the unmapped trail up the river canyon and the trail down to Camp Irene.

Turning right here, our route descends to a stream not shown on the map and follows it down to the river, passing a 1974 burn shortly before reaching Camp Irene. This camping area has a sandy beach, fine granite slabs, lovely pools—and a lot of campers, since it is a popular overnight stop along the Tahoe-Yosemite Trail. Those who need solitude will find it up or down the river. Fishing in the Mokelumne is good for brown and rainbow trout (to 14").

3rd and 4th Hiking Days: Retrace your steps, 12.5 miles.

Silver Lake to the Mokelumne River **6**

Distance   28.2 miles
Type   Shuttle trip
Best season   Mid
Topo maps   Silver Lake
Grade (hiking days/recommended layover days)
   Leisurely 6/2
   Moderate 5/1
   Strenuous 4/0
Trailhead   1, 2

HIGHLIGHTS This tour visits examples of all the landscapes of the Carson Pass region—volcanic peaks, rounded granite domes, deep-cut river canyons and lake-dotted plateaus. Anyone in good condition who has the basic skills for hiking cross country will enjoy this long shuttle trip.

DESCRIPTION (Moderate trip; would be leisurely but for the 4th hiking day)

1st, 2nd and 3rd Hiking Days: Follow Trip 3 to the **Mokelumne River**, 14.5 miles.

4th Hiking Day (**Mokelumne River** to **Long Lake**, 7.2 miles): (This trail description as far as the junction with the trail to Camp Irene is quite detailed because the multiplicity of trails and paths in the region west of Summit City Creek makes route finding a problem.) From the *Cedar Camp Trail* sign, retrace your steps 300 yards to the unsigned junction in a sandy flat and turn left. A bare hundred yards south of this junction, very noticeable ducks lead up a granite slab, more or less straight ahead. Don't follow them. Instead, veer right, and when you top the crest of granite a few feet above you, you will (if it's still there) see a duck which will lead you onto the little-used trail on which you came here from the Tahoe-Yosemite Trail. If you do accidentally follow the prescribed ducked route, you will soon find yourself going down beside the river. Eventually you will have to leave the riverside and climb some cliffs above a gorge, perhaps using rope to haul your pack once or twice. Finally you will arrive at Camp Irene, and from there you can take the Tahoe-Yosemite Trail north 1 mile to its junction with the Munson Meadow Trail, a junction described in later paragraphs.

Back at the Tahoe-Yosemite Trail where we left it yesterday, we turn left, top a small ridge, cross a tributary stream, and descend into a dense forest of second-growth ponderosa pine and incense-cedar with a few delicate ferns on the level forest floor. Then, emerging from this forest, we see that we are close under granite cliffs on the right (north). From here a gentle downgrade takes us past a 5-foot-thick ponderosa, burned through at the base, into a fine forest of first-growth sugar pines, their great cones strewn about the forest floor.

After crossing a stream that flows in early season, our route soon leaves the forest and climbs more than 100 feet on rocky-dusty underfooting, leveling off under a sparse-to-moderate cover of Jeffrey pines, incense-cedars and black oaks. In ⅛ mile after the climb, the eastbound hiker would notice a fork veering right, but he should keep left. From this junction our path makes a steep, sandy ascent for several hundred yards, then drops slightly across exposed granite outcroppings. Just after it swings right, there is another unofficial junction that might beguile an eastbound hiker; he should keep right at this junction. Then one arrives at the signed junction of the trails to Camp Irene (left) and Munson Meadow (right). From here, retrace the steps of most of the 2nd hiking day, Trip 5, to Long Lake. The ascent you will make out of the Mokelumne River canyon is very stiff indeed, and the earlier you start this hiking day, the better.

5th Hiking Day: Reverse the 1st hiking day of Trip 4, 6.5 miles.

Carson Pass to Showers Lake   7

Distance	10.2 miles
Type	Round trip
Best season	Mid
Topo maps	Silver Lake

Grade (hiking days/recommended layover days)
  Leisurely 2/1
  Moderate 2/0
  Strenuous ---
Trailhead   4

HIGHLIGHTS Showers Lake is one of the best camping places between U.S. 50 and State Highway 88, with numerous campsites and good angling for brook trout. En route, the trail through the upper Truckee Valley offers panoramic views of immense volcanic formations and promises potential close-up glimpses of many birds and mammals.

DESCRIPTION

1st Hiking Day (**Carson Pass** to **Showers Lake**, 5.1 miles): From a parking area (8350′) 0.9 mile west of Carson Pass our dusty route climbs steadily northward on a slope moderately forested with red fir, lodgepole pine and clumps of aspen. Leaving the tree cover behind, we climb steeply up a corrugated slope covered by fragrant sagebrush and mule ears. In the warm sun of this open slope the sage odor adds spice to the thin, clear air.

After ⅓ mile of climbing, we join the Pacific Crest Trail coming in on our right from Carson Pass. Views southward expand, and after ascending 400 feet in ½ mile, the trail reaches a pond-dotted saddle on the divide between Truckee River drainage and American River drainage. From this saddle views southward of Round Top Peak and its snow-draped satellites are excellent. In the north, we see Mt. Tallac, Dicks Peak and Jacks Peak, all west of Tahoe. Here we begin a descent down the long, green, tree-dotted valley of the upper Truckee. Nearby on the east, Red Lake Peak is topped by slablike volcanic outcroppings resembling a stegosaur's back plates. An easy scramble to its summit would yield panoramic views.

Down here, little runoff streams that spring from porous volcanic rocks trickle their water onto flower gardens of iris, yarrow milfoil, Mariposa lily, sulfur flower, lupine and paint-brush. Descending moderately to steadily from the summit, we cross three runoff streams (dry in late season), then a westward-flowing tributary, and finally the infant Truckee River—all via easy fords.

Just past another easy ford are the buildings of a cow camp, and near them the Round Lake Trail branches right. The meadows here are full of little gray Belding squirrels, com-monly called picket-pins, and often a Swainson hawk soars overhead, hoping to surprise one of them. Continuing the level walk from the Round Lake junction, we pass an unsigned trail to Meiss Lake, visible as a meadow-fringed blue sheet in the northeast. Then one last time we ford the river, on boulders, and a few feet beyond the ford an old jeep road forks right toward Meiss Lake, as our route bears left.

We pass a trail to Schneider Camp (marked by a blazed **S** on the lodgepole), and ascent out of Dixon Canyon on a gentle grade. From the crest of this little ascent, the trail dips past a shallow, weedy pond and continues on the old two-track jeep road. After crossing two runoff streams (dry in late season), we begin a steady-to-steep ascent of ¼ mile, first up a wash filled with smoothed, round rocks, and then on a rocky-dusty trail, under moderate-to-dense forest cover of red fir, hemlock, silver pine and lodgepole pine. Sixty yards after the jeep tracks emerge from this forest onto a meadowy slope lush with lupine and mule ears, a trail veers slightly left and uphill from the tracks, and we take the trail. (The old jeep road also goes to Showers Lake.) This trail section traverses a bountifully flowered, meadowy slope to a forested saddle overlooking Showers Lake, from where it descends to the fair-to-good campsites on the west and east sides of the lake (8650'). Fishing is good for eastern brook (to 12"). From a base camp here, one may easily walk cross country to Four Lakes, where fishing and swimming are often good in mid-to-late season.

2nd Hiking Day: Retrace your steps, 5.1 miles.

Carson Pass to Echo Summit 8

Distance	12.6 miles
Type	Shuttle trip
Best season	Mid
Topo maps	Silver Lake, **Fallen Leaf Lake**

Grade (hiking days/recommended layover days)

Leisurely 2/1
Moderate 2/0
Strenuous ---

Trailhead 4, 3

HIGHLIGHTS This trip offers one of the easiest ways in the whole northern Sierra to get away from the crowd, and it is an excellent choice for a two-party shuttle. With a minimum of effort, the hiker can traverse some high, scenic, little-used country, where the wildlife is as plentiful as the people are scarce.

DESCRIPTION

1st Hiking Day: Follow Trip 7 to **Showers Lake**, 5.1 miles.

2nd Hiking Day (**Showers Lake** to **Echo Summit**, 7.5 miles). Heading northwest from the southwest shore of Showers Lake, we soon find the trail, and then ascend gently for several hundred yards through mixed conifers. Coming out onto open slopes, we ford a year-round stream fed by the snow cornice that drapes the ridge of Little Round Top above. Where we cross this stream, its banks are lined with thousands of blossoms of the showy yellow flower *Arnica chamissionis*. In fact, this whole open bowl is laced with runoff streams and lavishly planted with colorful bushes and flowers: blue elderberry, green gentian, swamp whiteheads, mountain bluebell, aster, wallflower, penstemon, spiraea, cinquefoil, corn lily and columbine. As we walk around this bowl on the boundary between volcanic rocks above and granite below, we have good views of Stevens Peak and Red Lake Peak, both built up of layers of richly colored volcanic flows.

Finally, the trail ascends out of the bowl and enters a sparse cover of lodgepole and silver pine. At the crest of this ascent, the pine gives way to hemlock as we pass a cattle drift fence (close the gate) and level off through open high country. Reaching a willowy meadow, one may lose the trail momentarily, but it is easy to find if one continues straight across the meadow. A short distance beyond is a junction with a signed trail to Schneider Cow Camp, which leads west. One third of a mile beyond this junction our route crosses, at right angles, an unsigned but well-grooved trail which is used by local stockmen, and then continues its almost level, winding course northward under a sparse-to-moderate mixed forest cover.

We then pass a collapsed stock fence and make a short, steep descent down a hemlock-covered hillside to a meadowy slope where marsh marigolds, their white and yellow petals set off by their rich green leaves, bloom in the wetness of melting snows until late in the season. Our sandy footpath soon passes a trail that winds down Sayles Canyon, and then we continue north to a summit from where views of the Crystal Range, including Pyramid Peak, are good. From here it is a gentle descent under hemlock and silver and lodgepole pine to Bryan Meadow. Here one may camp except in late season, when the stream is dry. A collapsed log cabin in the meadow sprawls near the confluence of routes leading to Showers Lake, U.S. 50 and Benwood Meadow.

Heading for Benwood Meadow, we ascend a gently rising sandy trail through meadowy, open stands of lodgepole pine, with some sagebrush. The alert hiker here may spot a redshafted flicker on one of its characteristic undulating flights between trees. At the top of this sandy climb the trail levels off and becomes indistinct, but the route is well marked by blazes. A short, steep descent then brings us to a willow-filled bowl where an unnamed stream rises. We cross the young stream and on the far slope veer right, on a trail that soon switchbacks steeply down a red-fir-covered slope. At the foot of the slope is another willowy meadow, and shortly beyond that another steep downslope, also shaded by red fir, where following the route may require attention to the occasional ducks. The trail then levels out in a large meadow that was once a lake, skirting the west side of it.

The trail from this meadow to Benwood Meadow is some-times indistinct, but there are sufficient blazes and ducks. At Benwood Meadow the flora is quite noteworthy: along the wet meadow margin the flower-spotter is kept busy by the pleni-tude of aster, corn lily, snow plant, alpine lily, monkey flower, penstemon, false Solomon's seal, squawroot, pennyroyal, groundsel, columbine, larkspur and mountain bluebell, to say nothing of the ferns, grasses and sedges.

Past Benwood Meadow, our nearly level trail meets a junc-tion with a trail that goes left to a ski resort near Echo Summit. Then it dips to cross the outlet of a lily-filled pond, and ascends gently up a rather exposed slope, where a few mixed conifers partially shade a ground cover of huckleberry oak, pinemat manzanita and Sierra chinquapin. Finally, the rocky-dusty trail ends at a graded road (7520') that serves a small tract of sum-mer homes ⅓ mile south of Echo Summit.

Ebbetts Pass

The wilderness flanking Ebbetts Pass is probably the least-used area in the whole Sierra Nevada. One reason is that it doesn't have a lot of lakes. But it does have volcanic formations aplenty, and many year-round streams. The East Fork of the Carson River is a just-barely-discovered beauty.

Hikers who want to let their bodies acclimate overnight before hitting the trail can stay in style at Lake Alpine Lodge or at the accommodations in Bear Valley. Markleeville is not far away, and just south of Markleeville is the East Fork Resort— although these places are not as high as one might wish for acclimating.

Highway 4 provides the best access to the 160,871-acre Carson-Iceberg Wilderness, goal of most of the trips in this chapter. Few people know the name of this wilderness, and as a result you are likely to find solitude in it.

Mosquito Lake to Bull Run Lake **9**

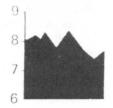

Distance	8 miles
Type	Shuttle trip
Best season	Mid
Topo maps	Markleeville, Dardanelles Cone

Grade (hiking days/recommended layover days)

    Leisurely 3/0
    Moderate 2/0
    Strenuous ---

Trailhead   8, 9

HIGHLIGHTS   Two of the better, scenic, trout-stocked lakes of the Lake Alpine area are visited on this easy hike. Dayhikers and fishermen may wish to hike only to Heiser Lake via the Heiser Lake Trail or only to larger Bull Run Lake via the Bull Run Trail, thereby avoiding the short 2½-mile shuttle.

DESCRIPTION (Leisurely trip)

1st Hiking Day (**Mosquito Lake** to **Heiser Lake**, 2 miles): At the west end of Mosquito Lake in a picnic ground, look for a faint trail that follows old blazes southeast, directly up a forested slope. In about 30 yards, the trail becomes obvious, leading up granitic bedrock that has a veneer of volcanic rocks. The steep trail quickly levels off, then makes a short, moderate descent and winds south close to a pond that is erroneously labeled "Heiser Lake" on the *Markleeville* topo map.

Leaving the pond's environs, we climb steeply through a thinning forest of silver and lodgepole pine and mountain hemlock, and surmount a granitic ridge at its low point. On fresh-looking, glacially scoured rock we descend from the ridge and follow a winding route that takes the path of least resistance down slabs. After leveling off in deep forest, we climb ⅓ mile to a junction on a little flat. Tomorrow we'll head south-west from here down a creekside trail, but since our immediate goal is Heiser Lake, we turn east, hike a short ¼ mile uphill, then switchback and climb south over a low granitic ridge that hides the shallow lake. Dotted with several small islands of granitic rock, this conifer-fringed lake presents the fisherman with a picturesque distraction while he contemplates a meal of fresh brook trout. Campsites lie on the north and south shores under a pleasant canopy of red fir, lodgepole pine, silver pine and mountain hemlock.

2nd Hiking Day (**Heiser Lake** to **Bull Run Lake**, 2.5 miles): First, retrace your steps ½ mile to yesterday's trail junction. From here our route, usually well blazed and ducked, takes us southwest to the brink of a rocky slope, and then down the slope via very steep switchbacks. We then stay fairly close to Heiser Lake's outlet creek, paralleling it west across a flat basin shaded by mountain hemlocks. Approaching the basin's west edge, we cross four closely spaced branches of a tributary that joins the outlet creek just south of the trail. After a brief climb west, our trail turns south and leads to a signed junction with the Bull Run Trail.

From the junction, this route almost immediately fords Heiser Lake's outlet creek, a ford that could require a little doing in early season when it is a small torrent of white water. After following an almost level granitic bench for ⅓ mile, this route angles south and crosses the first of many creeklets. Our winding route goes from slab to granitic slab as it climbs and gyrates up toward the lake. Were it not for a superabundance of blazes and ducks, some hikers would get off route. This climb is broken into distinct ascents, the first one trending southeast up and around a secondary ridge, the second one trending south-west past a trailside pond before it approaches Bull Run Lake's outlet creek and ascends near it to the lake's bedrock dam.

Although not large by Sierra standards, this popular lake can accommodate dozens of campers, particularly on the spacious flats beneath large red firs. Swimming in the lake is good in early August, and fishing is often good for brook trout.

3rd Hiking Day (**Bull Run Lake** to **Stanislaus Meadow**, 3.5 miles): After backtracking to the trail junction just west of Heiser Lake's outlet, our route stays on the Bull Run Trail as it winds, steeply at times, 350 vertical feet down rock slabs covered with lodgepole and silver pine, red fir and mountain juniper, well above the outlet creek from both lakes before it eases off in a shady flat. A short forest traverse brings us to a crossing of this creek, which in early season can entail a cold, wide, knee-deep ford. Beyond the ford we follow the creek a shady, long ⅓ mile to a refording of two branches of it, which will give early-season hikers another challenge. The trail from the ford maintains a westbound course for 100 yards to an even wider ford, the headwaters of North Fork Stanislaus River. As usual, look for logs across the stream, which may make fording drier and perhaps much quicker.

Immediately beyond the North Fork we cross a seasonally dry wash before turning north and roughly paralleling the North Fork upstream. A wide path leads up this moderate grade, and, near its top, we may be greeted by a chorus of cowbells, which incessantly ring as their wearers munch away in Stanislaus Meadow. A fence keeps the cattle in the meadow and us in the forest while an easy ½ mile hike along its west side brings us to the Bull Run Lake trailhead.

Bull Run Lake *Jeff Schaffer*

Wolf Creek Meadows to Soda Springs

10

Distance	20.5 miles
Type	Semi loop trips; part cross-country
Best season	Mid
Topo maps	Topaz Lake

Grade (hiking days/recommended layover days)
  Leisurely 3/1
  Moderate 2/0
  Strenuous ---
Trailhead 6

HIGHLIGHTS One can acquire a good feeling for eastside Sierra flora and geology on this trip, ideally suited for weekend backpackers. Because the landscape is viewed from a crest route going and a canyon route returning, the hiker sees it from two very different perspectives.

DESCRIPTION (Moderate trip)

1st Hiking Day (**Wolf Creek Meadows** to **Soda Springs Guard Station**, 9.5 miles): At the edge of a volcanic slope covered with sagebrush, mule ears and bitterbrush, the High Trail climbs upward into an open forest of Jeffrey pine and white fir. With the brief views of Wolf Creek Meadows behind us, we now enjoy the shade that the forest provides on this steep climb. Beyond a large split boulder and its surrounding mountain mahogany bushes, the High Trail parallels the ridge up to a level crest, then climbs steeply to a small, grassy flat. Just beyond this flat, we start an uphill traverse across a grassy, gentle slope that contains a curious combination of water-loving, white-barked aspens almost next to drought-resistant, mangy-barked junipers. Jeffrey pines, white firs, willows, mule ears and sagebrush complete the cast of principal plants. Here, taking a break, one can easily fall asleep to the soothing sounds of rustling aspen leaves.

Up these shady slopes we climb, and about ½ mile beyond the meadow, the steep trail eases up and then levels off as it comes to an open slope. Here the trail provides a momentary view of the Vaquero Camp buildings in the east, down in Silver King Valley, and more enduring views of the granitic Freel Peak area, in the northwest, beyond whose summits lies Lake Tahoe.

Along our short, open traverse we find a good exposure of a type of blocky volcanic rock that is common to this "land of fire and ice." It is called an *autobrecciated* ("self-broken") lava flow. From the middle Miocene epoch through the late Pliocene epoch, thick andesitic lava flows poured from summits that probably resembled today's Oregon Cascades, and they covered an area of the Sierra Nevada that extended from Sonora Pass north to Lassen Park and from east of the present Sierra crest westward to the Central Valley. When the thick lava flows cooled as they flowed along their downward paths, they became less and less able to move, particularly along their rapidly cooling edges, and eventually these edges solidified. But then the pressure of the still-flowing internal material fractured the edges, creating the broken-up texture we see here.

At the base of an autobrecciated flow decorated with vine maples, we enter a shady white-fir forest and encounter a refreshing, flowery, mossy, spring-fed creeklet. Beyond it our trail climbs moderately eastward, then descends slightly to a low knoll covered with ragged mountain mahogany. Leaving the knoll, we pass through a forest of pines and firs, and descend steeply south into two seasonal, parallel creeklets that drain Snowslide Canyon. Volcanic rocks give way to granitic ones as we leave this broad, brushy canyon, descend through a shady forest, round a jagged, granitic ridge, and then reach another seasonal creek.

One-fourth mile beyond this creek, our trail tops out at a bedrock saddle on a ridge above the East Carson canyon. From it, short switchbacks lead steeply down a brushy slope covered with huckleberry oak and manzanita; then our trail diagonals southwest down to a gentle slope on which we cross an unsigned east-west trail. Soon we reach a bubbling creek, and cross it only 90 yards before arriving at East Fork Carson River. If you don't like river fords, you can camp along or near the riverbank, and later backtrack ⅓ mile to the east-west trail and follow it east ¼ mile to another river ford. (Those who ford the East Carson southbound on this trip will reford it here.)

Before mid-July, the river is usually waist-deep, about 50°F at most, and swift, but by Labor Day it has dropped to knee depth. A rope helps in an early-season traverse across the river's bouldery bottom, but it is unnecessary for the experienced backpacker, since there are no dangerous rapids downstream.

For those who fish this river, a likely catch is the mountain whitefish, which looks like a cross between a trout and a sucker. A small mouth on the lower part of its head is the sucker characteristic, but the presence of an adipose fin on the lower back identifies it as a close relative of trout and salmon. Like these fish, it is good to eat. This river also contains the Tahoe sucker, whose protractile mouth, on the bottom of its head, is ideally suited for scavenging the river bottom. Although bony, it is tasty.

Across the river, the High Trail ends in 80 yards at a signed junction with the East Carson River Trail—an old jeep road closed to motor vehicles. On this gravelly road we parallel the river ⅓ mile upstream to the north edge of a sagebrush flat. Here the river angles west, but our tracks head south through dense sagebrush. Reaching a dry wash debouching from a small, very bouldery gorge, we climb up it to a low bedrock saddle. From the saddle we make a short descent past a small, steep cliff, on the right, then reach a larger, longer, steeper one, on the left. This cliff we parallel southeast, then continue to three close-spaced Jeffrey pines in a sagebrush flat. From between the west and south pines, the main route goes 200 yards southwest to a ford of the East Carson, then south along jeep tracks through a shady forest to a refording of the East Carson one mile later. This refording takes place at the "bottom" (south) curve of a large meander, whose west half dries up late in the summer, when the lower river shoots directly east 150 yards to the ford (see the accompanying map). Eventually, the meander will disappear as the river establishes a more efficient, more direct course. About 250 yards south of this ford, in a field of granitic boulders left by a glacier, an indistinct trail heads east-southeast through the grass another 250 yards to Poison Creek, just beyond whose east bank is a path that leads south 300 yards to the Soda Springs Guard Station.

Most hikers, when they arrive at the three Jeffrey pines, will prefer not to ford and reford the East Carson, even though these two fords are considerably easier than the High Trail ford. For them there is a dry route to the Soda Springs Guard Station. After leaving between the south and east pines, follow a path south-southeast for 100 yards. If you're on the right path—there are many cow paths—it will bend south and soon reach a

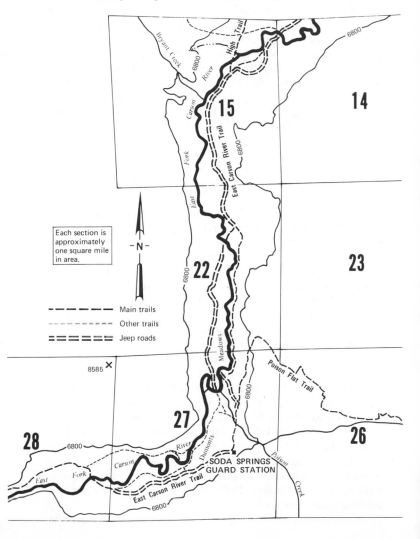

granitic cliff that plunges down to the East Carson only ¼ mile
due south of the three pines. Once around the bouldery base of
this small cliff, you have an easy, open walk southward that
parallels the East Carson.

About ¾ mile beyond, the river bends west and you follow it
on a faint trail through sagebrush to the northeast corner of the
large meander mentioned in the alternate route. From this
corner a set of jeep tracks leads southeast 1/5 mile across a flat
to a signed junction with the Poison Flat Trail, just within forest
cover. Trip 13 heads north along this trail, and trips 15 and 16
head south along it to this junction. We turn south, up-canyon,
and follow the jeep tracks, which quickly reduce to a path in the
100 yards it takes to reach the first of as many as half a dozen
distributaries of Poison Creek. Between two of them, the alternate route—a footpath from the west-northwest—ends at our
broad path. A little beyond we meet the fenced-in compound
around Soda Springs Guard Station. You can camp by multibranched Poison Creek, or a small creek ⅓ mile along the trail
west of the guard station provides another possibility.

2nd Hiking Day (**Soda Springs Guard Station** to **Wolf
Creek Meadows**, 11 miles): First, retrace your steps 2¾ miles
to the signed High Trail junction. This day's route continues on
a jeep road going northeast from the junction, then quickly
curves right as it rounds an open flat. In 0.4 mile from the High
Trail junction, we arrive at an East Carson ford which is almost
as difficult as the High Trail ford. Our next segment of jeep
road starts northeast up a flat and crosses it, then is almost cut
in two by a river's meander that has eroded deeply into the flat.
Beyond the meander, a traverse across an equally long flat ends
at the East Carson one mile below the High Trail junction.

Here, look for two large Jeffrey pines just north of you, between which a barbed-wire gate marks the start of a trail. From
the gate this trail stays on the west side of the East Carson,
paralleling the river at first, but gradually veering away from it.
We cross two long, but not high, moraines—those bouldery,
sandy ridges left by a glacier before it retreated back up the
East Carson canyon and into extinction. Beyond the second
moraine is a seasonal creeklet which we cross only 70 yards
west of the East Carson. The trail now parallels the river to a
junction with some jeep tracks.

We follow these north almost ½ mile up to a low ridgecrest

of a rocky moraine that marks the northernmost extent of a former glacier in Silver King Valley. Atop this moraine is a barbed-wire fence across the jeep tracks. Our challenging route leaves the jeep tracks atop the moraine, follows the fence west about 300 yards to a gate, descends to the entrance of the gorge, and follows the river's west side 2½ miles.

The difficulty of this gorge route varies, the hardest part occurring in the scenic first half. When the water is low—after Labor Day—you can walk along the river's edge, but in early season you'll have to climb above it many times. Nevertheless, a rope is not necessary. At first, you'll pass by impressive, deeply cut cliffs of autobrecciated lava flows. Farther down, you're likely to see columnar flows in addition. Campsites in this isolated gorge are plentiful, but unfortunately the best ones are on the opposite bank. This route ends at the official trail, which fords the East Carson at Gray's Crossing, directly west of a low gap.

From the crossing, the East Carson River Trail heads west, then climbs steeply up to gentler slopes above the river. Soon we reach a gate, pass through it, and gradually curve westward into Railroad Canyon. Up this canyon we hike, seemingly too long to be on the right route, and then we cross its creeklet. From here, the last permanent source of fresh water, our trail climbs north out of the canyon, circles along the edge of a flat-topped autobrecciated lava flow, then traverses ⅓ mile northwest to the south tip of shallow Wolf Creek Lake.

From the lake's southeast corner, our trail climbs west up to the base of steep volcanic slopes, then ascends to the ridge above the trailhead, along which runs a fence. On the other side of its gate, we meet the end of a jeep road, and on it walk west a short distance to a saddle, recognizing that the large, scattered granitic boulders resting on the volcanic bedrock are "erratics"—boulders carried here by a large glacier that once flowed north down Wolf Creek canyon. From the saddle we can look up-canyon and imagine how impressive this canyon would have appeared about 6,000 years ago, when a river of ice, hundreds of feet thick, slowly flowed past this spot, quite likely reaching, and occasionally damming, the East Fork Carson River. After a moment's reflection on this subject, we leave the saddle and descend 100 steep yards to our trailhead, which is beside the trailhead of the High Trail.

11 Wolf Creek Meadows to Wolf Creek

Distance   24 miles
Type   Shuttle trip
Best season Mid or late
Topo maps   Topaz Lake, Sonora Pass
Grade (hiking days/recommended layover days)
   Leisurely 3/0
   Moderate   2/0
   Strenuous ---
Trailhead   6, 5

HIGHLIGHTS Like Trip 2, this trip starts as a scenic crest route, then it proceeds through parts of three glaciated canyons. Plenty of creekside campsites await anglers who would like to try their skill at trout fishing.

DESCRIPTION (Moderate trip)

1st Hiking Day (**Wolf Creek Meadows** to **Murray Canyon Trail junction**, 12 miles): First, follow Trip 10 to Soda Springs Guard Station, 9.5 miles. Leaving the shady campground at the guard station, we hike west on a jeep trail and after ⅓ mile cross a spring-fed creeklet. Just beyond this creeklet is a well-used campsite under lodgepole pines, only 20 yards downslope. Immediately below it is a trail coming from the larger meander mentioned in Trip 10 (see the map in Trip 10). Westward, this trail parallels our jeep trail, dying out in a grassy meadow. Our easy route through sagebrush reaches this meadow in ½ mile and the jeep tracks, like the trail, die out in it. They quickly reappear at the northwest end of the meadow and lead us 200 yards northwest to a wide ford of the East Carson.

Continuing northwest we arrive at an unsigned junction. From here our route goes 1½ miles over a trail that is often a multilane cowpath. The trail tends to stay away from the river as it ascends gently through Jeffrey-pine forest. After the canyon heads south, the trail emerges on the edge of a large, cow-infested meadow, on the northwest side of which is a signed junction about 50 yards beyond Murray Canyon creek. Several fair campsites can be found near the cottonwoods along the creek. This creek, and the river provide fair-to-good fishing for rainbow and paiute-rainbow hybrid (to 10").

2nd Hiking Day (**Murray Canyon Trail junction** to **Upper Wolf Creek Meadows**, 12 miles): At the signed trail junction, we leave the gentle gradient of the East Fork Carson River Trail and climb, steeply at times, up 15 switchback legs that lead high on a brushy, open-forested slope and then into Murray Canyon. Like virtually every tributary canyon of the East Carson above Soda Springs, this one usually had a glacier in it when there was one in the main canyon. Being much smaller, however, the Murray Canyon glacier was unable to keep pace with the tremendous excavating power of the East Carson glacier, which in this area was sometimes more than 800 feet thick. As a result, the East Carson glacier cut down faster, leaving Murray Canyon as a hanging valley—which we have just entered at the top of the switchbacks.

From the top of these switchbacks we go another 200 yards to the verdant banks of clear Murray Canyon creek. After 100 steep yards, the trail resumes a moderate grade and takes us past the first of many flower-lined creeklets. One-third mile up from the creek crossing, we pass through the gate of a cattle fence, then continue up the flowery path. At a trail junction where Murray Canyon splits in two, our trail, the main one, bends right and climbs steeply west up the canyon.

About ¼ mile above the junction is a permanent creek, lined with willows and alders; then in another ¼ mile the trail crosses a second creek. Beyond it the route steepens, on a few short switchbacks up a granitic slope. Talus that has fallen from volcanic formations above has buried much of the granitic bedrock, and it becomes very widespread as the grade eases and the trail enters a small gully flowered with mule ears. Beyond this gully, we climb steadily north ½ mile to a crest saddle, where, a few yards northwest of the actual crest, there is a junction with a fairly new trail. Trip 15, which has coincided with this hiking day up to this saddle, departs south along this crest path.

As we switchback northwest down rather open volcanic slopes, ahead is a flat-topped ridge composed of several thick, horizontal lava flows, below which lies a huge talus slope. This rocky slope was built up after the last glacier retreated up-canyon when water, freezing and expanding in the flows' cracks, pried off countless blocks.

At the bottom of the descent into deep, long Wolf Creek Canyon, we encounter a cattle fence, pass through its gate, and follow the trail as it widens to a jeep road. Joining this short stretch is a jeep spur from the south and, merged together, they head 100 yards northwest to a signed junction, near a conspicuous snow-depth marker, with the Asa Lake Trail. Our route, a jeep road for the remainder of this hike, starts north and quickly reaches a ford—usually a wet one—of Wolf Creek. Across the creek, we amble along an easy path ⅓ mile to a meadow and a signed junction.

Continuing northeast on the jeep road around the fenced meadow, we descend to a creeklet and then parallel Wolf Creek at a short distance, staying above the small gorge it has cut through volcanic rock. Small, tempting pools can be seen in the creek, particularly just before a gate on a low, descending ridge. Beyond the ridge gate, our route descends very steeply to a crossing of Bull Canyon creek, a wet ford except in late season. At this alder-lined crossing, granitic bedrock once again is evident and it becomes more abundant down-canyon.

Strolling down-canyon to Dixon Creek, we approach and veer away from Wolf Creek several times. A long, wide, rocky stream bed has formed behind a constriction in the canyon created by a prominent granitic ridge on the east side and by Dixon Creek's alluvial fan on the west. Since the *Topaz Lake* topo was made, Dixon Creek has shifted its course to a more northern position down across this fan. For most of the summer Dixon Creek runs too high to ford without getting wet feet. Once across it, though, you'll keep your feet dry the rest of the way. The jeep road first parallels the creek, then veers northwest away from it, skirts a grove of aspens and cottonwoods, and curves east around a well-weathered granitic knob. From here it is an easy 1 mile stroll to the trailhead, the Wolf Creek Meadows Undeveloped Camping Area.

Wolf Creek Meadows to Sonora Pass **12**

Distance	30 miles
Type	Shuttle trip
Best season	Mid
Topo maps	Topaz Lake, Sonora Pass

Grade (hiking/recommended layover days)
>   *Leisurely* 5/1
>   *Moderate* 4/0
>   *Strenuous* 3/0

Trailhead	6, 15

HIGHLIGHTS One of the longest and deepest canyons east of the Sierra crest, the East Fork Carson River canyon at times contained glaciers up to 19 miles long. Our trip heads south up this spectacular canyon, stops at scenic Wolf Creek Lake, then passes through a sculptured volcanic "badland" on the south slope of Sonora Peak. This peak—the highest summit between State Highway 108 and Mt. Shasta—is easily climbed in a short side trip.

DESCRIPTION (Strenuous trip)

1st Hiking Day: Follow Trip 11 to **Murray Canyon Trail junction**, 12 miles.

2nd Hiking Day (**Murray Canyon Trail junction** to **Wolf Creek Lake**, 13 miles): Next to granitic bedrock just south of the Murray Canyon Trail junction is a fair campsite. At this campsite Murray Canyon creek blocks our path in early and mid season. During these seasons you may have to wade several yards downstream before you can resume your brief

walk along the west side of this creek. In about 200 yards,
Murray Canyon creek bends east and joins the meandering
East Fork Carson River. Immediately south of the creek's
bend, we join the main path from our starting point. This path,
obvious to northbound hikers, makes four fords of Murray
Canyon creek and, due to willows and grass, is difficult for
southbound hikers to locate. Staying along the East Carson
canyon's meadowy west edge, we now hike about ½ mile south
to a usually flowing creek, cross a very low ridge, and make a
very steep but short ascent, 200 yards to a junction. Here, a ¼-
mile-long alternate route leads east to Carson Falls before
turning south and rejoining the main route. Since both routes

East Fork Carson River   *Jeff Schaffer*

are equally strenuous, the more scenic Carson Falls Trail is certainly recommended.

Midway along this short trail you'll descend briefly to almost level granitic slabs near the lip of the river's gorge. Take your pack off here and then *cautiously* explore the falls and pools of the gorge. Over a period of thousands of years large potholes have been drilled into the bedrock as strong currents have swirled large boulders round and round. When the river's water is low, some potholes make brisk, invigorating swimming holes. If you climb to the top of an almost isolated granitic mass just downstream, you can get the best view of the main falls.

After the Carson Falls Trail rejoins the main trail, we walk through a flat that is being "logged out" by beavers. Entering an aspen grove at the edge of this flat, we curve southeast along a granitic base just above the sometimes swampy flat, and soon reach a ford of the East Carson. If you don't find any dry logs, cross at a wide, shallow place just downstream. A short ½-mile farther, where the river—trapped in a small gorge—turns abruptly west, we leave its company and hike up-canyon to a junction with the Golden Canyon Trail. From the junction our route curves southeast and quickly becomes a steep, brushy climb 400 vertical feet to the top of a granitic mass that has withstood repeated efforts of past glaciers to eradicate it. Leaving its southeast end, our route rollercoasters for ½ mile and touches upon a river meander just before it starts a fairly long climb.

This winding climb crosses a few creek beds before going south up the gully of a north-flowing seasonal creek. Beyond the top of the gully, junipers together with Jeffrey, lodgepole and silver pines are momentarily left behind as we descend into a shady red-fir forest, home of the red squirrel, or chickaree. Our path levels off at a year-round creek and beyond it we parallel the East Carson—usually at a small distance—for 3 miles upstream. The shady path crosses many creeklets as it progresses gently to moderately up-canyon, and along the way one has glimpses of the high cliffs along the canyon's east side.

At the south end of the cliffs, a descending ridge forces our route across the East Carson, which can be a slippery and wet ford in early and mid season. On the west bank, we hike south and in about 150 yards arrive at a junction with the Pacific Crest Trail. One mile from the PCT junction we cross the path of a recent avalanche which built up so much force on its descent of the west slope that it swept across the snow-covered East Carson River and knocked down trees on the east slope.

Beyond a second avalanche path we enter a forest of mature lodgepole pines and in it see more evidence of glaciation. Here, erratics—boulders transported by a glacier—were left behind as the glacier melted back some 12,000 years ago. The glacier that left these erratics was perhaps only 2½ miles long, a midget compared with the massive giant that flowed 19 miles down-canyon perhaps 60,000 years ago. The granitic bedrock over which the more recent one flowed is polished smooth and remains little changed from the day the glacier left it.

A ⅔-mile walk leads to a crossing of a permanent stream, tricky in early season. Then the trail's gradient increases noticeably. Unfortunately, when we sight the windswept saddle we're puffing up to, there is still ⅔ mile of climbing—now up a steep gradient—ahead. Whitebark pines and even late-season snow patches become evident as we make the final push. Finally struggling up to the 10,240-foot-high saddle, we take a well earned rest to pause and admire the view down the glaciated, U-shaped canyon of East Fork Carson River.

From the saddle, the Pacific Crest Trail leads southwest along Sonora Peak's northeast slopes, but this day's hike ends by descending ⅓ mile south to campsites at the west edge of the grassy, frog-inhabited meadow that contains shallow Wolf Creek Lake. A post marks the start of the ducked path down to the lake. In 200 yards along it you'll see the lake, and can take one of several ducked routes down a moderately deep slope to it. At 10,090 feet, the lake is usually pretty cold for swimming, and fishing would yield only frogs. The lake's serene setting, however, renews one's spirit, and while relaxing, you may be fortunate enough to see a large marsh hawk glide across the meadow.

3rd Hiking Day (**Wolf Creek Lake** to **Sonora Pass**, 5 miles): After retracing the steps back to the saddle, we follow the Pacific Crest Trail south. Winding among fractured granitic blocks, we reach a steep, conspicuous ramp. The ramp, unfortunately, is narrow, leaving the trail pitifully small latitude to switchback up it, and snow can obscure parts of this climb well into August. Emerging from it, we encounter two creeklets on a slope covered with wind-cropped willows. View-seekers wishing to climb Sonora Peak can leave the trail here for a stiff but technically easy 1000-foot climb up to its lofty, dark summit.

Granitic bedrock gives way to volcanic rocks and talus as we now traverse south along the east slopes of Sonora Peak. Along this easy stretch one can see how the whitebark pines have been reduced to shrub height by winter's freezing winds. To the east, the effects of glaciation are evident in Wolf Creek canyon, but they are negligible in the distant Sweetwater Mountains. At times, you may see camouflaged U.S. Marines from the nearby Mountain Warfare Training Center. In the field from May through October, these troops participate in war games in an area that includes the Sonora Peak environs, Wolf Creek canyon and Silver Creek canyon. From the saddle southeast of Sonora Peak, the high peaks on the Yosemite border are seen on the distant southeast horizon.

Our trail, now well graded, winds in and out of bleak gullies before coming to the tops of a conspicuous group of volcanic pinnacles that sit right on the Alpine-Mono county line. A 30-yard scramble south to one of their summits permits a sweeping panorama, north-to-east-to-south, of the Pacific Crest Trail and the slopes it traverses, and it also provides a panorama of the Sierra peak summits in the south.

More gullies lie ahead as we descend west. In ½ mile we reach a ridge and double back eastward. Then, hiking south near the crest, we again cross many gullies, so typical of this eroded volcanic landscape. Several of them have good water all year. The sunny slopes between are coated with sagebrush, mule ears, creambush, and a scattering of lodgepole and whitebark pines. Overhead, Clark nutcrackers flap and caw, and red-tailed hawks wheel and soar. Finally, we descend gently to a Pacific Crest Trail parking lot just north of where Highway 108 crosses Sonora Pass.

13 Wolf Creek Meadows to Poison Lake

Distance	36.5 miles
Type	Semiloop trip
Best season	Mid
Topo maps	Topaz Lake, Sonora Pass

Grade (hiking days/recommended layover days)
    Leisurely 5/1
    Moderate 4/0
    Strenuous 2/0
Trailhead   6

HIGHLIGHTS Good fishing and swimming await hikers who backpack into Poison Lake. Along the way, they'll obtain numerous panoramas of large, glaciated canyons and visit several carbonate and soda springs.

DESCRIPTION (Moderate trip)

1st Hiking Day: Follow Trip 10 to **Soda Springs Guard Station**, 9.5 miles.

2nd Hiking Day (**Soda Springs Guard Station** to **Poison Lake**, 8 miles): From the campground at Soda Springs Guard Station, we head north on the trail we hiked in on. In ¼ mile we arrive at a signed junction with the Poison Flat Trail. This trail we follow north as it hugs the east edge of Dumonts Meadows and then begins to climb above the canyon floor. Behind us, the west wall of the East Carson canyon becomes ever more impressive as we climb moderately to steeply up to a ridge just north of Poison Flat creek. From the ridge, we head east up toward a small exfoliating dome that at first resembles those of Yosemite, but closer up is seen to be volcanic. Our trail's gradient eases off as it passes the dome and comes to a signed spur trail to Soda Cone, which is about 100 yards away on the south bank of Poison Flat creek.

The conifer-lined meadow that we follow beyond the Soda Cone spur trail is often inhabited by cattle, which give Poison Flat creek a disagreeable taste and odor. The hike through the meadow is an easy one up to a low, shady divide. Then, under the canopy of the forest's edge, we parallel the south side of the meadow eastward, cross an aspen-lined gully, and come to a barbed-wire gate, then another. Immediately beyond, we reach the signed Poison Lake Trail. Travelers who are hiking this trip at a very leisurely pace may want to descend 100 yards on the Silver King Trail to a junction with the Driveway Trail, near Silver King Creek. Between this junction and a crossing 300 yards upstream you can find many good, shady, creekside campsites beneath lodgepole pines. Along this creekside route Trip 14 descends before turning east up the Driveway Trail.

Our trail up to Poison Lake starts steeply, then eases as it climbs up to a ridgecrest. It stays on or near the ridge for about a mile. Where the ridge ends at the base of a steep slope, we climb steeply southwest to a minor ridge that provides a major, sweeping view of rounded hills in the north, granitic cliffs in the east, Silver King canyon in the south, and the ragged Sierra crest in the southwest. From the ridge our trail continues to climb through thick brush. Soon, short, very steep switchbacks lead up into the forest's shade once again, and the gradient becomes pleasant.

Another climb leads to a small, rocky flat, dense with sagebrush and bitterbrush, from whose south end we can look upcanyon into Lower Fish Valley, Upper Fish Valley and Fourmile Canyon. From the flat our trail makes an undulating traverse west toward a small canyon and nearly reaches it at its top. Here the trail turns northwest and goes past several meadows before leveling off on a broad ridge above Poison Lake. A short, steep descent down this ridge leads to the lake's willow-clad south shore. Good campsites lie under lodgepoles and hemlocks on its northwest shore and fishing is good for brook trout.

3rd Hiking Day: Retrace your steps to **Soda Springs Guard Station**, 8 miles.

4th Hiking Day: Follow the 2nd hiking day of Trip 10, 11 miles.

14 Rodriguez Flat to Lower Fish Valley

Distance   14 miles
Type   Semiloop
Best season Mid or late
Topo maps   Topaz Lake, Sonora Pass
Grade (hiking days/recommended layover days)
   Leisurely 2/1
   Moderate ---
   Strenuous ---
Trailhead   11

HIGHLIGHTS A fine weekend selection, this two-day trip
visits five subalpine valleys. The country traversed contains some of the largest Sierra junipers to be found anywhere. In addition, over half a dozen side trips can be made from the Silver King Trail.

DESCRIPTION

1st Hiking Day (**Rodriguez Flat** to **Lower Fish Valley**, 7.5 miles): Our trail, the Snodgrass Canyon-Fish Valley Trail, makes a moderate climb southwest and shortly passes two trails from the Little Antelope Pack Station. A forest cover of white fir, silver pine and lodgepole pine persists for the next ⅓ mile of steep ascent, then yields to sagebrush as the old, metamorphosed sediments of Rodriguez Flat give way to much younger volcanic rocks. The view here is quite spectacular, and on a clear day you can see desert ranges northeast well beyond broad, open Rodriguez Flat.

The short, open ascent soon curves around the base of a volcanic hill and gives us new views—of Slinkard Valley below in the north, and the Sierra crest in the northwest. A traverse across broad, gentle, sagebrush-covered slopes leads to a signed junction, at which the Driveway Trail—our returning route—forks right (southwest). Our trail, the smaller of the two, soon passes through a fence gate and descends moderately past sagebrush and bitterbrush to the well-used grazing lands of spacious Corral Valley. On the valley floor, we cross two branches of Corral Valley Creek. The north branch, which drains the area most used by cattle, tends to be muddy, but the south branch, which drains more-forested slopes, looks and is drinkable. In it you'll see piute trout, which, like those in Coyote Valley and upper Silver King Creek, are an endangered and protected species. Please, no fishing here!

Beyond Corral Valley Creek, our southbound trail goes into the forest, curves west, parallels the valley a short distance, and then climbs an ever-increasing slope up to a dry saddle. From here the descent into Coyote Valley is a steep one, but it is made easy by the cushioning effect of the deep gravel. Near the bottom of a gully, the trail crosses a seasonal creek and goes but a short distance southeast before coming to an enormous, two-trunked juniper. With a diameter of 12 feet and a girth of 36, this specimen just might be the largest juniper in the Sierra. Beyond it, our trail winds south down toward Coyote Valley, reaching its sagebrush-covered floor beside a large, five-foot-diameter lodgepole (the key landmark to look for if you're hiking this trail in the opposite direction).

On the valley floor we walk a level ¼ mile to an easy ford of Coyote Valley Creek. Beyond the ford, the trail veers away from the creek and gradually climbs south. Near the crest above Upper Fish Valley, the forest becomes more dense and the aspens more dominant. At the crest's broad saddle a fence greets us, and from its gate we descend, usually past grazing cattle, steeply down to Upper Fish Valley. On the valley floor, a signed trail junction lies near a tall, orange snow-depth marker. Our trip proceeds north about 300 yards beyond the junction to a meeting of three fences, each with its own gate. Go through the north gate and follow the path that parallels the west side of the north-northeast-heading fence. Our trail soon starts to curve northwest, climbs over a low moraine left by a retreating glacier, and then comes to within hearing range of unseen Llewellyn Falls, just southwest of us. Let your ears direct you to this significant 20-foot-high cascade.

Llewellyn Falls creates a barrier trout cannot get over. As a giant glacier slowly retreated up Silver King Canyon, perhaps

50,000 years ago, cutthroat trout followed its path. They were able to swim into Upper Fish Valley and higher valleys before Silver King Creek eroded away bedrock to form the falls. Once isolated, they evolved into a subspecies known as the piute cutthroat trout (*Salmo clarki seleniris*), or simply piute trout. These trout became endangered not through overfishing but rather through the introduction of Lahontan cutthroats and rainbows, which then bred with the piutes to form hybrids. Once this miscegenation was discovered, Fish and Game workers removed purebreds and in 1964 treated Silver King Creek with rotenone to kill the hybrids. After the purebreds were reintroduced above the falls, their numbers grew from about 150 in the late 1960s to about 600 in the early 1970s. By 1975 the population had changed very little more, and it appears to be stable. Fishing, nevertheless, is strictly prohibited, for the piute trout could be easily fished out of existence.

From Llewellyn Falls gorge, our trail descends briefly northeast into Lower Fish Valley. The trail approaches Silver King Creek several times before reaching the north end of this overgrazed grassland, where you can cross the creek (wet in early season) and camp among the trees wherever people and cattle have not made too much of a mess. Fishing along Silver King Creek is good-to-excellent for rainbow, piute and rainbow-piute hybrid (to 9″).

2nd Hiking Day (**Lower Fish Valley** to **Rodriguez Flat**, 6.5 miles): Continuing downstream, we walk northwest toward a low ridge that hides the forested, little-visited valley of Tamarack Creek. Our path leaves Lower Fish Valley, turns northeast and climbs a low granitic saddle before entering the south end of Long Valley. To avoid springs and boggy meadows, take the trail that circles around the valley's east side. Part way down the flat valley, the trials join and then approach Silver King Creek. This creek meanders lazily through the glacial sediments that long ago buried its canyon's bedrock floor, and our trail approaches several of these meanders before leaving the valley's north end.

Following Silver King Creek, our trail passes its confluence with Tamarack Creek. After ½ mile of easy, shaded descent along the creek, we ford it about where granite outcrops force the trail to the north bank (wet in early season). About 200 yards downstream we meet the Driveway Trail near a large gate.

Our route then descends to cross Silver King Creek just below its confluence with Corral Valley Creek (wet in early season). Climbing steeply, we ascend a brush-covered slope where the thin soil supports only a few scattered junipers for shade. Soon the grade eases to moderate and then gentle, and after 2½ miles we reach a junction with the Snodgrass Canyon-Fish Valley trail, from where we retrace the first part of the previous hiking day. Before hiking the last mile along this familiar trail back to the trailhead, stop and look at the oversized cairn just before this junction. Built seven feet high by careful hands, this cairn stands as a monument to the loneliness of the Basque shepherds who once tended flocks in the area. Called *arri mutillak*, or "stone boys," monuments like this were built by lonely shepherds for lack of any other way to pass the time. Today, hikers *seek* to be alone and *look* for places of solitude in this east Sierra landscape

an arri mutillak *Jeff Schaffer*

15   Rodriguez Flat to Ebbetts Pass

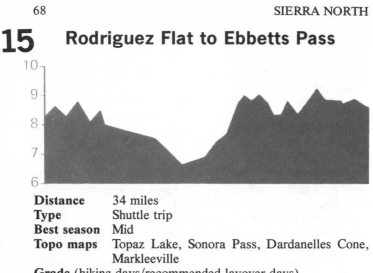

Distance	34 miles
Type	Shuttle trip
Best season	Mid
Topo maps	Topaz Lake, Sonora Pass, Dardanelles Cone, Markleeville

Grade (hiking days/recommended layover days)
  Leisurely 5/1
  Moderate 4/0
  Strenuous 3/0
Trailhead   11, 7

HIGHLIGHTS Ridges and canyons east of the Sierra crest wait to be explored along this scenic route. You'll encounter mammoth junipers, a rare trout, soda and carbonate springs, diverse scenery and good fishing. The last 11 miles are along the famous, ridge-hugging Pacific Crest Trail.

DESCRIPTION (Moderate trip)

1st Hiking Day: Follow Trip 14 to **Lower Fish Valley**, 7.5 miles.

2nd Hiking Day (**Lower Fish Valley** to **Murray Canyon Trail junction.** 9.5 miles): Follow the 2nd hiking day, Trip 14, to the Driveway Trail junction and walk 100 yards up the Silver King Trail to the Poison Lake Trail junction. From it, reverse the steps of the first half of the 2nd hiking day, Trip 13, to Soda Springs Guard Station, and then follow the 1st hiking day, Trip 11, to the Murray Canyon Trail Junction.

3rd Hiking Day (**Murray Canyon Trail** to **Asa Lake**, 10 miles): Follow the first part of the 2nd hiking day, Trip 11, up Murray Canyon to the crest junction. Our trail starts southeast from the crest, crosses a pebbly flat, and then returns to the crest to follow it a short distance. Through the thinning forest we see Highland Peak and other volcanic summits to the north-west, and in the southwest are the volcanic cliffs of Arnot Peak. Our trail soon leaves the crest and then contours ½ mile south across a brushy slope to a saddle just north of a low knoll. We cross the saddle, descend southeast, and gradually curve south-west through lodgepole forest over toward a grassy meadow south of the knoll. At the east end of this meadow our trail disappears, but you'll find it again at the west end. From here, you can look down across a large, open bowl. Our route, very vague, starts southwest down into the bowl, contours south just below the forest's edge, and then climbs southeast toward a saddle on the southwest side of a very prominent summit of highly broken volcanic rock. Just before the saddle, you'll reach a new segment of the Pacific Crest Trail.

Choosing the Pacific Crest Trail at the junction, we de-scend northwest along the west side of the bowl. As the bowl gives way to steeper slopes, the PCT circles west around a ridge, descends southwest and momentarily enters and then leaves a small but deep side canyon before reaching the slightly cloudy east fork of Wolf Creek, flowing down a wide, rocky wash. The cloudy color is due to fine volcanic sediments suspended in the water. A ⅓-mile traverse west past caves and fingers of a cliff of deeply eroded volcanic deposits gets us to the wide, silty middle fork of Wolf Creek.

Leaving this stream, we curve west briefly, then climb steadily northwest up to several branches of the west fork of Wolf Creek. The Pacific Crest Trail climbs north up a slope just beyond the main, east-flowing branch, switchbacks west, and climbs more steeply through a thinning forest. Rather than traversing west to a forested saddle, our trail continues to climb northwest above its east end—a route designed to avoid cattle-grazing lands on the other side. On reaching the west slopes of summit 8960+, we diagonal northwest down them, then curve north down to a small, flat saddle that lies at the base of the summit's northwest ridge. Here, it is important that you not continue north and cross the saddle. Rather, head west down a small gully, then parallel a low ridge, staying on its southwest side. A large cow meadow will quickly appear below you, and you'll almost touch it just before reaching a small gorge. The meadow's creek joyfully cascades down the resistant, volcanic end of the gorge, then flows out into Lower Gardner Meadow. The Pacific Crest Trail descends to a jeep road at the east end of this meadow, and on this road Trip 14 parallels the creek westward. At this junction, situated on a broad, low ridge known as Wolf Creek Pass, the road curves north immediately into a grassy, boggy meadow.

From the jeep road, the Pacific Crest Trail climbs northwest up a low ridgecrest, then curves north above the boggy meadow. The trail crosses the old Asa Creek Trail, then in ¼ mile arrives at a small pond just southeast of unseen Asa Lake. A minute's walk upstream off trail from the pond leads to the lake's east shore, where it is apparent why this small lake stays full and clear even in late summer: refreshing springs rush from the volcanic rocks above its east shore, and with the aid of a canal, their water is continually channeled into the lake. Under shady red firs above its northeast shore are some good campsites, and brook trout await the skillful—or lucky—angler.

4th Hiking Day (**Asa Lake** to **Ebbetts Pass**, 7 miles): Get back on the Pacific Crest Trail by walking about 150 yards upslope from Asa Lake's northeast corner. Once on the trail, follow it moderately to steeply up around a ridge, then through a small cove shaded by red firs. On the climb out of the cove, the forest of hemlocks and pines gives way to sagebrush as the trail traverses northwest toward a saddle. Tryon Peak looms ahead, and in the southwest, the large popular Highland Lakes stand out clearly in their broad, glaciated canyon. At the often windy saddle we encounter whitebark pines, which, better than any other conifer in this area, thrive in the harsh winter climate of this high elevation (9300').

We cross a crest-line fence, then follow a descending path that diagonals through tight clusters of whitebark pines and mountain hemlocks before crossing the willow-lined headwaters of Nobel Creek to intersect the faint Nobel Canyon Trail. Beyond this intersection the Pacific Crest Trail skirts above the east edge of a meadow and descends gradually southwest. Then our route curves north to a low saddle above the southwest corner of Nobel Lake. Staying high above the lake, the route curves northwest across a low ridge. The trail here is vague over the next hundred yards. It quickly dies out, but can be found again on the east side of the small gully immediately below. From the gully, the trail curves east to Nobel Lake's outlet creek, crossing it about 200 yards below the lake. Now the obvious trail heads north and soon switchbacks down a bizarre landscape of eroded, broken-up, *autobrecciated* lava flows (see Trip 10) that support only a few hardy junipers. We recross Nobel Lake's creek, head west briefly to a ridge of glacial sediments, and follow it north ¼ mile to a fork. Here, just east of the ridge crest, the Nobel Canyon Trail leaves the PCT.

The PCT rounds the ridge, descends to the bouldery main arm of Nobel Creek, and begins a traverse northwest. After ⅓ mile it starts climbing in earnest and momentarily leaves volcanic rock behind as it approaches granitic knobs atop a northeast-trending ridge. Our trail climbs north to the ridge's crest, curves around one knob back to the crest again, and then starts southeast around a second knob. At its south side we cross the crest for good and commence a winding traverse west along the base of some impressive, deeply eroded, volcanic cliffs. Northeast across Nobel Canyon is Silver Peak (10,774'), site of hectic mining activity beginning in 1863.

A brief climb north leads to the top of another northeast-trending ridge, this one just east of State Highway 4. Then a ¼-mile descent southwest from it brings the hiker to a junction, from which the PCT winds ⅓ mile southwest to a crossing of State Highway 4 only 200 yards north of Ebbetts Pass. From the junction, our route leads north and descends a spur trail ¼ mile to the Pacific Crest Trail parking lot.

Nobel Canyon from above Nobel Lake   *Jeff Schaffer*

16   Rodriguez Flat to Lake Alpine

Distance	49 miles
Type	Shuttle trip
Best season	Mid or late
Topo maps	Topaz Lake, Sonora Pass, Dardanelles Cone (Markleeville optional)

Grade (hiking days/recommended layover days)
    Leisurely 8/2
    Moderate 6/1
    Strenuous 4/0
Trailhead   11, 10

HIGHLIGHTS This exciting route traverses several major Sierra ridges along its westward course. As you progress west, the vegetation changes dramatically, sagebrush and juniper giving way to dense forests of pine and fir. Sections of two famous trails are hiked along this route: first, the 2600-mile-long Pacific Crest Trail, then later, the 180-mile-long Tahoe-Yosemite Trail.

DESCRIPTION (Moderate trip)

1st, 2nd and 3rd Hiking Days: Follow Trip 15 to **Asa Lake**, 27 miles.

4th Hiking Day (**Asa Lake** to **Hiram Meadow**, 9 miles): From Asa Lake, retrace your steps ½ mile south down the Pacific Crest Trail to the jeep road at Wolf Creek Pass. This road we take ½ mile west, following a creek through spacious, cow-inhabited Lower Gardner Meadow. Leaving the creek we traverse southwest across undulating country for another ½ mile to a north-flowing creek. In 150 yards we reach a signed fork, then turn northwest, and wind ¼ mile up to a gap, 100 yards beyond which our road is joined by a faint trail from Upper Gardner Meadow. In another 80 yards, this trail resumes its course, veering left. We follow it northwest ¼ mile up to a low crest, on which we cross a north-leading jeep road. From this junction the hiker will follow the trail about 200 yards to a reunion with the road 70 yards before a creek crossing. Draining lower Highland Lake, this creek can be a wet ford in early season. A trailhead parking lot is seen just above the west bank, and from it our road curves west 100 yards to the Highland Lake Road.

Wide, level Highland Lake Road contours around the west shore of lower Highland Lake, popular with fishermen for its population of brook trout. Beyond the lake, our road climbs gradually to Highland Lakes Campground, just north of the upper lake, which is divided into two camps. Backpackers will usually find quieter sites in the camp at the end of a short, eastbound spur road.

At the far end of upper Highland Lake the road ends and the well-signed Highland Creek Trail to Lake Alpine begins with a steep descent along the lake's outlet creek, then bends more westward away from it. Beyond a small knoll on the left, we descend west ½ mile down a steep, winding trail, passing a small gorge before we reach upper Highland Lake's outlet creek. In early season large boulders just downstream will make the crossing a dry one. Heading south, we pass through two small meadows, each with an abundant garden of corn lilies, then in ¼ mile approach a creek that drains what the map calls "Poison Canyon." (Poison Canyon is incorrectly called "Champion Canyon" on the topo map. All the canyon labels on the topo map from "Poison Canyon" to "Slaughter Canyon" should be moved one canyon to the southwest; the canyon labeled "Poison" on the map is actually unnamed.)

We follow the creek ¼ mile downstream, cross it near its union with Highland Creek, and in another ¼ mile come to a good campsite, under large cottonwoods, on the east bank of Highland Creek. At times, logs placed by hikers make this wide-creek crossing a dry one, but if you are here before mid-July, you can expect to wade. Then we round the base of a granitic ridge, enter a lodgepole flat, traverse the west side of a damp meadow, and return to forest cover as the trail and the nearby creek both bend south. In this part of the canyon, Highland Creek has several shallow pools that are ideal for a quick bath.

Our trail soon reaches a second ford of Highland Creek—

just as wide as the first and a little deeper. Once across, we veer away from the creek on a minor climb, then descend to the stream that drains Champion Canyon ("Hiram Canyon" on the topo map). Its ford is an easy one, and on a moderately descending trail we head down to the sunny flats of Hiram Meadow. Only 80 yards south of Highland Creek's union with Weiser Creek is a third, usually wet ford of the former.

Late-season hikers will note that this ford is a wet ford long after most Sierra snow has melted. This is because Highland Creek canyon and its tributary canyons have abundant volcanic sediments that act as a reservoir to hold water well into September. Good campsites lie across the ford on the west bank.

5th Hiking Day (**Hiram Meadow** to **Rock Lake**, 8.5 miles): About 100 yards west of the Highland Creek ford is a junction with the Weiser Trail. At the start of the deer-hunting season on the last weekend of September, hunters will descend this trail on motorcycles, bringing noise and pollution with them. Plan accordingly. From the junction we hike west across wide, flat Hiram Meadow, re-enter lodgepole cover, and quickly arrive at a cabin. Our path turns southwest, soon reaches willow-lined Highland Creek, and then crosses some low knolls of highly fractured, fine-grained igneous rock. One mile southwest of Hiram Meadow the Highland Creek Trail briefly climbs away from the creek just before it turns south and cascades down a sizable gorge. Our trail parallels the watercourse at a distance as we descend steeply to a junction with the Woods Gulch Trail. This trail east—part of the Tahoe-Yosemite Trail—crosses Highland Creek in 60 yards, just north of its union with the creek from Jenkins Canyon ("Slaughter Canyon" on the topo). Westward, the next 13-mile stretch of the Tahoe-Yosemite Trail coincides with the Highland Creek Trail.

Leaving the junction, our route turns west and in a few minutes brings us beside some small, lovely Highland Creek pools. We follow the creek only momentarily, then gradually veer away and climb up a brushy, granitic slope to an open forest of Jeffrey pines. In it, we descend quickly to a shady flat from which our trail descends moderately to the canyon bottom, where we cross a usually trickling creek that originates in a small, shallow lake northwest of Hiram Meadow. Traversing around the east shore of this lake is the Bull Run Creek Trail, which we meet only ¼ mile west of the trickling creek. Although motor vehicles are allowed on this trail, few successfully make it up or down due to its excessively steep, very sandy nature. In 100 yards we cross refreshing Bull Run Creek, shaded by cottonwoods and white firs.

Now our route is on a trail segment built above the shore of the new Spicer Meadow Reservoir, which drowned Gabbott Meadow. Soon the trail climbs steeply northwest, but then turns southwest and almost levels off, giving one a chance to catch one's breath on the traverse through a shady forest of white fir and Jeffrey pine. Emerging from the forest, we begin to climb steeply again, this time up brushy slopes to a small gap in the granitic bedrock.

Almost immediately, we pass through a second gap, then start a short traverse southwest, from which we can admire the dark, volcanic formations called the Dardanelles. This monumental ridge, composed of lava hundreds of feet thick, is only a small remnant of a long lava flow that originated near Bridgeport, California, about nine million years ago. From that source it flowed about *100 miles* down-canyon, stopping at the western edge of the Sierra foothills. In the ensuing millions of years, the walls of the canyon it flowed down were eroded away while the canyon bottom it buried was preserved beneath the flow. Two million years of glacial attacks further eroded the Dardanelles landscape until the granitic floor of Highland Creek lay a good 1000 feet below the base of the Dardanelles. We can expect future glaciers to excavate Highland Creek's canyon even more. Visible up-canyon are Iceberg, Airola and Hiram peaks—all with volcanic summits but none of them related to the Dardanelles flow.

Crossing the crest, which stands 550 feet above Highland Creek, we hike southwest just west of the crest. That the last Highland Creek glacier was *at least* as thick as the crest is high is obvious from the fresh polish it gave the granitic bedrock here. The glacier was, in fact, about 1300 feet thick. At a point where one could head south cross-country 1 mile down to Highland Creek, our trail turns northwest and climbs to a glaciated saddle. Then, midway along the mile-long roller-coaster path to Wilderness Creek, we cross one of its tributaries. The ford of Wilderness Creek is difficult in early season, but the stream disappears in late season. Beyond this creek our trail passes the Sand Flat Trail, climbs north to a gravelly, barren flat, and then briefly parallels Wilderness Creek. Continuing a moderate-to-easy climb north, we reach the east end of Rock Lake in ¾ mile. Grassy and unappealing at this end, Rock Lake provides good swimming and fishing (brook trout) near its southwest end. Along its south shore are several forested campsites.

6th Hiking Day (**Rock Lake** to **Lake Alpine**, 4.5 miles): From the lake's end, our route starts northwest along the old Highland Lake Trail, and then, just out of sight of the lake, turns northeast and follows a new tread ¼ mile up a granitic ridge. Then, from the slightly higher main ridge, we curve north, cross a small, dry wash, and descend to a flat ¼ mile east of North Fork Stanislaus River. From it, a short climb north and then a steep descent bring us to the river (difficult ford in early season).

Beyond this ford we climb steeply northwest to cross a ridge, and then wind ½ mile down glacier-polished slabs to a large, forested flat with a trail junction. From here the old trail goes 1¼ miles west past the south shore of Duck Lake to a cabin-side junction with a jeep road. Through July and part of August the mosquitoes along this swampy route are almost unbearable. Turning right on the new trail, we immediately cross a creek, and wind west along the north edge of this forested flat. When the trail reaches a point about 200 yards north of Duck Lake, it abruptly turns north and climbs up a ridge. After 300 yards it turns abruptly west and then climbs more moderately ⅓ mile west up to a switchback in the jeep road that ascends northward from the Duck Lake basin. On this closed road we climb west briefly up to a saddle, pass through a gate, follow the crest southwest, and then descend ½ mile to the trailhead at the east end of Lake Alpine's Silver Valley Campground.

Sonora Pass

Southward from Tahoe, each highway pass over the Sierra crest is higher than the previous ones, and at Sonora Pass we are 9624 feet above sea level. Whatever the altitude, the scenery is magnificent. The volcanic reds and browns of Sonora Peak, Leavitt Peak, and Relief Peak contrast with the bright granite of Whitecliff Peak, Forsyth Peak and Tower Peak, and all over the area we find places where volcanic rocks and igneous rocks have collided.

Highway 108 is almost the only access to the 117,596 acre Emigrant Wilderness, an area of many lakes that is one of the most popular trout-fishing regions in the country. Thousands of anglers have had the time of their lives fishing these waters.

East of the Sierra crest is a large area of *de facto* wilderness in the drainage of the West Walker River which some day, we hope, will be given wilderness status by Congress as an addition to either Emigrant Wilderness or Hoover Wilderness.

Considering the altitude, it would be well to spend a night before hiking at a campground or at a resort such as Kennedy Meadows or Leavitt Meadows, to allow your red-blood count to increase.

17 Kennedy Meadow to Summit Creek

Distance	13.6 miles
Type	Round trip
Best season	Early or mid
Topo maps	Sonora Pass, Tower Peak

Grade (hiking days/recommended layover days)

  Leisurely ---
  Moderate 2/0
  Strenuous ---

Trailhead 12

HIGHLIGHTS A part of this route follows the historic Emigrant Trail used by the pioneers in crossing the Sierra from the area around Bridgeport to Columbia and points west. Relief Peak was a major landmark for these early travelers, and the terminus of this trip lies in this unusual formation's shadow. The scenery along the way is an absorbing study in glacial and volcanic terrain.

DESCRIPTION

1st Hiking Day (**Kennedy Meadow** to **Summit Creek**, 6.8 miles): The trailhead (6400') is located alongside Middle Fork Stanislaus River at Kennedy Meadow resort. Amid a dense forest cover of Jeffrey pine, incense-cedar, sugar pine, juniper and white fir, the trail crosses a small ridge to Kennedy Meadow itself and skirts the east side of the meadow, offering sweeping views of the lush grasslands. Beyond the meadow, the trail crosses the river via a bridge and immediately veers west. Now the footpath ascends gently past the foot of a small granite dome and then switchbacks up a steeper grade between this dome and its larger neighbor. Under a sparse-to-moderate forest cover of mixed conifers, the route ascends steadily up a little canyon to a saddle, where it turns eastward to descend a sandy, multi-tracked slope to Summit Creek. After paralleling the creek for a few steps, the trail crosses it on a bridge and meets the old abandoned trail a few yards south of the Kennedy Lake Trail junction, near the PG&E dam-maintenance station.

Our route then contours high above the east side of Relief Reservoir. The trail section paralleling the shore offers excellent views to the south and west before it descends to the timbered shallow at the Grouse Creek ford. From Grouse Creek, the trail ascends steadily over a series of rocky switchbacks, and then veers southeast to pass the Lower Relief Valley Trail after one mile. Then we begin a steady-to-steep uphill climb as it leaves the shaded riparian zone and enters the brush-covered volcanic rubble above Summit Creek. This steady ascent is relieved when the trail drops into the little pocket encompassing Saucer Meadow. The gravesite indicated on the topo and Forest Service maps was that of a passing immigrant.

The section of trail beyond this point was part of a major trans-Sierra route, used during the middle of the 19th century—the Emigrant Trail. With the many-hued volcanic rock of Relief Peak on the left, and white, glaciated granite on the right, the trail climbs along Summit Creek to several fair campsites. Fishing along the creek is poor.

2nd Hiking Day: Retrace your steps, 6.8 miles.

South of Grouse Creek

Kennedy Meadow to Emigrant Meadow

18

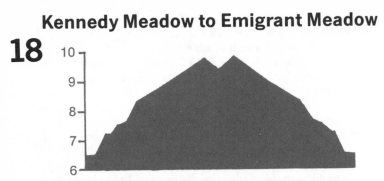

Distance	25.2 miles
Type	Round trip
Best season	Mid or late
Topo maps	Sonora Pass, Tower Peak

Grade (hiking days/recommended layover days)
  Leisurely 4/1
  Moderate 4/0
  Strenuous 2/0
Trailhead 12

HIGHLIGHTS A good part of this trail follows the historic Emigrant Trail, and travelers today have an excellent opportunity to identify with these hardy pioneers. Scenically, this route splits the terrain into two distinctly different parts. To the north, the basaltic and pumice slopes vividly disclose the vulcan overlay that gives the country its colorful reds and blacks. To the south, mirrorlike stretches of glacially polished granite add contrast and interest.

DESCRIPTION (Leisurely trip)

1st Hiking Day: Follow Trip 17 to **Summit Creek**, 6.8 miles).

2nd Hiking Day (**Summit Creek** to **Emigrant Meadow Lake**, 5.8 miles): Our level trail continues up-canyon on red-fir-dotted slopes for a mile, then makes a rocky 400-foot ascent to a little saddle which is the portal of the camping area called Sheep Camp, a very overused area. Winding above Summit Creek beyond Sheep Camp, the trail soon leaves timber cover, and crosses a pumice slope above Lunch Meadow. This large meadow is subalpine, dotted with sparse stands of lodgepole and mountain hemlock. At the east end of Lunch Meadow our route passes the trail to Emigrant Lake, branching right. North of our trail, red and black volcanic columns thrust up from the otherwise smooth, red, pumice slopes, and punctuate the skyline with their tortured shapes. Directly to the east the traveler can discern the shallow saddle that is Brown Bear Pass.

The trail to the pass is a gradual but steady ascent offering colorfully contrasting views of Granite Dome and Relief Peak to the west. It is easy to see why the emigrants who used this same route relied upon the distinctive outline of Relief Peak as a landmark. At the summit of Brown Bear Pass (9700'), the grassy expanses of historic Emigrant Meadow begin to present themselves, and the serenity of this pioneer waystop is enhanced by the placid blue waters of Emigrant Meadow Lake.

As the trail descends from Brown Bear Pass on a long traverse, the visitor cannot help being impressed by the gigantic scale of this grassy, granite-walled basin. It seems a fitting stage for the enactment of the "great move westward," and it doesn't take a great deal of imagination to hear boisterous shouts, the creaking of wagons, the barking of dogs, and the tired, hungry lowing of trail-weary stock. This great meadow saw the frenzied summertime travel of thousands of pioneers headed for the western slope, but of their passing all that remains is an echo in the wind. Fair but exposed campsites may be found along the west side of Emigrant Meadow Lake (9400'). Fishing for rainbow (8–13") is good, with a midseason slowdown.

3rd and 4th Hiking Days: Retrace your steps, 12.6 miles.

At Brown Bear Pass

19 Kennedy Meadow to Emigrant Lake

Distance   26.8 miles
Type   Round trip
Best season   Mid or late
Topo maps   Sonora Pass, Tower Peak
Grade (hiking days/recommended layover days)
    Leisurely 4/1
    Moderate 3/1
    Strenuous 3/0
Trailhead   12

HIGHLIGHTS A long-time favorite of anglers, Emigrant Lake
is often used as a base camp for short fishing
trips to the surrounding lakes. This route to Emigrant Lake
allows the traveler to take in the geological variety of the country. Alpine meadows surrounding isolated melt-off tarns compete for attention with vast slopes of red pumice and fields of
polished granite.

DESCRIPTION (Leisurely trip)

1st Hiking Day: Follow Trip 17 to **Summit Creek,** 6.8
miles).

2nd Hiking Day (**Summit Creek** to **Emigrant Lake**, 6.6
miles): First follow Trip 18 to the trail junction at the east end of
Lunch Meadow. Here our route branches right (south), fords
Summit Creek, and ascends through a sparse mountain-hemlock cover to a long, low saddle. Views along this segment
of trail present a wide range of colors. The superimposed
vulcanism of Relief Peak and the ridge to the east are a potpourri of pastel shades of reds, blacks, yellows and ochres.
Black Hawk Mountain to the west is granite in varying shades
of dun, gray, and buff-brown.

The long saddle through which our trail winds is a series of granite fields that are delightfully broken by tiny, wildflower-filled meadows. Many of these meadows are further enhanced by one or two small melt-off tarns. The long, shallow valley on the other side of the saddle contains a tributary of North Fork Cherry Creek, and from it there are excellent views across the Cherry Creek watershed south to Michie and Haystack peaks.

The trail descends on the east side of this tributary for ½ mile and then fords to the west side. This ford is the correct place from which to head east cross country to reach Mosquito Lake, which has pink-fleshed rainbow trout. Continuing down the east bank, we ford a little tributary and then recross the main stream to the west side. From here our trail descends to the large meadow at the inlet to large (230-acre) Emigrant Lake (8800'). There are several good-to-excellent campsites at the inlet, on the north side, and at the outlet. This popular lake is glacial in character, with a sparse forest cover, and fishing for rainbow (8–18″) is good (excellent in early and late season).

3rd and 4th Hiking Days: Retrace your steps, 13.4 miles.

Granite Formations near Lunch Meadow

20 Kennedy Meadow to Emigrant Lake

Distance   30.4 miles
Type   Semiloop trip
Best season Mid or late
Topo maps   Sonora Pass, Tower Peak
Grade (hiking days/recommended layover days)
   Leisurely 5/2
   Moderate 4/2
   Strenuous 3/2
Trailhead   12

HIGHLIGHTS Like the previous trip this route tours a part of the historic Emigrant Trail and visits large Emigrant Lake. In addition, linking Emigrant Lake with Emigrant Meadow Lake, this route makes a good fisherman's loop and takes in more scenic variety.

DESCRIPTION (Leisurely trip)

1st and 2nd Hiking Days: Follow Trip 19 to **Emigrant Lake**, 13.4 miles.

3rd Hiking Day (**Emigrant Lake** to **Emigrant Meadow Lake**, 4.4 miles): Beginning at the trail junction above the inlet to Emigrant Lake, this route crosses a log bridge over North Fork Cherry Creek and ascends a moderately forested slope to Blackbird Lake (9000') and a junction with a trail to Middle Emigrant Lake, where we turn left and follow part of the 5th hiking day, Trip 21.

4th and 5th Hiking Days: Reverse the steps of the 2nd and 1st hiking days, Trip 18, 12.6 miles.

Kennedy Meadow to Cow Meadow Lake **21**

Distance	45 miles
Type	Semiloop trip
Best season	Mid or late
Topo maps	Sonora Pass, Tower Peak

Grade (hiking days/recommended layover days)
   Leisurely 7/2
   Moderate 5/2
   Strenuous 4/2
Trailhead 12

HIGHLIGHTS This is a fine choice for a midseason fishing trip, as it circles the lake-dotted Cherry Creek watershed. A day's walking from one or another base camp will permit the fisherman to sample almost 100 lakes. The route also tours some of the finest scenery in Emigrant Wilderness, which should provide adequate incentive for the nonfisherman as well.

DESCRIPTION (Leisurely trip)

1st and 2nd Hiking Days: Follow Trip 19 to **Emigrant Lake,** 13.4 miles.

3rd Hiking Day (**Emigrant Lake** to **Cow Meadow Lake**, 6 miles): From the trail junction at the inlet to Emigrant Lake, our route traverses the long, timbered north side of the lake, and passes a junction with a poorly maintained trail to Cow Meadow Lake via North Fork Cherry Creek. It then crosses a low, forest-covered saddle and descends to ford Buck Meadow Creek. After crossing the long meadow at the north end of upper Buck Lake, the trail circles the west side of that lake, passing a trail to Deer Lake, crosses the isthmus separating the two lakes, and follows the east side of lower Buck Lake, often being back in the trees away from the lakeside. Upper Buck Lake is a good-sized (50-acre) glacial lake with numerous good campsites around the shore. Fishing for rainbow (to 18") is good. Lower Buck Lake is somewhat deeper and rockier, though about the same size, and fishing is usually about the same as the upper lake. About ¼ mile beyond the south end of Lower Buck Lake, the trail passes the Wood Lake lateral, and amid a nice forest cover of lodgepole descends steeply (600') to the Emigrant Lake Trail junction and lovely Cow Meadow Lake (7840'). There are excellent campsites along the north edge of the lake. This 55-acre lake is connected by lagoons with overhanging banks. A DF&G dam at the south end keeps the water level fairly constant, and fishing for rainbow and some brook is excellent (8–18"). Angling on the stream above the lake is good.

4th Hiking Day (**Cow Meadow Lake** to **Maxwell Lake**, 7.5 miles): From the east side of Cow Meadow Lake, the trail ascends 560 feet via a frequently blasted, usually cobbled trail to the bench containing rocky, deep Lertora Lake (8400'), passing a trail to the west and Huckleberry Lake before arriving at Lertora. This 25-acre lake offers only fair angling for brook and rainbow (7–13"). From the west end of Lertora Lake this route veers east along the south side of the lake, and descends over a very rough trail to the northeast end of large (200-acre) Huckleberry Lake (8000'). This subalpine lake provides good fishing for brook and rainbow (8–18"), and East Fork Cherry Creek above the lake often provides excellent angling.

From the meadows at the northeast end of Huckleberry, the trail heads upstream and soon fords East Fork Cherry Creek as it ascends the canyon. Views of the unusual granite island known as Sachse Monument dominate the northern skyline as the trail passes an abandoned tungsten mine. At this point the trail joins the mining road, and then it refords the stream before passing the Twin Lakes Trail lateral. At the south end of Horse Meadow our trail branches northwest up a timbered slope to Maxwell Lake (8700', 46 acres). This emerald-green gem with a tufty meadow fringe affords excellent angling for brook trout (8–14"). The polished granite of Sachse Monument towers over the south side of this charming lake, and the choice campsites on the north side of the lake have an uninterrupted view of both the lake and the peak.

5th Hiking Day (**Maxwell Lake** to **Emigrant Meadow Lake**, 5.5 miles): From Maxwell Lake the trail climbs by a series of switchbacks through a moderate forest cover of lodge-pole pine and then winds through a long, rock-lined meadow past several beautiful lakelets to Blackbird Lake and a junction with a trail to Emigrant Meadow Lake. Here our route branches right (north) past several small tarns that are usually dry by late season. The trail soon becomes faint, since this lateral is unmaintained, and one must keep a sharp eye out for ducks and blazes.

This footpath ascends along the south side of wandering North Fork Cherry Creek for about 1½ miles, and then fords the creek. From the ford onward, the trail is rutted into meadowy turf, but has become overgrown due to lack of maintenance. The trail becomes a little steeper just south of Middle Emigrant Lake, and then levels out at the wet meadows at the foot of the lake. Anglers who wish to try their luck on this fair-sized, granitic lake will find the fishing fair-to-good for rainbow (7–10″). The trail rounds the west side of the lake, fords the inlet stream, and crosses a low, rocky ridge to the Emigrant Meadow Lake basin (9400′). This huge meadow was the traditional stopping place for emigrant trains on the first leg of their Sierra crossing. This hiking day terminates at the open and exposed fair campsites on the west side of the lake. Fishing in Emigrant Meadow Lake is good for rainbow (8–13″).

6th and 7th Hiking Days: Reverse the steps of the 2nd and 1st hiking days of Trip 18, 12.6 miles.

Maxwell Lake

22 Kennedy Meadows to Hetch Hetchy

Distance   44 miles
Type   Shuttle trip
Best season   Mid or late
Topo maps   Sonora Pass, Tower Peak, Pinecrest, Lake
                  Eleanor
Grade (hiking days/recommended layover days)
  Leisurely 7/2
  Moderate 5/1
  Strenuous 4/0
Trailhead   12, 16

HIGHLIGHTS This is a trip of contrasts. The route begins by
bisecting the volcanic and glacial terrain north
of Bond Pass. This terrain is, as one writer aptly described it, "a
land born of fire and ice." As beautiful as the terrain is northwest of Bond Pass, the primitive, unspoiled beauty of Jack
Main Canyon has to be the high point of this trip. Glacial, subalpine meadows like those around Emigrant Meadow Lake
impress the visitor, but it remains for the lower grasslands of
Grace Meadow, with its meandering Falls Creek, to claim the
heart.

DESCRIPTION (Leisurely trip)

1st and 2nd Hiking Days: Follow Trip 18 to **Emigrant
Meadow Lake**, 12.6 miles.

3rd Hiking Day (**Emigrant Meadow Lake** to **Dorothy
Lake**, 5 miles): From Emigrant Meadow the route climbs over
a rocky ridge to Grizzly Meadow (9700') and two unnamed
lakes. Fishing here is fair-to-good for rainbow (to 10"). This
area is subject to the Forest Service's Multiple-Use land pro-

gram; hence the traveler may encounter summer-grazing steers. Further evidences of this program mar the serenity of this wilderness just beyond the lakes, where the trail encounters a mining road. Our route follows this road as it descends to the Summit Meadow "trail" junction, a distance of about 2 miles. From here our route follows another mining road across the northern fringe of the meadow, and then ascends by a series of switchbacks to the gentle saddle called Bond Pass (9700'). Amidst a clump of red fir marking the summit, the trail leaves the dirt road and crosses into Yosemite National Park. There are excellent views, east from the summit, of Saurian Crest and Tower Peak.

The descent on the east side winds through dense lodgepole and fir to a junction of the trail to Dorothy Lake (9440'). After turning north on it, a ½-mile gentle ascent brings the traveler to the scattered campsites on the west shore. Anglers should ready their tackle for the good-to-excellent fishing for brook and rainbow (8–15"). Dorothy Lake, with its pleasant meadow fringes and bunched stands of lodgepole, makes an excellent base camp from which to explore the surrounding lakes and terrain. Of particular interest is the "rock glacier" beneath nearby Forsyth Peak. A discovery side trip to the lake just south of Dorothy Lake provides excellent views of this geologic wonder. Like their ice counterparts, rock glaciers are moving masses.

4th Hiking Day (**Dorothy Lake** to **Grace Meadow**, 3.2 miles): First, retrace your steps ½ mile to the first junction, then continue down-canyon. Jack Main Canyon begins at Dorothy Lake, and from the start it is a great hiker's route. A whole spectrum of wildlife may be found along this trail, and the abundance of the wildlife is testimony to the effectiveness of the National Park system. In the meadowed fringes of Dorothy Lake, the piping of the Belding ground squirrel ushers the traveler past the marmot-inhabited opposite slopes. If one is on the trail early enough, deer still out grazing will keep him entranced with their graceful movements. Ample signs of the black bears that roam this section of the park will be found along the trail—particularly during gooseberry season.

Scenically, this short stretch of trail is an idyllic series of tiny meadows alongside murmuring Falls Creek. To the east, somber Forsyth Peak and abruptly divided Keyes Peak (juxtaposed black gabbro and white granite) cap the canyon walls. The trail gradually descends through a dense forest cover to the north end of long, rolling Grace Meadow (8620'). In contrast to the wide-open, windy stretch of Emigrant Meadow, Grace Meadow has a soft, intimate feel that makes it a favorite base camp. Anglers should be ready for excellent brook and rainbow (to 13") along Falls Creek.

5th Hiking Day (**Grace Meadow** to **Paradise Valley**, 8 miles): From Grace Meadow our trail heads south through more meadows and lodegpole-pine stands on an almost level descent. During breaks in the trees you can get a good view back up-canyon at the straight, glaciated valley, while ahead is rounded Chittenden Peak. As we come abreast of Chittenden Peak, the grade steepens and becomes a bit rocky. We pass the trail to Tilden Lake and wind gently down slabs, sometimes near now-dashing Falls Creek.

Where we climb onto a sandy flat, we meet a junction where we leave the Pacific Crest Trail. Continuing down-canyon, we rejoin the languid creek opposite lovely Wilmer Lake, which is separated from the creek by a natural levee. Just below the lake, the canyon narrows and the grade steepens. Along this stretch the trail parallels the creek, which is a series of rapids, falls and pools in smooth granite. Where the canyon bends south, we descend to a lodgepole-pine-and-meadow-covered valley that was a lake in the recent geologic past. The glacial lakes in this canyon will all eventually fill with sediment or another glacier, whichever comes first.

The next section of Falls Creek is very tranquil, winding through willowy marshes from pool to pool. The trail, sometimes near the creek, sometimes climbing over bedrock ridges, leads through ferns and aspens at the base of the steep north canyon wall. After leaving the creek for ⅓ mile, we arrive at a small lake bordered by an aspen grove on the north and a cliff on the south. At the west end of this brook-trout-filled lake is a good campsite, strategically located near both this lovely lake and Falls Creek, which is several hundred feet to the south.

6th Hiking Day (**Paradise Valley** to **Beehive**, 8 miles): A short distance west of the lake beside a large pool our trail meets a signed trail to Tilden Canyon. Continuing west we pass some "improved" campsites and cross a large, overgrazed meadow. Beyond this seasonally wet meadow our trail climbs over sun-baked slabs and descends to join the creek again by a large pool, where it begins yet another slow-moving stretch. Along this section the trail goes between the creek and a nearby lake on a narrow, aspen-covered levee. Leaving the creek again, we pass another, smaller lake and skirt the marshy north shore of a larger one. For the next two miles our trail winds down glacially modified Jack Main Canyon, sometimes on slabs, sometimes through trees and sometimes near Falls Creek. From where the creek turns south to cascade down into the valley containing Lake Vernon, we climb a rocky stairway up a gully and onto the timbered flanks of Moraine Ridge. After a 500-foot ascent we leave forest cover and arrive at the ridge's summit. From the summit we can look back at much of northern Yosemite. Most of what you see was covered with ice at various times during the Pleistocene Epoch. Now we see the glacial aftermath of rounded ridges, polished domes and scoured valleys.

Following the crest of Moraine Ridge, we descend along a very wide, dusty trail through an open forest of Jeffrey pine and white fir. After we cross a burned section, we pass the trail to Lake Vernon, and the grade eases. Back in denser forest now, we cross a very low saddle where we can find lodgepole pine, Jeffrey pine, aspen, incense-cedar and black oak—species rarely found together. A little farther on we make a short, steep descent, and then a gentle descent through a wet area to the forest-bound meadow at Beehive (6500'). The water supply here is a small spring west of the junction with the trail to Laurel Lake. As this lovely meadow is popular with people, there are usually bears around.

7th Hiking Day (**Beehive** to **O'Shaughnessy Dam**, 7.2 miles): Leaving Beehive, we descend gently though a burned area past a second trail to Laurel Lake. Fire is an important parts of the life of this forest. You will notice that most trees survived this fire, proving it was not very hot. In areas where fire is suppressed, large amounts of fuel accumulate, and the fire that eventually occurs will be devastating. Soon we pass a marshy pond on the crest of a moraine and begin the steep 2500-foot descent to Hetch Hetchy. As we wind down the rocky, dusty trail, the forest cover changes to reflect the elevation loss. We leave sugar pine behind, white fir is replaced by Douglas-fir and black oak gives way to canyon live oak.

About 600 vertical feet down this hill we round a ridge where we can pause to take in the views of Hetch Hetchy Reservoir and the surrounding uplands. Descending farther, we cross a small creek and soon join the service road to Lake Eleanor. The last 2½ miles to the trailhead take one down the steep canyon wall via a series of long switchbacks under canyon live oak and California bay. Cutting switchbacks along this descent has caused severe erosion. Natural erosion is also evident where the last switchback begins next to a large landslide. Here, tall trees have been broken off and carried a long way downslope. Beyond the last switchback the trail from Rancheria Creek joins the road, and we stroll 0.7 mile to the dam.

Mule ears   *Jeff Schaffer*

Gianelli Cabin to Y Meadow Lake **23**

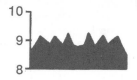

Distance	10 miles
Type	Round trip
Best season	Mid or late
Topo maps	Pinecrest

Grade (hiking days/recommended layover days)
Leisurely 2/0
Moderate ---
Strenuous ---

Trailhead	13

HIGHLIGHTS Except for the short distance from Gianelli Cabin to Burst Rock, this trip is within beautiful Emigrant Wilderness, and the route parallels a segment of the historic Emigrant Trail. En route to Y Meadow Lake, anglers can try their luck on two small but fairly productive lakes, and early-trip views, from Burst Rock, are panoramic.

DESCRIPTION

1st Hiking Day (**Gianelli Cabin** to **Y Meadow Lake**, 5 miles): At Gianelli Cabin (8560')—now only part of the log cabin's base remains—the trail begins in a meadow and soon ascends a steep slope covered with red fir and silver and lodgepole pine. This segment has been used as a jeep trail, so it is somewhat eroded. The trail tops the ridge at Burst Rock (9161'), a landmark for the old Emigrant Trail, and crosses the Emigrant Wilderness boundary (no motorized vehicles allowed). This vantage point offers excellent views to the north of Liberty Hill, Elephant Rock, the Dardanelles, Castle Rock, and the Three Chimneys. You can see as far as Mt. Lyell on the southeast border of Yosemite Park. As the trail bears east along the ridge, the traveler also has excellent views of the Stanislaus River watershed to the north and the Tuolumne River watershed to the south.

The trail descends gradually to a low saddle overlooking granitic Powell Lake. This small lake offers fair fishing for

brook trout in early and late season, and the fine views to the
northeast make this an attractive spot for a lunch break. The
trail then crosses a small ridge, descends through a forest of
lodgepole, fir, and mountain hemlock, and arrives at the open
stretches of meadowy Lake Valley. A faint fisherman's trail
(0.7 mile) to Chewing Gum Lake turns south through the
meadow. Anglers with a yen will want to try the fair-to-good
fishing for brook on this small (5-acre) lake before continuing.
From Lake Valley it is 1½ miles across another broad ridge to
the turnoff to Y Meadow Lake. Here our route turns south for
one winding mile to the fair campsites at the north end of Y
Meadow Lake (8600'). Unfortunately, the water level fluc-
tuates so much that the lake cannot support fish life. However,
anglers accustomed to cross-country walking may elect to try
the waters of Granite Lake (0.7 mile south) for the good fishing
for brook (8–13"). There are some poor-to-fair campsites at
Granite Lake.

2nd Hiking Day. Retrace your steps, 5 miles.

Remains of Gianelli Cabin

Gianelli Cabin to Wire Lakes   **24**

Distance   24.8 miles
Type   Round trip
Best season Mid or late
Topo maps   Pinecrest
Grade (hiking days/recommended layover days)
  Leisurely 4/1
  Moderate 4/0
  Strenuous 2/1
Trailhead   13

HIGHLIGHTS This round trip penetrates the heart of
Emigrant Wilderness as it wends through a
delightful series of meadows and over high, open ridges. Wire
Lakes, the destination for this trip, is a stepladder set of three
memorable high-mountain lakes that afford excellent angling
and several fine choices for secluded camping.

DESCRIPTION (Leisurely trip)

1st Hiking Day: Follow Trip 23 to **Y Meadow Lake**, 5
miles.

2nd Hiking Day (**Y Meadow Lake** to **Upper Wire Lake**,
7.4 miles): First retrace your steps from Y Meadow Lake to the
trail junction of the Gianelli Cabin/Whitesides Meadow Trail.
Here our route turns right (northeast) toward very large
Whitesides Meadow. Travelers should be prepared for the
probability of seeing summer-grazing cattle on these broad
expanses (Forest Service Multiple-Use land program) but these
bovine occupants should not detract too much from an appreciation of this subalpine grassland. At the east end of the
meadow our route passes the Eagle Pass Trail, and then
ascends the moderately timbered slope at the northeast end. On
this ascent our rough path passes a trail to Upper Relief Valley
and Kennedy Meadow, and another one after 1½ miles of

descent. Then it dips down to ford West Fork Cherry Creek (sometimes dry in late season) at Salt Lick Meadow (8520').

From here the trail climbs to a tarn-dotted bench and then descends past several picturesque tarns to Spring Meadow. Tiny lakes sprinkle the green expanse of the meadow, and early-to-mid season trailpounders will find the grassland areas spiced with lupine, paintbrush and buttercup. Anglers will find the fishing for brook trout fair-to-good along the tributary (Spring Creek) flowing through Post Corral Canyon. A short mile farther southeast, a signed trail leaves the main trail and winds the remaining 0.4 mile along a ridge to the excellent campsites on the northwest side of upper Wire Lake (8800'). Equally good campsites may also be found at Banana Lake (middle Wire Lake), 0.3 miles southwest via a cross-country route. Fishing on the Wire Lakes is good-to-excellent (with a midseason slowdown) for brook (8–14"). Campers will find any of the several secluded campsites on these high montane lakes an idyllic setting for a base camp.

3rd & 4th Hiking Days: Retrace your steps, 12.4 miles.

Crabtree Camp to Deer Lake **25**

Distance	22.6 miles
Type	Round trip
Best season	Mid or late
Topo maps	Pinecrest

Grade (hiking days/recommended layover days)
Leisurely 4/2
Moderate 4/0
Strenuous ---
Trailhead 14

DESCRIPTION

1st Hiking Day (**Crabtree Camp** to **Piute Creek**, 6.4 miles): Leaving the moderately forested flats of Crabtree Camp, we hop Bell Creek, making sure that our canteens are full for the waterless climb to Camp Lake, and quickly come to a junction with the Chewing Gum Lake Trail on a sandy bench. Our route ascends dustily through open mixed conifers, then contours south, undulating gently, to reach a segment of older trail. Here we assault a steep, much abused path, fortunately well-shaded, which levels out under aspens and lodgepoles at a lateral trail to Pine Valley. Open stands of mature Jeffrey pine, lodgepole pine, black oak, red fir, and Sierra juniper allow a viewful traverse above deeply forested Pine Valley; then the trees close in as we follow a red-fir corridor around a grassy pond and gently ascend to the Emigrant Wilderness boundary. Four hundred yards later we reach the west end of shallow, green Camp Lake. This sparsely forested, sorely trampled lakelet supports a harried population of brook trout. At a saddle just past Camp Lake the trail to popular Bear Lake takes off to the left.

From the junction, the steep, dusty trail switchbacks down on deep sand flanked by dense manzanita and ceanothus to an easy ford of Lily Creek. Swinging southeast through a meadow sporting corn lilies, lungwort and groundsel, our path soon comes to a granite headwall, and makes a steep, rocky ascent. Now above most of the trees, we see, in the south, Pine Valley and the chaos of white domes in the Chain Lakes region. A parade of switchbacks leads to a lengthy traverse that passes through meadows south of black-streaked granite outcrops, and we soon reach a pretty lakelet, much larger than shown on the topo map, speckled with Indian pond lilies and backdropped by dancing aspens and lichen-dappled granite. Its clear, shallow waters support a thriving population of yellow-legged frogs, who might not mind if you took a dip.

After a short climb east of this tarn, we survey large Piute Meadow in the east, dome-guarded Toms Canyon in the north, Groundhog Meadow below in the southeast, and, on the eastern horizon, Bigelow Peak and the jutting prominence of Tower Peak. Bone-jarring dynamited switchbacks, esthetically ameliorated by a profusion of wildflowers, lead down to a sidehill traverse in glacial boulders west of Piute Meadow.

Keeping to the trees south of the willowed west arm of Piute Meadow, we pass a small campsite; then, where our route bends south to easily cross Piute Creek, there is another, larger site.

2nd Hiking Day (**Piute Creek** to **Deer Lake,** 4.9 miles): Only yards after Piute Creek the unsigned Groundhog Meadow spur trail comes in from the south. The dry slabs and lodgepole pines demarcating the lower margin of Piute Meadow are left behind when our path bends upward, switchbacking rockily up the east slope of Piute Creek canyon to a broad saddle southwest of Piute Lake. The trail then descends to the meadowed fringes of tiny (2-acre) Piute Lake (7900') and the good campsites on the north side. Fishing for rainbow (8–12") in this shallow lake is fair to good.

From Piute Lake the trail drops to ford West Fork Cherry Creek and then strenuously ascends a steep, rocky, washed-out section to an overlook just above warm little Gem Lake. Less steep than the previous climb, the trail from Gem to Jewelry Lake is nonetheless a rocky ascent. Our route skirts the north side of the meadow fringes surrounding Jewelry Lake, and anglers will want to try their luck for the fair-to-good fishing for rainbow (to 10") in the lake and the lagoons around the inlet. From the east end of Jewelry Lake, it is a short mile by rocky, gently ascending trail to the excellent campsites on the north side of Deer Lake (8540'). This long, granite-bound lake has nice meadow fringes on the north side. The forested campsites look out over the lake's island- and rock-dotted surface. Fishing for nice-sized rainbow (8–16") is good-to-excellent on both the lake and the inlet stream.

3rd and 4th Hiking Days: Retrace your steps, 11.3 miles.

Deer Lake *Luther Linkhart*

26   Gianelli Cabin to Crabtree Camp

Distance	27.3 miles
Type	Shuttle trip
Best season	Mid or late
Topo maps	Pinecrest

Grade (hiking days/recommended layover days)

    Leisurely 5/1
    Moderate 4/1
    Strenuous 3/0

Trailhead   13, 14

HIGHLIGHTS This route has proved popular with angler, naturalist, photographer and hiker alike. High, coldwater lakes and streams vie with deep fir forests and alpine meadows for the attention of the visitor. The shortness of the shuttle for this trip makes it a near-loop.

DESCRIPTION (Leisurely trip)

1st and 2nd Hiking Days: Follow Trip 24 to **Upper Wire Lake**, 12.4 miles.

3rd Hiking Day (**Upper Wire Lake** to **Piute Lake**, 5.5 miles): From upper Wire Lake the traveler has the option of circling to Deer Lake by the longer trail route or descending through the Wire Lakes basin and going cross country to the west end of Deer Lake. The trail route, after retracing the short angler's lateral, rejoins the Spring Meadow/Deer Lake main trail and turns south. After a slight climb, the remaining distance to Deer Lake is a steady descent over a forested streamcourse that passes several small, unnamed lakes. At Deer Lake this route passes the Buck Lakes trail and turns right (southwest) toward Jewelry Lake.

The cross-country route from upper Wire Lake to this point first leads southwest to Banana Lake (middle Wire Lake), where all semblances of trail vanishes. The easiest descent from here is to take the clear route through the meadowed area east of Banana Lake and then descend via the usually dry streamcourse to the Jewelry Lake/Deer Lake Trail about 0.3 mile west of Deer Lake. The trail from Deer Lake to Jewelry Lake is a ½-mile rocky descent that brings the traveler to the pleasant meadow fringes surrounding Jewelry Lake. This lake has placid lagoons forming its inlet which provide fair-to-good fishing for rainbow (to 10"). Crossing the inlet stream, the route descends a rocky trail to warm little Gem Lake (8240'). From this viewpoint the trail descends steeply to a ford of West Fork Cherry Creek and then climbs gently to tiny Piute Lake. Fishing for rainbow (8–12") in this shallow lake is fair-to-good.

4th and 5th Hiking Days: Reverse the steps of part of the 2nd and all of the 1st hiking days, Trip 25, 9.4 miles.

27 Gianelli Cabin to Kennedy Meadow

Distance   33.3 miles
Type   Shuttle trip
Best season   Mid or late
Topo maps   Pinecrest, Tower Peak, Sonora
Grade (hiking days/recommended layover days)
  Leisurely 5/2
  Moderate 4/2
  Strenuous 3/2
Trailhead   13, 12

HIGHLIGHTS This trip journeys through a cross section of Emigrant Wilderness. The route touches some justly popular base-camping lakes, and from these points the traveler has access to the unusual and exciting surrounding country. Taken at Leisurely pace, this route affords one of the best possible week-long excursions in the region.

DESCRIPTION (Leisurely trip)

1st and 2nd Hiking Days: Follow Trip 24 to **Upper Wire Lake**, 12.4 miles.

3rd Hiking Day (**Upper Wire Lake** to **Emigrant Lake** via Deer and Buck Lakes, 7.5 miles): The traveler going to Deer Lake has a choice of going by trail or cross country. The trail route entails retracing the short fisherman's trail to its junction with the main trail from Spring Meadow. There our route turns right (south), and descends gently past several unnamed tarns to Deer Lake. The cross-country route goes south through the Wire Lakes basin to Banana Lake (middle Wire Lake), and then veers east a short distance through a meadowed basin. At the end of this meadow a long, usually dry streamcourse descending to the south gives access to the trail 0.3 mile west of Deer Lake (8540'). This is a large, granitoid, meadow-fringed lake offering good-to-excellent fishing for nice-sized rainbow (to 16"), and anglers who have had an early start will want to try these waters.

The trail to Buck Lakes continues east over a low rocky ridge, and then descends steeply to join the Emigrant Lake/Cow Meadow Lake Trail on the west shore of Buck Lakes. At this junction our route turns left (north) along the west side of upper Buck Lake, and follows Buck Meadow Creek as it crosses the long meadow at the lake's north end. Our route then veers east, fords Buck Meadow Creek, and crosses the steep, low ridge separating the Emigrant Lake and Buck Lakes basins. At Emigrant Lake (8800') the trail follows the long north shore to the several good-to-excellent campsites near the inlet. Emigrant Lake is the largest lake (230 acres) in this Wilderness, and is a long-time favorite of fishermen because of the good-to-excellent rainbow fishing (8–18") in its deep waters. Those who prefer stream fishing will find the lagoons near the inlet exciting sport, but the fish are smaller.

4th and 5th Hiking Days: Reverse the steps of the 2nd and 1st hiking days, Trip 19, 13.4 miles.

Lower Buck Lake *Luther Linkhart*

28 Kennedy Meadow to Gianelli Cabin

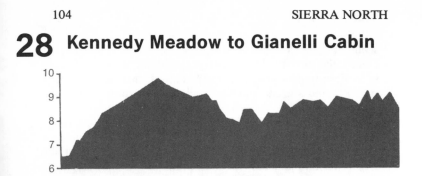

Distance   43.1 miles
Type   Shuttle trip
Best season Mid or late
Topo maps   Sonora Pass, Tower Peak, Pinecrest
Grade (hiking days/recommended layover days)
   Leisurely 7/3
   Moderate 5/2
   Strenuous 4/2
Trailhead   12, 13

HIGHLIGHTS After visiting the north side of Emigrant Wilderness, this route turns south and traverses the beautiful, lake-dotted country of the Cherry Creek watershed. At Emigrant Meadow the trail joins the old Emigrant Trail, and history buffs will have the opportunity of seeing this historic crossing as the pioneers did.

DESCRIPTION (Leisurely trip)

1st and 2nd Hiking Days: Follow Trip 13 to **Emigrant Meadow Lake**, 12.6 miles.

3rd and 4th Hiking Days: Reverse the steps of the 5th and 4th hiking days, Trip 21, 13 miles.

5th Hiking Day (**Cow Meadow Lake** to **Deer Lake**, 3.5 miles): Leaving Cow Meadow Lake, the trail passes a junction with a trail from East Fork Cherry Creek and then ascends steeply 600 feet amid a dense, predominantly lodgepole forest cover to a junction with the Wood Lake lateral. Lower Buck Lake (42 acres) is a rocky, deep, glacial lake that is separated from upper Buck Lake by a narrow isthmus. Fishing on both lakes for rainbow (to 18″) is good. Our route crosses the isthmus and turns north, where it strikes the Deer Lake Trail. Here our route turns left (west) and climbs steeply for ½ mile.

Then it descends more gently for a mile past the Wood Lake Trail to the excellent campsites on the north side of Deer Lake (8540'). This long lake has the same kind of subalpine meadow fringing as upper Buck Lake. The fine campsites, situated in small stands of lodgepole, look out across the lake's island-dotted surface. Fishing for rainbow (to 16") is good-to-excellent.

6th Hiking Day (**Deer Lake** to **Y Meadow Lake**, 9 miles): From the trail junction at the middle of Deer Lake's north shore, our route climbs north beside an unnamed stream and past a series of inviting tarns. About 1.7 miles from Deer Lake we pass the Wire Lakes Trail going left (west) and then descend a densely forested slope to the east end of Spring Meadow. This meadow is a vast, lakelet-dotted grassland that is lush with buttercups, lupine and paintbrush. One frequently sees cattle grazing here, allowed by the National Forest multiple-use land program.

From Spring Meadow the trail crosses a small ridge containing more tarns and then descends moderately-to-steeply through a wooded section to Salt Lick Meadow, where it crosses tiny West Fork Cherry Creek (sometimes dry in late season). Then the route ascend through lodgepole pine and mountain hemlock, passing the first of two trails leading north to Upper Relief Valley and Kennedy Meadow and, 0.6 mile later, an unsigned trail leading south to secluded Toejam Lake. Our trail tops the ridge and then descends to sprawling Whitesides Meadow. At its head we pass another trail to Upper Relief Valley and, soon after, a trail to Cooper Meadow, both leading north. The green expanse of this meadow is broken by the flow of an unnamed tributary of South Fork Stanislaus River. Our trail touches this stream at the meadow's west end, then veers away southwest to the Y Meadow Lake Trail junction. Here we branch left and walk one winding mile to the fair campsites in the timber fringe at the north end of Y Meadow Lake (8600').

7th Hiking Day: Reverse the steps of the 1st hiking day, Trip 23, 5 miles.

29 Leavitt Meadow to Fremont Lake

Distance   18 miles
Type   Round trip
Best season Mid or late
Topo maps   Sonora Pass
Grade (hiking days/recommended layover days)
   Leisurely 2/1
   Moderate 2/0
   Strenuous ---
Trailhead   17

HIGHLIGHTS Along this well-traveled route the traveler is introduced to the contrasts of the North Boundary Country. Here the dark rock thrown up by volcanoes meets the lighter, more typical Sierra granite. Cameras for the photo-bug are a must, and the angler can look forward to good rainbow-trout fishing at Fremont Lake.

DESCRIPTION

1st Hiking Day (**Leavitt Meadow Campground** to **Fremont Lake**, 9 miles): The trail leaves the Leavitt Meadow Campground (7120') via a metal bridge across the West Walker River. Beyond the bridge our trail ascends briefly, and in ¼ mile we meet a junction just beyond a mountain juniper on the left and a Jeffrey pine followed by an uprooted stump on the right. Here we veer right onto the Walker River Trail on a sagebrush-covered arid slope, and traverse over to the wide valley of Leavitt Meadow. Far up the river canyon Forsyth Peak stands majestically on the border of Yosemite.

As we ascend gently just above the valley floor, it does not take a great deal of imagination to picture emigrant wagons working their way southwest toward Emigrant Pass, at the headwaters of this river. Close beside the trail are many tall specimens of a bush-tree called mountain mahogany. Despite its dry, tough appearance, the foliage of this desert plant is relished by the local mule-deer population. The plant is particularly striking in the early fall, when the styles (part of the flowers) are white, silky, 3-inch-long plumes growing by the hundreds on each bush.

On this steady ascent we meet several trails, coming in at acute angles, that lead back north to the pack station in Leavitt Meadow. Then, after the meadow disappears from sight, and just beyond a pond, we pass the unsigned Poore Lake Trail branching left and continue to the north shore of algae-bottomed Roosevelt Lake, ringed with a sparse fringe of Jeffrey pines. There are some undistinguished campsites on the west side of the lake, and sometimes fishing is good for brook trout to 13".

Then our trail leads over a granite shoulder and down to the outlet of Lane Lake, nearly a twin of Roosevelt and only a few yards from it. This outlet usually dries up by midsummer, but the dead lodgepole pines southwest of the ford are testimony to flooding earlier in the season. From the ford, the trail ascends briefly southeast and then levels off as it passes several lovely aspen groves, some with lush grass floors even into late season.

Over a mile from Lane Lake, our trail descends to the willow-lined banks of the river, crossing a small but vigorous tributary ⅛ mile before reaching the main stream. We ascend gently near the riverside for ¼ mile through a cool forest of mixed conifers, aspens and cottonwoods, then veer away on a steeper ascent that fords another tributary. The rocky-dusty trail then steepens to surmount a saddle crested with junipers and Jeffrey pines, which offers fine views up the West Walker valley to Forsyth Peak and the Sierra crest. Descending over a sandy trail, our route passes the marked turnoff to Hidden and Red Top lakes, and then resumes its moderate ascent along the east bank of the West Walker River. The rocky stretch of trail alongside the river gives access to many pleasant, granite-bottomed potholes. Here the river tumbles along in a series of small falls and cascades that have carved a narrows through the white granite that typifies the middle of the West Walker River Valley. The upper walls are of barren, metavolcanic rock that ranges the color spectrum from black to reds and yellows.

Where the narrows opens out onto a forest flat, rife with mosquitoes in early season, we come to a junction with the Fremont Lake Trail, just off the *Sonora Pass* topo map. Turning right, we follow this trail to the riverbank and find a good log crossing less than 100 yards downstream. Across the river are many well-used campsites, and we stroll downstream past several to reach the signed Fremont Lake trail continuation. This we follow westward and ascend steeply to cross a saddle topped with juniper and Jeffrey pine. This saddle offers **V**'d views south to Tower Peak. The trail then descends gently, passes the trail to Chain of Lakes, and in 100 yards reaches Fremont Lake (8240'). The forest cover around this generous-sized lake is moderate-to-dense lodgepole and juniper, most of it around the south end of the lake. Here in the timber are fair campsites, and fishing for rainbow (to 12") and eastern brook (to 10") is good.

2nd Hiking Day: Retrace your steps, 9 miles.

West Walker River above Leavitt Meadow

John Muir Trail, Mt. Lyell

30   Leavitt Meadow to Cinko Lake

Distance   28 miles
Type   Round trip
Best season   Mid or late
Topo maps   Sonora Pass, Tower Peak
Grade (hiking days/recommended layover days)
   Leisurely 3/1
   Moderate 3/0
   Strenuous 2/0
Trailhead   17

HIGHLIGHTS This interesting route traces West Fork West Walker River to its headwaters cirque beneath the Sierra crestline. From the sagebrush and Jeffrey pine belt it ascends to the Boreal belt, passing through three life zones. Of the several trips in this drainage, this offers one of the best exposures to the geological, topographical and biological features of this country.

DESCRIPTION (Leisurely or Moderate trip)

1st Hiking Day: Follow Trip 29 to **Fremont Lake**, 9 miles.

2nd Hiking Day (**Fremont Lake** to **Cinko Lake**, 5 miles): After retracing our steps back to the Chain of Lakes junction described in Trip 29, we turn right (south) and ascend steadily near, but out of sight of, Fremont Lake. This ascent steepens as it crosses open, granite-sand slopes with only a few junipers and pines for shade. Near the top of this ascent one has uninterrupted views to the south of Forsyth and Tower peaks, and one encounters his first silver pines of this trip. The first of three large granite domes that tower over the east side of Chain of Lakes comes into view, and the trail crosses to the north of it. Then, on a gently descending path through an increasingly dense forest cover, we pass the marked trail to Walker Meadows and arrive at the first of several tiny, green, lily-padded lakes. These lakes reflect the verdant forest cover that extends to their willow-lined shores, and by late summer their shallow depths teem with the biota that typifies near-stagnant waters.

The trail leaves the last and largest of the Chain of Lakes and ascends gently over sand and duff through a moderate forest cover of lodgepole and silver pine past a small, unnamed lake north of Lower Long Lake. A few yards past this lily-padded lake, the trail veers right, around the north side of Lower Long Lake. The "blancoed" rock in the center of the lake is a favorite midday resting place for the sandpipers that inhabit the area. Fishermen seeking the pan-sized rainbow here will enjoy the sandpiper's low, skimming flight, which seems to trim the fringe of rushes. Fair-to-good campsites dot the north and west sides of the lake. More extensive campsites are found a few yards farther up the trail, at Upper Long Lake.

The trail jogs around the lower end of Upper Long Lake, fords the intermittent outlet stream and meets the Piute Meadows lateral, going left. Our route turns right past a picturesque tarn to the banks of West Fork West Walker River. Here at another junction our route branches left alongside this tumbling stream. Good campsites dot both sides of the West Fork near the junction, marred only by the cowflops incident to the Multiple-Use grazing permit for nearby Walker Meadows. Occasional hemlocks with their gracefully bowed tops occur along the pleasant, granite-ledged, timber-pocketed ascent from the campsites. Many wildflowers, including shooting star, penstemon, bush lupine, aster, columbine, goldenrod, heather, Mariposa lily, wallflower, woolly sunflower and fleabane, decorate the stream's edge and complement the cheerful splashing of the nearby stream.

This gentle-to-moderate climb continues along the southeast side of the stream to the foot of a large, white granite dome (Peak 10010), where it fords via boulders to the northwest side of the creek. Contrasts of the dark volcanic rock and the white granite underlayment of this part of the Sierra are nowhere more marked than in this valley, and the viewer is assailed with dark battlements of multihued basalt, and sheer escarpments of glacially smoothed batholithic granite. William H. Brewer, head of the Brewer Survey party that passed near here in July 1863, took note of the volcanic surroundings, saying ". . . in the higher Sierra, along our line of travel, all our highest points were capped with lava, often worn into strange and fantastic forms—rounded hills of granite, capped by rugged masses of lava, sometimes looking like old castles with their towers and buttresses and walls, sometimes like old churches with their pinnacles, all on a gigantic scale, and then again shooting up in curious forms that defy description."

This ascent takes the traveler to timberline and to alpine climes as the surrounding forest cover becomes stunted and comes to include occasional altitude-loving whitebark pines. At a signed junction our route turns southeast along a clear trail to Cinko Lake. This trail fords West Fork West Walker River and passes a charming meadow with a tiny tarn in its upper reaches. Then it makes a brief moderate ascent to the intermittent north outlet of arrowhead-shaped Cinko Lake. There is another outlet on the south side of the lake. The trail emerges at the lake's edge (9200'), adjacent to the north outlet, where there are several good campsites. Fishing for rainbow and eastern brook (to 12") is good.

3rd Hiking Day: Retrace your steps, 14 miles.

Leavitt Meadow to Dorothy Lake **31**

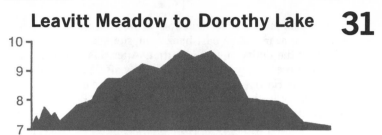

Distance	34 miles
Type	Semiloop trip
Best season	Mid or late
Topo maps	Sonora Pass, Tower Peak

Grade (hiking days/recommended layover days)

Leisurely 6/1

Moderate 4/1

Strenuous 3/1

Trailhead 17

HIGHLIGHTS Touring the headwaters of the West Fork West Walker River and the headwaters of Cascade Creek and Falls Creek would be an ambitious undertaking in any one trip, but this trip boasts more. Near Dorothy Lake, the culmination of the trip, the visitor can take in the unusual Forsyth Peak "rock glacier."

DESCRIPTION (Moderate trip)

1st and 2nd Hiking Days (**Leavitt Meadow** to **Dorothy Lake**, 18 miles): First follow Trip 30 to **Cinko Lake**, 14 miles. From the southeast side of Cinko Lake our trail winds down a lodgepole-and hemlock-clothed hillside to the unpopulated banks of an unnamed stream. Then it climbs slightly, veering east away from the water. A very short, steep descent then takes the hiker to a beautiful lakelet. About ⅛ mile past the lake, we reapproach the stream and then veer away again eastward. In another ⅛ mile the trail crosses this persistent tributary on a wooden bridge, then ascends for a moment, levels off, and passes three snowmelt tarns on the right. Continuing level through a tarn-filled saddle here, our southbound trail soon meets the Dorothy Lake Trail, which is also the Pacific Crest Trail here, we turn right (south), following the trail on a gentle ascent through a thinning forest cover of lodgepole, hemlock and whitebark pine.

One-half mile from the junction we cross Cascade Creek on a large log near a large east-bank campsite, and in another ⅓ mile ford the outlet of Lake Harriet. After this ford the trail ascends more steeply, and becomes rocky after passing island-dotted Lake Harriet. This ascent levels through a meadowy section and fords the stream joining Stella and Bonnie lakes. Ahead, the low profile of Dorothy Lake Pass is fronted by another moderate, rocky ascent, and the trail then levels past the grassy north arm of Stella Lake. At the northeast end of this arm, a ducked cross-country route to Lake Ruth and Lake Helen departs from our route.

The long, low saddle on which Stella Lake sits terminates at Dorothy Lake Pass, where there is an excellent view of Dorothy Lake (9400'). To the southeast, the hiker has V-notched views of Tower Peak, and to the south, the granite grenadiers of multi-turreted Forsyth Peak dominate the landscape. From the pass, the trail descends steadily over a rocky slope that is the territory of numerous conies and marmots.

As the trail skirts the north side of this beautiful lake, it winds through lush grass and willow patches with spots of color provided by shooting star, elephant heads, goldenrod, paintbrush, whorled penstemon, pussy paws and false Solomon's seal. This stretch of the north shore was not so lush when the first recorded explorer of this lake walked here. Lt. N. F. McClure, of the 4th Cavalry, came this way in 1894 noting, "Grazing here was poor, and there had evidently been thousands of sheep about." The trail passes three windy campsites along the north shore before arriving at the good campsites at the west end of the lake. Fishing for rainbow and occasional eastern brook is good-to-excellent except during a midsummer slowdown. This lake makes an excellent base-camp location for exploring and fishing the nearby lakes in the upper Cascade Creek basin, and for viewing the Forsyth Peak "rock glacier."

This phenomenon can be viewed from the unnamed lake south of Dorothy Lake. Seen from here, it is a prominent "river" of rock flowing in a long northwest-curving arc. This arc begins on the northeast face of Forsyth Peak, then curves down the easternmost ravine and points its moving head toward Dorothy Lake. Composed of coarse rock that tumbled from Forsyth Peak's fractured face, it hides an underlayment of silt, sand and fine gravel, and it depends upon ice caught between larger boulders for its mobility.

3rd Hiking Day (**Dorothy Lake** to **Fremont Lake Trail Junction**, 8 miles): First retrace the steps of the previous hiking day as far as the Cinko Lake Trail. Then continue to descend on the north side of tumbling Cascade Creek. Switchbacks are needed to convey the hiker down past the cascades of this namesake creek. Near the bottom of this descent the forest, now including stately red firs, becomes thicker. As the trail nears the West Walker River, the moderate descent levels, and then the route fords near an old corral. Beyond the wading ford is a **Y** junction, and here our route turns left (downstream). The trail continues north along the east side of the West Walker River, fords an unnamed tributary of the river, and skirts a large meadow before beginning a gentle-to-moderate ascent. The sand-and-duff trail then crosses a saddle and descends to ford Long Canyon Creek. About ¼ mile beyond this stream is the Fremont Lake Trail junction, and we take this trail across the river to the campsites passed on the first hiking day. Alternatively, one may continue downstream on the east side of the river to other good campsites. Fishing in the deeper holes of this section of the river is good for rainbow (to 11").

4th Hiking Day: Reverse the steps of most of the 1st hiking day, Trip 29, 8 miles.

Dorothy Lake and "rock glacier" on Forsyth Peak

32 Leavitt Meadow to Tower Lake

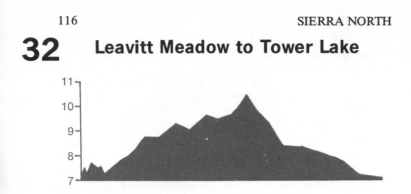

Distance   40 miles
Type   Semiloop; part cross-country
Best season Mid or late
Topo maps   Sonora Pass, Tower Peak
Grade (hiking days/recommended layover days)
   Leisurely 7/2
   Moderate 5/2
   Strenuous 4/2
Trailhead   17

HIGHLIGHTS The cross-country segment of this trip makes it a choice for experienced backpackers only. The strenuousness of the route guarantees the walker a proportionate measure of solitude, and views of the alpine crest on this trip are seldom seen by anyone except the cross-countryer.

DESCRIPTION (Moderate trip)

1st and 2nd Hiking Days: Follow Trip 31 to **Dorothy Lake**, 18 miles.

3rd Hiking Day (**Dorothy Lake** to **Tower Lake**, 5 miles): From the campsites at the west end of Dorothy Lake, retrace the steps of the previous hiking day to Stella Lake, to where the ducked cross-country route to Lake Ruth rounds the northeast end of the lake. This route ascends over a rock-and-grass ledge system along the east side of the intermittent stream joining Stella Lake and Lake Ruth, and arrives at the outlet end of Lake Ruth. Here, nestled in the sparse whitebark-pine fringe of the lake, are good campsites that make a fine alternative to the more crowded environs of Dorothy Lake. The route from the outlet skirts the east side of the lake for a short distance and then ascends a long, gentle swale to the southeast. Several small melt-off tarns mark the crossover point to the Lake Helen drainage. Keeping to the south side of this large, granite, circular lake, the route fords the tiny but noisy southwest inlet, and then crosses the rocky slope directly south of the lake.

At the southeast inlet our route fords and ascends moderately to a lovely grass bench. The remaining ascent to the obvious saddle in the southeast crosses steeper sections, and route-picking is best accomplished on the left (north) side of the cirque wall. This steep pitch brings one to a sparsely dotted whitebark-pine saddle offering incomparable views. Included in the views to the north and west are, from north to west, Wells Peak, White Mountain, Sonora Peak, Stanislaus Peak, Leavitt Peak, Kennedy Peak, Relief Peak and Forsyth Peak. To the east and southeast the view encompasses, from east to south, Flatiron Butte, Walker Peak, Buckeye Ridge, the Kirkwood Creek drainage, Grouse Mountain, Hunewill Peak, Hawksbeak Peak, Kettle Peak, Cirque Mountain and Tower Peak. From the summit of this saddle one can also see most of the lakes of the Cascade Creek drainage, as well as Tower Lake at the foot of Tower Peak. Tower Peak, the most spectacular peak of the North Boundary Country but not the tallest, is the goal of most climbers in this region. Visible from most of the drainages to the south, it has served mountaineers as a landmark for more than a hundred years.

Descending from the saddle on the southeast side entails crossing rock and scree to a rocky bench, and thence a grass-and-ledge system to a small lakelet just north of Tower Lake. The route then rounds the south nose of granite ridge to the willowed outlet of Tower Lake, where it fords to the fair campsites, centered in the only stand of timber found here on the east side of the outlet (9600'). There is fair-to-good fishing for the golden trout (to 11") that inhabit this lake. Good alternative campsites can be found ½ mile down the outlet stream.

4th Hiking Day (**Tower Lake** to **Fremont Lake Trail Junction**, 9 miles): From Tower Lake the trail descends over a rocky slope close to the north side of the outlet stream from Tower Lake. This steep, rocky descent affords a view of a dramatic avalanche chute that slices the slope on the northeast side of Kirkwood Creek canyon. To the rear, back toward Tower Peak, the view is dominated by the climactic, phalluslike northern extension of Tower Peak. This classic white-granite pinnacle soon obliterates views of Tower Peak itself, and it stands as mute testimony to the obdurate granite's resistance to glacial erosion.

The rocky descent soon reaches timberline, where hemlock and lodgepole pine appear, and then refords the outlet stream in a willowed section at the confluence of the Tower Lake outlet and the tiny stream draining the glacier at the foot of the granite column to the south. This new section of trail from Tower Lake keeps to the east side of the creek as it descends gently over duff and rock, and fords an unnamed tributary.

Beyond the ford, the new trail rejoins the old trail, winding through a dense forest cover of lodgepole and hemlock. Then the trail refords Tower Lake's outlet stream and ascends above the narrowing canyon. These narrows show almost vertical granite walls, between which the stream becomes a plummeting ribbon. Ahead, the valley of the West Walker River can be seen through the trees, and a short, easy descent over a duff trail soon brings us to a trail junction just north of the confluence of the Tower Lake outlet and Kirkwood Creek.

Our route turns right, fords the West Walker River, and then skirts the oxbows of the river where it serpentines through Upper Piute Meadows. At the north end of the meadows the sandy trail passes a turnoff to Piute Cabin, a Forest Service trail-maintenance station, and then veers away from the river as it continues to descend gently. The cattle seen in some years in Upper Piute Meadows are part of the Forest Service's "Multiple Use" administrative concept. Cowflops have been reported as far away as the head of Thompson Canyon—and it may be logically assumed that they were a result of allowing grazing here. After jogging around a marshy section, the trail again comes within sight of the river, and then joins the trail from Dorothy Lake. From the junction we proceed as described in the 3rd hiking day, Trip 34.

5th Hiking Day: Reverse the steps of most of the 1st hiking day, Trip 29, 8 miles.

Upper Piute Meadows

Leavitt Meadow to Buckeye Creek **33**

Distance	39.9 miles
Type	Shuttle trip; part cross-country
Best season	Early or mid
Topo maps	Sonora Pass, Tower Peak, Matterhorn Peak

Grade (hiking days/recommended layover days)

    Leisurely 7/2
    Moderate 5/2
    Strenuous 4/1

Trailhead   17, 18

HIGHLIGHTS Using two major eastside drainages this trip circumnavigates Walker Mountain and Flatiron Ridge, and is about evenly split between high country and lower, forested areas. This is a superlative choice for the novice who has a couple of shorter trips behind him, and who is looking for a longer trip with some of the challenge of cross-countrying.

DESCRIPTION (Moderate Trip)

1st, 2nd, and 3rd Hiking Days: Follow Trip 32 to **Tower Lake**, 23 miles.

4th Hiking Day (**Tower Lake** to **Buckeye Forks**, 7.5 miles): First, descend to Upper Piute Meadows as described in the 4th hiking day, Trip 32. Just below the confluence of Kirkwood Creek and the creek draining Tower Lake, ford to the northeast side of the stream and turn right, up Kirkwood Creek. Here at the southernmost extension of Upper Piute Meadows our route ascends moderately through a dense forest cover of lodgepole and occasional silver pine that sees the inclusion of hemlock near the top of the climb. This route passes below the spectacular avalanche chute noted on the previous hiking day.

On a moderate ascent that steepens as it turns east and then northeast, the trail rises to the saddle marking the divide between the Walker River and Buckeye Creek. The startling eminence of Hawksbeak Peak to the south vies for the traveler's attention with the rich volcanic reds and blacks of the slopes to the north. After reaching a small pond at the headwaters of Kirkwood Creek, the trail descends moderately on duff and rocky surfaces to the head of North Fork Buckeye Creek. This descent through a sparse-to-moderate forest cover of lodgepole, hemlock, and occasional whitebark and silver pine crosses back and forth over the splashing creek. Then, in a final steep descent, the trail drops to "Buckeye Forks," where it meets the trail descending from Buckeye Pass to the south.

Here at the forks is a meadow-set snow-survey cabin of log-tenon construction. It is believed that this well-made cabin was constructed in 1928, and is the oldest U.S. Snow Survey shelter. When built, the cabin was surrounded by open meadow, which has since been overgrown with the ubiquitous lodgepole and willow. This dense growth is undoubtedly due to the strong evolutionary contribution of the nearby colony of beavers. As is clearly seen just downstream, these beavers have repeatedly flooded this section between Buckeye Forks and The Roughs, and the consequent buildup of sediments and high water table were conducive to forest reproduction. However, what the beaver giveth he also taketh away. Were this dense forest to be flooded again, these healthy trees would be drowned. That happened downstream, where the bleached white ghost snags make skeletal reminders of the beaver's potent niche in the evolutionary web. Of the mammals, excepting man, the beaver is far and away the greatest single alterer of the natural environment.

There are good campsites near the old cabin, and fishing in Buckeye Creek is good for rainbow and eastern brook (to 9").

5th Hiking Day (**Buckeye Forks** to **Buckeye Roadend**, 9.4 miles): From the cabin, the trail continues to descend steadily over alternating duff, sand and rock. On each side, gnawed and fallen aspen show the beaver's dietary preferences, but despite this rodent's industrious efforts (some naturalists would say "because of it") the forest cover along the creek is dense, and it serves as a foraging grounds for all manner of birdlife, including flickers, chickadees, juncos, robins, William-son's sapsuckers, hummingbirds and nuthatches.

As the canyon narrows between high, glacially polished granite walls, the trail enters the section known as The Roughs. Here the sometimes swampy trail winds along the left bank of Buckeye Creek, overshadowed by sheer, rounded granite to the north and polished spires to the south. Good campsites can be found in The Roughs. The first one is one mile from the forks, and there is another ¼ mile farther. Then, ¼ mile beyond, we make a steep 200-yard ascent over black metasedimentary shale to a juniper-topped saddle and the boundary of the Hoover Wilderness. From just beyond the saddle views down Buckeye Canyon are spectacular. The lush grasslands of Big Meadow provide a soft counterpoint to the ruggedness of Flatiron and Buckeye ridges.

A few hundred steep yards down beyond the saddle, we ford the vigorous creek that drains the basin between Ink Rocks and Hanna Mountain, and the tumultuous sounds of the cascades above and below the ford furnish soul-satisfying background music for a fine rest stop. From this viewpoint the trail descends over a rocky, exposed slope on a long traverse to rejoin the trail shown on the topo map just upstream from the confluences of Buckeye Creek and the tributaries draining the slopes of Hunewill and Victoria peaks. This steady descent is the last of the precipitous terrain, and the remainder of the walk is over long, gradual slopes covered with sagebrush, mountain mahogany, bitterbrush and mule ears. Occasional clumps of aspen occur where the trail crosses a tributary or where it veers close to Buckeye Creek, and they provide welcome shade on a hot mid-summer afternoon. In these well-watered sections the traveler also encounters colorful clumps of monkey flower, goldenrod, lupine, shooting star, paintbrush and penstemon.

Big Meadow itself is a charming two-mile-long grassland replete with Belding ground squirrels and morning-feeding deer. At one time, around 1870, this meadow rang with the sounds of axes and the whirring of a sawmill blade. Here the Upper Hunewill mill operated to provide mining timber. Near the fence at the bottom of the meadow, the observant passerby can make out the signs of an abortive effort to construct a flume to carry water from Buckeye Creek to Bodie.

We pass through a gate in this fence and immediately head

right, downhill, for the ford of Buckeye Creek, marked by two posts about 6 feet tall, about 30 yards downstream from the fence. This ford can be difficult in early season. From the creek our trail leads up a small ridge and then undulates over several more ridges, generally within sight of the stream. Beyond a viewpoint for seeing a beaver dam, the trail traverses along a hillside clothed by many head-high aspen trees and many flowers (in season), including scarlet gilia, with its red, trumpet-form blossoms. After crossing two little runoff rills, we can look through the trees down upon a large meadow, which we skirt on a level trail under aspen, juniper, red-fir and lodge-pole-pine trees. About ½ mile farther we cross the tip of a tongue of that meadow, and an unmapped stream that flows late into summer. Soon the trail becomes a two-track abandoned vehicle way, and we stroll through a sagebrush field squeezed between the lodgepole pines that border the creek and a large stand of aspen trees on the nose of a ridge that protrudes onto the canyon bottom.

The next section of trail passes through alternating green meadows and gray sagebrush fields, with constant good views of the towering north and south walls of Buckeye Canyon. Past one last, fairly large meadow we come to a fence with both a hiker's gate and a stock gate, where we begin the last mile of this 7-day journey under the shade of Jeffrey and ponderosa pines, red firs and quaking aspens. This last mile is a gentle downhill stroll that ends at a parking area just up-canyon from a Forest Service campground.

Yosemite

Yosemite—a magic name, famous world-wide.

But when most people think of Yosemite, they think Yosemite Valley, which is all too crowded. Hardly anyone knows that it is possible to spend a week in the backcountry of northern Yosemite and *not see anyone*. We don't guarantee you would see no one, but it is possible, especially if you spend the week off-trail somewhere in the drainage of Rancheria Creek, Piute Creek, Stubblefield Canyon or Thompson Canyon.

Most of the acres in Yosemite National Park are officially declared wilderness, where man is only a visitor and his works are absent. You should take advantage of that fact. Almost a thousand miles of trail will help you do so.

Those who would prefer a little bit of civilization in the backcountry can reserve—far in advance—a bed in a tent plus dinner and breakfast at any or all of the five High Sierra camps run by the Park concessionaire. These camps form a loop that makes a good week-long itinerary. (For reservations, write High Sierra Camps, Yosemite National Park, CA 95389.) Each camp also has a backpacker camping area near it.

Of course there are plenty of places to stay in the Valley, but its elevation of 4000 feet won't do much to acclimate you for hiking. Prefer the campgrounds at Bridalveil Creek or Tuolumne Meadows for hikes near those places.

Twin Lakes to Peeler Lake

Distance   16 miles
Type   Round trip
Best season   Mid or late
Topo maps   Matterhorn Peak
Grade (hiking days/recommended layover days)
   Leisurely ---
   Moderate 2/1
   Strenuous ---
Trailhead   19

HIGHLIGHTS Despite a stiff 2500-foot climb, this trip makes a fine choice for the city-weary hiker with a "long weekender" trip-selection problem. An early start will allow the hiker to enjoy the morning freshness on the steeper uphill parts, and to be in camp soon enough for a pleasurable swim or some afternoon angling. Peeler Lake, as a destination, is a delightfully unique Sierra experience in that one camps literally on top of the mountain chain, for this lake pours its waters down both sides of the Sierra.

DESCRIPTION

1st Hiking Day (**Twin Lakes** to **Peeler Lake**, 8 miles): This trip begins in the Mono Village Campground at the west end of Twin Lakes. First, follow signs saying *Barney Lake* through the campground to find the wide, level, shaded trail. Travelers setting out in the fall season should take a few minutes at the outset for a side trip to view the colorful Kokanee salmon spawning in the shallows of Robinson Creek south of the campground.

Beyond the campground our sandy trail winds through a moderate-to-dense forest of Jeffrey pine, juniper, lodgepole pine, aspen and cottonwood along Robinson Creek. In late summer, cottony catkins from the cottonwood trees here litter the initial section of trail, leaving the ground surface the gray-white of spring snow. Crossing several small tributaries, the trail then ascends gently, and within ¾ mile encounters the first fir trees, but the forest cover soon gives way to a sagebrush-covered, gently sloping bench, from where one can see the great headwall of the valley in the west.

As one makes his way up this open bench through thigh-high sagebrush, rabbitbrush, chamise and mule ears, one has unobstructed views of Victoria, Hunewill and Robinson peaks on the right, and some ragged teeth of the Sawtooth Ridge on the left. About halfway up this bench the trail passes a "ghost forest" of drowned trees caused by beaver dams downstream. Beavers still share this fine Sierra stream with us. On the right, somnolent marmots are likely to be seen dozing among piles of scree that flow from the feet of the avalanche chute scarring Victoria Peak; on the left, the dramatic, unbroken granite wall of Blacksmith Peak at the top of Little Slide Canyon dominates the view. A sign here proclaims this area as part of Hoover Wilderness. On the left, Robinson Creek becomes a willow-lined cascade that is frequently heard but seldom seen.

About ½ mile into the wilderness, the ascent resolves into switchbacks that ford several small tributaries. In their moist banks one encounters monkey flower, monkshood, red columbine, swamp onion and shooting star scattered among clumps of bracken fern. Along the drier stretches of trail the severity of the rock is alleviated by colorful patches of Indian paintbrush. Mariposa lily, scarlet gilia, yarrow milfoil, whorled penstemon, pussy paws, streptanthus and goldenrod.

After the ascent levels out, the trail veers south, fords another tributary, and arrives at the outlet point of arrow-shaped, overused Barney Lake. Anglers wishing an interlude of fair-to-good fishing for eastern brook and rainbow trout will want to tarry around the deeper east and northeast shores of the 9-acre gem. Others may elect to take a cool, quick dip, or merely to lie on the sandy beach and watch the play of the local water ouzels.

The remainder of the trail to the top of the watershed is not marked on the topo map, but is patently clear on the scene. This trail skirts the west side of the lake in a steady, long, hot ascent that takes one onto the canyon wall well above the "ghost forested" delta inlet of Barney Lake. Once above the wetter sections of the delta, the trail descends to a wildflower-decorated ford of Robinson Creek. Here amid the willows can be found lavender swamp onion, red columbine, orange tiger lily and yellow monkey flower. The moderate forest cover now shows the transition to higher climes with the introduction of hemlock and some silver pine.

About ¼ mile upstream the trail refords Robinson Creek, and after fording the outlet creek from Peeler Lake just above its confluence with Robinson Creek, it rises abruptly by steep, rocky switchbacks. Leveling off somewhat, it then comes to a bench junction with the Crown Lake Trail. This junction is ¼ mile northwest of Robinson Lakes (the two tiny lakes downstream from Crown Lake). Here our route turns right and ascends moderately for about ½ mile near the south outlet from Peeler Lake, and then steeply up the draw just northeast of the lake, to reach this outlet. Beautiful Peeler Lake (9500') sits astride the Sierra crest, contributing water to Robinson Creek on the east and Rancheria Creek on the west. Large (about 60 acres), it has abrupt, rocky shores, and the deep-blue color characteristic of deeper Sierra lakes. There are good-to-excellent campsites almost all around the lake. The best lie on the east shore, reached by leaving the trail where it starts to descend to cross the south outlet. Fishing for eastern brook and rainbow trout (to 14") is sometimes good.

2nd Hiking Day: Retrace your steps, 8 miles.

Switchbacks on the Crown Lake Trail

Twin Lakes to Crown Lake   **35**

Distance   16 miles
Type   Round trip
Best season   Early, mid or late
Topo maps   Matterhorn Peak
Grade (hiking days/recommended layover days)
  Leisurely ---
  Moderate 2/1
  Strenuous ---
Trailhead   19

HIGHLIGHTS Like the previous trip, this one entails considerable "up," but it is still a good two-day trip
selection. This route follows Robinson Creek all the way to
Crown Lake, and in its course exposes the traveler to some of
the finest east-side scenery available anywhere along the
Sierra. Crown Lake itself is set in the heart of the Sierra crest,
and consonant with its name, it forms a royal diadem of blue in
a regal setting of forest greens.

DESCRIPTION

1st Hiking Day (**Twin Lakes** to **Crown Lake**, 8 miles):
First follow Trip 34 to the junction of the Peeler and Crown
Lake trails. From this junction our route leads south, undulating gently between large outcroppings of glacially polished granite. As the trail ascends moderately below Robinson Lakes
(unlabeled on the topo map; they are the lakes downstream
from Crown Lake) it winds through one near-pure stand of
hemlock—unusual for this part of the Sierra. Just before you
reach Robinson Lakes is an inviting natural, deep pool that is
colored bright aqua. Robinson Lakes are two small, shallow,
placid lakes with a sparse forest cover of lodgepole pine, silver
pine and hemlock, separated by an isthmus.

The trail rounds the south side of the larger Robinson Lake, fords Robinson Creek, and turns south on a steady ascent. Just below Crown Lake we reford the creek and then switchback up to the good campsites (9500') just downstream from the lake along the outlet, where there are excellent views of Kettle Peak and Crown Point. Fishing for rainbow and some eastern brook (to 9") is fair.

2nd Hiking Day: Retrace your steps, 8 miles.

The Sierra crest over Crown Lake

Twin Lakes to Upper Piute Creek **36**

Distance 23 miles
Type Round trip
Best season Mid or late
Topo maps Matterhorn Peak
Grade (hiking days/recommended layover days)
   Leisurely ---
   Moderate 4/1
   Strenuous 3/1
Trailhead 19

HIGHLIGHTS This trip is a satisfying one for the hiker who has viewed the Sawtooth Ridge from the north side only. Following Robinson Creek nearly to the crest of the Sierra, this route circles the west end of the Sawtooth Ridge, and then drops down into the scenic upper reaches of Piute Creek. For those who appreciate spectacular mountain scenery of alpine character, this trip is almost a must.

DESCRIPTION (Moderate trip)

1st Hiking Day: Follow Trip 35 to **Crown Lake**, 8 miles.

2nd Hiking Day (**Crown Lake** to **Campsites, Upper Piute Creek**, 3.5 miles): From Crown Lake's outlet the trail ascends along the west side, offering fine views of the meadowed inlet. The ascent soon steepens as the trail begins a series of short, rocky switchbacks that terminate just east of Crown Point. Here the trail levels out in a willowed meadowy area with several small lakelets, and meets the Snow Lake Trail just beyond. Our route turns left (south), fords the stream draining Snow Lake, and climbs over an easy talus-and-scree pile. This rocky ascent levels briefly within sight of another small lakelet; then the trail cuts across a bench and ascends steeply by rocky switchbacks. In most years there is a large snowbank across this slope well into summer, and one should exercise some caution here. After one more bench this ascent terminates at a tundra-topped saddle on the divide north of Slide Mountain. Here sparse whitebark pine and hemlock stoop to alpine climes, and the traveler taking a breather at this unnamed pass is likely to hear the scolding of a disturbed cony.

From this pass the trail stepladders down through a series of sandy tundra pockets, serpentining its way north and then east before beginning the long traverse down to Piute Creek. This traverse strikes timberline just below the cross-country turnoff to Ice and Maltby lakes, which is at the ford of the stream draining the swale that gives access to Ice Lake. Fishermen will find the excellent fishing for eastern brook in these two lakes worth the side trip. On the lodgepole and hemlock that line the trail, one will encounter the historic **T** blaze typical of the older trails in Yosemite National Park—a sign emblazoned on these trails by the U.S. Cavalry in the early part of the century, when it was their responsibility to patrol the Park.

This hiking day terminates at the campsites upstream from the turnoff to the cross-country route down Slide Canyon, located on Piute Creek (9600') along the first ½ mile after the trail comes within sight of the creek. Fishing for eastern brook (to 8") is fair. This location makes a fine base-camp location for exploratory trips down Slide Canyon or over into Matterhorn Canyon, and it is a traditional base camp for climbers making ascents of Matterhorn Peak and other climbs along the Sawtooth Ridge.

3rd and 4th Hiking Days: Retrace your steps, 11.5 miles.

Twin Lakes to Buckeye Creek **37**

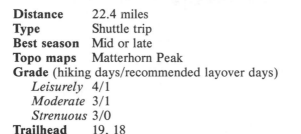

Distance	22.4 miles
Type	Shuttle trip
Best season	Mid or late
Topo maps	Matterhorn Peak

Grade (hiking days/recommended layover days)
  Leisurely 4/1
  Moderate 3/1
  Strenuous 3/0

Trailhead   19, 18

HIGHLIGHTS This circle trip around Buckeye Ridge visits nearly the entire range of Sierran environments, from the sagebrush-scrub of the east side to the sub-alpine grassland of Kerrick Meadow. In between, it winds through pure stands of hemlock, past water-loving clumps of quaking aspen and amidst windblown, gnarled whitebark pine. In its variety it is indeed an "everything trip for everyone."

DESCRIPTION (Moderate trip)

1st Hiking Day: Follow Trip 35 to **Peeler Lake**, 8.0 miles.

2nd Hiking Day (**Peeler Lake** to **Buckeye Forks**, 5.0 miles): From Peeler Lake the trail descends along the lake's west outlet, crossing and recrossing this outlet as it flows down into the marshy upper reaches of Rancheria Creek in Kerrick Meadow. In the meadow, we meet the Kerrick Canyon Trail, turn right (north) on it, and then ascend a gentle slope above the north end of the meadow. A moderate forest cover of mostly pines lines the rest of the gently ascending sand-and-duff trail to the summit of Buckeye Pass. This pass (9580') in a small, lodgepole-encroached meadow is on the Yosemite Park boundary.

Then the duff trail drops down the northeast side of the pass, and soon fords the infant rill of Buckeye Creek. From here to the next ford, this descent skirts a series of charmingly meadowed steps on the northwest side of the creek. These pockets of grasslands have rich gardens of flowers whose full, splashy colors invite the passerby to linger and enjoy the aster, goldenrod, paintbrush, penstemon, shooting star, larkspur, lupine, buttercup, columbine and monkey flower. Owls hunt these meadows at night, and the daytime traveler should keep a lookout for large convoctions of agitated birdlife. At the core of such gatherings, frequently, is a large owl seeking protection in dense foliage.

The series of meadows terminates at a ford where the trail crosses to the east side of the creek. About ¼ mile beyond this ford is a snowcourse, and from it an unmaintained trail takes off over the ridge bound for Barney Lake. For the next ½ mile our trail continues to descend moderately through an area where the trees are much avalanche-broken, and then we jump across an unnamed tributary that tumbles down from Hunewill Peak. In another ½ mile we reach the first of several fair and good campsites located at places where the trail periodically touches the stream. Then a steep descending section followed by two less steep inclines bring us to the flat where the North and South Forks of Buckeye Creek conjoin. In this quiet flat we cross the South Fork on a log and 200 yards farther on wade the North Fork. There are good campsites in the vicinity of a snow-survey cabin here, and the junction with the main east-west trail is just beyond. Fishing in the forks for rainbow and brook (to 9″) is good.

3rd Hiking Day: Follow the 5th hiking day, Trip 33, 9.4 miles.

(Just 1.1 miles down the road toward Bridgeport a side road goes south across Buckeye Creek, but if you go straight ahead 0.4 mile and then park in a used-looking area beside the road, you can walk a few yards downhill to Buckeye Hot Springs. Here, right beside the singing brook, you can soak away the trip's dirt in a natural hot spa.)

Twin Lakes to Kerrick Meadow **38**

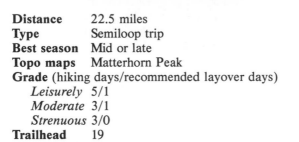

Distance   22.5 miles
Type   Semiloop trip
Best season   Mid or late
Topo maps   Matterhorn Peak
Grade (hiking days/recommended layover days)
    Leisurely 5/1
    Moderate 3/1
    Strenuous 3/0
Trailhead   19

HIGHLIGHTS To use a business metaphor, this trip gives a great return for a minimum investment. From the outset this route is enveloped in magnificent scenery. Along Robinson Creek, the skyline and the immediate surroundings are those of rugged grandeur, consonant with the physical expenditure of effort required on the uphill. As the trip circles Crown Point, it "levels out" both in physical terrain and in emotional impact. The ruggedness gives way to sweeping meadows and rounded summits, providing the traveler an opportunity to absorb some of the impact of this land of contrasts.

DESCRIPTION (Moderate trip)

1st Hiking Day: Follow Trip 35 to **Crown Lake**, 8 miles.

2nd Hiking Day (**Crown Lake** to **Peeler Lake**, 6.5 miles): Rounding the rocky west side of Crown Lake, the trail rises out of the lake basin by steep, rocky switchbacks that offer fine views back of the clear blue lake. This ascent levels out as it crosses a granite-flanked saddle and meets the Rock Island Pass Trail just west of a lakelet in a sandy-meadowed section. Our route turns right (southwest) and begins a long, steadily traversing climb toward Snow Lake. This traverse gives way to

switchbacks midway up the hill, and jogs southwest under
Crown Point before resuming its southward course on more
switchbacks by a little stream. Looking back from the top of
this climb, we have fine views to the east of the soldier-tipped
summit of Kettle Peak and the west end of the Sawtooth Ridge
(called Blacksmith Peak). Snow Lake itself, like Peeler Lake to
the north, is a crestal lake perched atop a divide, but in angling
circles it is best known for its fishery of golden trout. As the
trail rounds the rocky north edge of the lake, we see the
meadowy lake fringes, which are most extensive at the southwest end. Here the meadows extend from the lake's edge to the
low-profiled saddle called Rock Island Pass (10,150').

From Rock Island Pass the trail descends into the
Rancheria Creek drainage. The descent witnesses a change
from sparse whitebark pine to a conglomerate forest of lodgepole, hemlock and silver pine. After traversing above a sandy
meadow, the T-blazed trail here rises sharply over a sandy ridge
and then drops moderately on switchbacks through dense forest
cover to Kerrick Meadow and a ford of Rancheria Creek.

On the northwest side of the ford, the trail meets the Kerrick
Canyon Trail, where our route turns right and ascends gently up
Kerrick Meadow. Rancheria Creek winds its oxbowing way
through these sandy grasslands, and on the right we can see
large crestal sand accumulations indicating where the living
stream has moved across the meadow floor, leaving its spoor.
The meadow bottlenecks briefly into a canyon narrows, where
the creek tumbles over a silver cascade, and then opens into a
beautiful, open, wetter section near the headwaters. In the
middle of this marshy section the trail fords one arm of the
creek, and then continues on to meet the unsigned Peeler Lake
Trail at the meadow's head, where our route turns right (east).
From this junction the trail crosses the open meadow and winds
through a broken, moderate forest cover of lodgepole. This
route crisscrosses back and forth over the west outlet stream
from Peeler Lake and arrives at the good campsites along the
west shore of this large and beautiful lake (9500'). These campsites offer fine views to the east of Cirque Mountain, Kettle
Peak and Crown Point, and the deep waters near the west shore
offer fine bank fishing for eastern brook and rainbow (to 14").
Other good campsites lie on the east shore.

3rd Hiking Day: Reverse the steps of the 1st hiking day,
Trip 34, 8 miles.

Twin Lakes to Hetch Hetchy 39

Distance	43.8 miles
Type	Shuttle trip
Best season	Mid or late
Topo maps	Matterhorn Peak, Tower Peak, **Hetch Hetchy Reservoir**

Grade (hiking days/recommended layover days)
> *Leisurely* 8/2
> *Moderate* 6/1
> *Strenuous* 5/0

Trailhead 19, 16

HIGHLIGHTS This trip passes through the heart of the largest roadless area in the lower 48. After crossing the crest on the northern boundary of Yosemite, this route takes in a very large part of the Park before ending near its western boundary, 5700 feet lower. Few trans-Sierra crossings are less traveled or more scenic.

DESCRIPTION (Moderate trip)

1st Hiking Day: Follow Trip 34 to **Peeler Lake**, 8 miles.

2nd Hiking Day (**Peeler Lake** to **Arndt Lake**, 5 miles): Leaving Peeler Lake beside the west outlet, the trail drops down gently as it crosses back and forth over the outlet stream. This descent soon leaves the moderate forest cover and enters the north edge of Kerrick Meadow. At the head of this open, rank grassland the trail meets the Buckeye Pass Trail, where our route turns left (south) and begins a long, gentle descent. The trail on the west side of twisting Rancheria Creek is a narrow, sandy track lined with a wildflower collage of shooting star, penstemon, paintbrush, aster, goldenrod, buttercup, lupine, Douglas phlox, and pussy paws. In a timber-lined bottleneck, the meadows narrow briefly and then reopen. On the left one can see sand banks that were stranded when the oxbowing stream altered course sometime in the geologic past. The broad grasslands are alive with the scurrying and piping of alarmed Belding ground squirrels.

The trail then passes the Rock Island Pass Trail and continues to descend to a second timbered narrows. This brief stretch of lodgepole pine opens to yet another long meadow that is flanked on the southwest by the granite heights of Price Peak. On the descent through this meadow the canyon starts to narrow, and where the trail starts a gentle 200-yard ascent, our route leaves the trail.

Our short cross-country segment strikes out southward, fords Rancheria Creek, and ascends beside the tundra-lined outlet of Arndt Lake. A good route to the north shore of hidden Arndt Lake is via the saddle in the granite just east of where the outlet leaves the lake.

One will find good campsites at the outlet and around the north shore of Arndt Lake (9240'). Those with a tolerance for cool mountain water will enjoy the swimming off the granite that drops into this lake. Views of the polished granite domes flanking the south and east sides of the lake are soul-satisfying, and beckon the explorer to further investigation and discovery.

3rd Hiking Day (**Arndt Lake** to **Bear Valley Lake**, 7 miles): From Arndt Lake our route retraces the cross-country segment of the previous hiking day to the Kerrick Canyon Trail, and then continues down through a narrow, rocky canyon. The unseamed white granite canyon walls in this narrows show the glacial polish, smoothing and sculpting that reflect the geologic history of the canyon. Rancheria Creek on the left bumps and splashes down through a series of fine potholes offering swimming and fishing spots. Like all the older trails in the Park, this one is **T**-blazed, indicating that it was once a U.S. Cavalry patrol route—a route blazed when the Army was responsible for the integrity of the Park lands.

The sparse-to-moderate forest cover of mountain hemlock and whitebark and lodgepole pine in the narrows gives way to another meadow as the trail continues to descend. This meadow is surrounded by several magnificent examples of glacial domes—all unnamed. The clean, sweeping lines of the dome to the west are particularly impressive, and the passerby cannot help but feel the awesome power of the natural forces that created it. Near the foot of the meadow, the trail fords to the east side of Rancheria Creek, where it hugs the sheer, water-stained granite wall. Both the trail and the creek make an exaggerated **Z** before straightening out on a westward course and reaching the Pacific Crest Trail.

Turning west, the route undulates along the south wall of Kerrick Canyon. As it passes below the heavily fractured north facade of Piute Mountain, it is sometimes high above the creek and sometimes on the creek's banks. Many tributaries, varying in size from step-across to jump-across fords, break this route segment into lush gardens of monkey flower, tiger lily, shooting star, bush lupine, corn lily, columbine and goldenrod. (Most of these tributaries are not shown on the topo map.) As the canyon walls open, the trail descends close to the creek and meets the Bear Valley Trail. Here our route begins a steep switch-backing ascent up the south wall of Kerrick Canyon. Winding back and forth through a moderate forest cover of lodgepole pine, silver pine and hemlock, the trail near the top affords superlative views to the north and northeast.

A short distance beyond the lip of Kerrick canyon we come to Bear Valley Lake (9200′). There are excellent campsites near the outlet of this beautiful lake. Though fishless, this lake warms up enough by mid-summer to provide excellent swimming. Notwithstanding its name, Bear Valley has few bears. Of course it only takes one to eat your food, so, even in this remote spot it is best to store your supplies properly.

4th Hiking Day (**Bear Valley Lake** to **Pleasant Valley**, 5.5 miles): From Bear Valley Lake our trail crosses the outlet and descends a canyon to the southwest. After a short descent we cross the creek and turn south, passing a small lake. Beyond the lake we climb over a low moraine and descend to a meadow, signed BEAR VALLEY ELEV. 9400′. To the south is a saddle 700 feet above, to which we shall climb. After skirting this meadow on either side, we pick up the trail again and wind up through willow thickets, crossing a small, overgrown stream. Our trail, often muddy in places, is well appointed with wildflowers, including Sierra gentian, lupine and shooting star.

Soon the ground becomes drier as we pass a grove of large

hemlocks before the last, steep 200 feet to the saddle. From here we can look north over the heavily glaciated granitic landscape of northern Yosemite. To the south is a gently sloping valley that has seen glaciation only in the distant past, if at all. Much of our route to Rancheria Creek will now be through an island of forested, unglaciated upland, on Rancheria Mountain. We follow the faint, ducked trail, descending gently along an open grus-covered hillside above a small creek. Soon we swing south, drop down a sagebrush-covered hill and cross that creek. You may notice sharp boundaries between vegetation types by the creek. This indicates porous soil that drains very well, and grabbing a handful reveals mostly grus—granules of weathered granite. Such an accumulation could not develop here without a very prolonged absence of glaciation.

Beyond the creek we descend a hillside covered with tall wheatgrass and reach another small creek. Now we enter dense forest, and a short descent brings us to a wet, meadowy flat, beyond which we cross an indistinct moraine. After another short descent we arrive at a small, marshy lake. If you want to avoid the 1200-foot descent into and the return climb out of Pleasant Valley, you can camp at this mosquito haven. The sojourn would not be without its rewards, as the lake may contain mallards when you're there and the surrounding forest supports juncos, chickarees and deer.

From the lake we descend past an aspen flat to a broad, red-fir-covered saddle, where we meet the trail to Pleasant Valley. Turning south onto it, we descend gently and then steeply, as the trail winds down the side of Piute Creek canyon. Emerging from timber, we get good views up-canyon toward Sawtooth Ridge, while below us we can see some of the lakes around Pleasant Valley. To the south is the chasm of the Grand Canyon of the Tuolumne, flanked by Double Rock and Colby Mountain. The grade eases until we enter a gully and descend it to the forested floor of Pleasant Valley (6850'). Good campsites can be found along Piute Creek, and both the nearby lakes and the creek provide good fishing for rainbow trout.

5th Hiking Day (**Pleasant Valley** to **Rancheria Creek**, 11.8 miles): Though this day begins with an 1800-foot climb, the remainder is a 4000-foot descent of Rancheria Mountain to Rancheria Creek. First retrace your steps of the previous hiking day to the junction with the trail to Hetch Hetchy. Turning left, we ascend the dry slopes of Rancheria Mountain and gain its broad ridge. From the top of this ascent you can climb up volcanic talus to the left and enjoy the wonderful views from the actual summit of Rancheria Mountain. From there you can see Sawtooth Ridge, Piute Creek canyon, Mt. Dana, the Tuolumne River canyon and the Cathedral Range.

Heading southwest, we descend gently through open forest of silver pine and red fir, cross a dry hillside, and enter the lush meadows around the headwaters of an unnamed creek. Among the lodgepole pines along the creek are Bigelow sneezeweed, yarrow milfoil and elephant heads. Beyond the creek we cross over a low, dry hill that is covered with pussy paws and laced with gopher holes. Then we swing near a small creek, descend an eroded stretch of trail, and arrive at a campsite by the creek we crossed earlier. This may be the last water before Rancheria Creek, and it is a lovely spot to tank up before the upcoming 3000-foot descent.

Past the creek, the forest cover changes in response to lower elevation; we leave lodgepole pine behind and enter a white fir forest. After a series of switchbacks the grade eases as we pass through an alder thicket and enter drier environs inhabited by a sparse forest of Jeffrey pine, incense-cedar, sugar pine and white fir. Drought-tolerant ceanothus and manzanita dot the hillside between trees as we descend past a seasonal stream and climb over the east shoulder of LeConte Point.

The last 1400-foot descent to Rancheria Creek begins gently, and we get our first views of Hetch Hetchy Reservoir and Kolana Rock. Soon we begin a long series of switchbacks, where we see large numbers of black oak and perhaps a few of its associate, the California gray squirrel. When we arrive at the gorge above Rancheria Falls, we may or may not find a bridge across the creek. If there is no serviceable bridge, then crossing the creek *above the falls* can be extremely difficult and dangerous except during very low water. Beyond the creek we descend a rocky hillside past the trail to Tiltill Valley, and after ⅓ mile the trail levels off in a forested flat. Here we turn left onto a spur trail and walk over to the shaded creekside camping area below Rancheria Falls. Both bears and people frequent this area, so tend your supplies accordingly.

6th Hiking Day: Reverse the steps of the 1st hiking day, Trip 45, 6.5 miles.

40   Twin Lakes to Benson Lake

Distance	37.2 miles
Type	Round trip
Best season	Mid or late
Topo maps	Matterhorn Peak, Tower Peak

Grade (hiking days/recommended layover days)
   Leisurely 8/2
   Moderate 6/1
   Strenuous 4/1

Trailhead   19

HIGHLIGHTS This long trip penetrates to the heart of the North Boundary Country. In its course it surmounts the Sierra crest and traces a westside watershed to the Shangri-la basin of Benson Lake. Because of its moderate climes and its remote location, this lake is a favorite layover spot for parties traversing the Pacific Crest Trail, and its popularity is well founded.

DESCRIPTION (Moderate trip)

1st and 2nd Hiking Days: Follow Trip 39 to **Arndt Lake**, 13 miles.

3rd Hiking Day (**Arndt Lake** to **Benson Lake**, 5.6 miles): Proceed to the Pacific Crest Trail junction as described in the third hiking day, Trip 39. At this junction our route turns left (south) and ascends steadily by switchbacks through a moderate forest cover of hemlock. At the top of the first rise Piute Mountain comes into sight, and the trail levels briefly as it wends past a tiny snowmelt tarn. The trail then resumes climbing steeply through an increasingly sparse forest cover of hemlock and pine to Seavey Pass (9150′).

From the glacially polished granite setting of Seavey Pass the trail drops past another stately rockbound tarn just below the pass, and finally plummets down over steep, eroded pitches alongside a riotous unnamed stream that feeds the Benson Lake alluvial fan. This descent is rocky going, requiring a "grunt and bear it" attitude of the downhill-weary traveler, alleviated only by the fine views of Volunteer Peak across Piute Creek and of the splashing waterfall springing from the ridge south of Piute Mountain.

Where the trail levels out on the valley floor, it crosses the sandy alluvial sediments, and witnesses some drastic changes in the flora. The initial contact with the valley floor, with its solitary-standing specimens of Jeffrey pine towering amid gooseberry, gives the traveler the impression of sandy aridity. But within a few yards, the atmosphere changes as the trail becomes immersed in bracken fern, overflow freshets and dense forest. The trail is sometimes difficult to follow because of the rank growth and quagmire conditions of the valley floor. Two trails cut through this fertile area to Benson Lake. One, unmarked, turns right just after you enter the valley floor. The other departs just before the ford of Piute Creek. This lateral winds along the northwest bank of Piute Creek through fields of corn lily and bracken fern, with occasional clumps of tiger lily and swamp onion, to the good campsites along the east shore of the lake (7600'). Anglers can look forward to good fishing for rainbow and eastern brook trout (to 14"). Except in mosquito season, this lake makes a fine spot for a layover day.

4th, 5th and 6th Hiking Days: Retrace your steps, 18.6 miles.

Benson Lake

41 Twin Lakes to Smedberg Lake

Distance   49.6 miles
Type   Semiloop trip
Best season Mid or late
Topo maps   Matterhorn Peak, Tower Peak
Grade (hiking days/recommended layover days)
  Leisurely 8/3
  Moderate 7/2
  Strenuous 5/1
Trailhead   19

HIGHLIGHTS Making a grand loop through the center of the North Boundary Country, this trip traces three major watersheds, visits six major lakes, and views the finest scenery in the region. Layover days taken on this long route provide the opportunity of visiting any of the nearby lakes, over a dozen, or making side trips into any one of several other watersheds. It is a long trip with many stiff climbs that make it advisable for the hiker to first prepare himself by taking one or more shorter trips.

DESCRIPTION (Leisurely trip)

1st, 2nd and 3rd Hiking Days: Follow Trip 40 to **Benson Lake**, 18.6 miles.

4th Hiking Day (**Benson Lake** to **Smedberg Lake**, 4.5 miles): There is an old saying among those who have visited Benson Lake, "Everywhere from that hole in the ground is up," and one contemplating this hiking day must agree. Retracing our steps over the short lateral to the main trail, the route then fords Piute Creek and begins a long, steep climb through a moderate forest cover of lodgepole laced with occasional silver pine. Crisscrossing back and forth over the outlet stream from

Smedberg Lake, the trail then circles beneath the steep west facade of Volunteer Peak, and finally crosses over the shoulder of this peak past the first of two trail junctions to Pate Valley. On the north side of Volunteer Peak the trail drops to the south shore of Smedberg Lake (9220'), where excellent campsites may be found all along the south shore and along the southeast inlet about 200 yards from the lake. Fishing for rainbow and occasional eastern brook (to 13") is excellent. As a layover point this picturesque, island-dotted lake makes a fine central location for excursions to nearby Surprise and Sister Lakes.

5th Hiking Day (**Smedberg Lake** to **Matterhorn Canyon**, 6.5 miles): From the narrow valley holding Smedberg Lake, the trail is a steady climb to Benson Pass. It first follows up an inlet of Smedberg Lake on a southeast, meadowed course, then swings east on a stepladdering climb through moderate, then sparse, forest cover to an upper meadow above the main drainage feeding Smedberg Lake. After this brief respite the trail resumes its steep, rocky, upward course to Benson Pass (10,139'). The last climb is over a heavily eroded surface through sparse whitebark pine and hemlock. Excellent views to the northeast present themselves at the pass, and one can see Whorl Mountain, Twin Peaks, some of the pinnacles making up the Sawtooth Ridge, and the granite divide between Matterhorn Creek and Piute Creek.

The trail leaves Benson Pass on a descent that is steep, level and steep again as it drops to Wilson Canyon. Then the downgrade is gradual along the banks of Wilson Creek to the lip of Matterhorn Canyon. In this section the trail winds back and forth over Wilson Creek through an increasingly dense forest cover of lodgepole, with occasional whitebark pine near the top and silver pine near the bottom. Finally, the path is steep again to the floor of Matterhorn Canyon. On the canyon floor, Matterhorn Canyon Creek is a meandering stream flowing alternately through willowed meadows and stands of lodgepole mixed with silver pine. Our trail turns north and follows the stream a mile, then fords it to several campsites 200 yards downstream from the junction with the trail to Tuolumne Meadows. These canyon campsites (8480') boast several fine swimming holes just upstream in granite potholes. Fishing for eastern brook and rainbow trout (to 12") is good.

6th Hiking Day (**Matterhorn Canyon** to **Campsites,**

Upper Piute Creek, 8.5 miles): From these campsites our route goes northeast and leaves the Pacific Crest Trail behind. The route ascends moderately through alternately sandy and rocky sections. On both sides of the canyon, glaciated gray granite shoulders drop to the valley floor, and the black water-staining on their broad surfaces, particularly on Quarry Peak, makes eerie configurations. In a wet, muddy section where the trail fords several small tributary runoffs, it winds through wildflower displays that include lupine, elephant heads, monkey flower, paintbrush, goldenrod, aster and Mariposa lily. The trail then fords to the west side of Matterhorn Canyon Creek and then refords to follow the east bank through the latter part of the canyon narrows and well beyond. About ½ mile above a meadow it refords back to the west side.

From this ford the trail keeps to the west side of the creek, winding through meadow and tundra sections on a moderate ascent. Ahead, the pointed tops of Finger Peaks come into view, and later the massive granite of Whorl Mountain and Matterhorn Peak. Scattered lodgepole and hemlock trees dot the trail as it progresses up to the sky-parlor meadows of the upper basin. Some clumps of trees hold campsites (their protected location is testimony to the wind that often sweeps through the canyon), and the tree clumps are interspersed with stretches of grassland laced with sagebrush and willow.

Now the trail passes the last stand of trees, and ascends steadily on a long traverse below Finger Peaks. Views across the barren upper basin of Whorl Mountain are awesome, and its rugged massiveness contrasts sharply with the delicate wildflowers found underfoot as one nears Burro Pass. Here, scattered among sparse whitebark pines, one enjoys the spots of color provided by primrose, scarlet penstemon, wallflower and Douglas phlox. The final climb to the divide is accomplished via rocky switchbacks that terminate on the low saddle of Burro Pass (10,560'). Fine views of both the Matterhorn and Piute Creek canyons are to be had, but overshadowing all are the soldier-topped summits of the Sawtooth Ridge to the north.

The first recorded crossing of this pass was made by Lt. N. F. McClure in 1894. Today's traveler can compare his observations of the pass and its surroundings with those of McClure, who said, "The route now led for five miles through little meadows on each side of the stream, until a comparatively low saddle was seen to the left of us and near the head of the canyon. Investigating this, I found it was a natural pass. The scenery here was truly sublime. I doubt if any part of the main chain of the Sierra presents a greater ruggedness . . ."

As the trail descends on the north side of the pass, it affords fine views of the tiny, barren lakes at the foot of Finger Peaks. The basin of the pass is usually wet, and sometimes covered with snow, thereby making route-picking an instinctive matter. Here Piute Creek is a far cry from what was seen two hiking days ago. A mere stripling of a stream, it tinkles through meadow grass, and the traveler fords to the north side by an easy step. Belding squirrels pipe one's passage through the grassy tundra stretches, and the call of marmots on the nearby scree is a cacophonous accompaniment to the gentle descent into the moderate forest cover of lodgepole and hemlock. This hiking day ends at the good campsites (9600') found along that stretch of Piute Creek where the trail touches the creek banks northeast of Finger Peaks. Here fishing for eastern brook (to 8") is fair.

7th and 8th Hiking Days: Reverse the steps of Trip 36, 11.5 miles.

Looking up the Robinson Creek Trail

42   Green Creek to East Lake

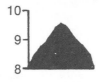

Distance   7 miles
Type   Round trip
Best season   Early, mid or late
Topo maps   Matterhorn Peak
Grade (hiking days/recommended layover days)
   Leisurely 2/0
   Moderate ---
   Strenuous ---
Trailhead   20

HIGHLIGHTS This is a fine beginner's weekend hike. East Lake offers one of the most colorful backdrops for a camping scene to be found in any wilderness. The trilogy of Gabbro, Page and Epidote peaks is composed of rocks varying in hue from vermilion reds to ochre, and these colors are set in metavolcanic blacks for contrast. Nearby Nutter, Gilman and Hoover lakes offer good fishing to supplement the angling in East Lake, and the general spectrum of scenery along the trail rounds out a rich diet indeed.

DESCRIPTION

1st Hiking Day (**Green Creek Roadend** to **East Lake**, 3.5 miles): The trailhead is just beyond the Green Lakes Pack Station at road's end. Amid moderate-to-dense Jeffrey, juniper, lodgepole and aspen forest cover, the trail ascends gently to a small step-across spring runoff. A ground cover of sagebrush, mule ears, serviceberry, western blueberry, wild lilac, lupine, wallflower, paintbrush, pennyroyal and buckwheat lines the trail in the initial drier stretches, and along the wetter spots one finds tiger lily, penstemon, shooting star, monkshood, monkey flower, columbine, rein-orchid and aster. The ascent then becomes steeper as it crosses an easy rocky ridge, and finally it begins a long series of steady switchbacks.

Crossing several intermittent runoff tributaries coming down from Monument Ridge, the trail keeps to the northwest side of West Fork Green Creek. While the creek itself is never out of hearing, it is often obscured visually by the sheath of willows that line its bank. Ahead, on the left, one can make out Gabbro Peak, and on the right the stream that falls from the hanging valley containing West Lake. Added to the wildflowers to be seen along the trail here are iris, corn lily, cow parsnip, stickseed, gooseberry, Douglas phlox and pussy paws.

The trail then climbs another dry slope by moderately ascending switchbacks to a junction just before Green Lake where the right fork leads to campsites on Green Lake and to West Lake. Anglers may wish to tarry here for the good fishing for rainbow and eastern brook (to 14"). Green Lake is large (about 50 acres), with a rocky west shore and a steep southeast shore. A mixed timber cover of lodgepole, hemlock and occasional silver pine surrounds most of the lake except for the meadowed inlet delta.

Our route, the left fork, fords West Fork Green Creek just below the lake and makes a long dogleg to the south before turning east to ford the outlet stream from East Lake. This outlet stream is a vigorous watercourse that follows the natural ravine shown on the topo map just north of East Lake. The trail makes a long loop away from the stream and then veers back to a second ford. The ascent is sometimes steep as it continues on to the meadowed outlet of East Lake. Fair-to-good campsites (9440') can be found around the outlet just below the flood-control dam, and on the north shore. Fishing for rainbow trout on this 75-acre lake is good. This lake makes a fine base-camp location for forays to nearby Nutter, Gilman and Hoover lakes.

2nd Hiking Day: Retrace your steps, 3.5 miles.

43 Green Creek to Tuolumne Meadows

Distance   26.2 miles
Type   Shuttle trip
Best season   Mid or late
Topo maps   Matterhorn Peak, **Tuolumne Meadows**
Grade (hiking days/recommended layover days)
   Leisurely 4/1
   Moderate 4/0
   Strenuous 3/0
Trailhead   20, 23

HIGHLIGHTS Three quarters of this scenic route travels
                    remote sections of Yosemite National Park that
are not frequented by day walkers. Solitude-seekers will find
the quiet of upper Virginia Canyon to their liking, and anglers
wanting a variety of lake and stream fishing for rainbow and
eastern brook will pronounce this trip ideal.

DESCRIPTION (Moderate trip)

   1st Hiking Day: Follow Trip 42 to **East Lake**, 3.5 miles.
   2nd Hiking Day (**East Lake** to **Lower Virginia Canyon**, 9
miles): From the outlet of East Lake the trail ascends above the
lake's waters as it rounds the east shore, affording superlative
views of Gabbro, Page and Epidote peaks foregrounded by the
deep blue of East Lake. The trail drops briefly across the gentle
ridge separating East Lake from the tiny lakelets to the east,
and then veers away from East Lake on an ascending traverse
before descending gently to the meadow-fringed shores of
Nutter Lake. Through a sparse forest cover of lodgepole and
hemlock, the trail then climbs above the west shore of beautiful Gilman Lake, passing a lateral trail down to it. Flanked by
the steep west face of Dunderberg Peak, and foregrounded by a

meadow and timber cover, this lake is a favorite of photographers. Anglers may also wish to linger—the better to sample the good fishing for rainbow.

From the Gilman Lake lateral our trail ascends past several small tarns, fords the stream joining Gilman and Hoover Lakes, and then rises steeply to the bench holding Hoover Lakes. These two alpine lakes are set between the dark rock of Epidote Peak and the burgundy-red rock of the magnificent unnamed mountain to the southeast. They are considerably colder than the lakes below, and they have been planted with eastern brook trout. The trail skirts the southeast side of the first, fords the stream between them, and passes by the northwest side of the second. After fording the inlet, it ascends steeply along the stream joining Hoover Lakes with Summit Lake. This rocky ascent through a thinning forest cover of lodgepole and occasional hemlock and whitebark pine meets the Virginia Lakes Trail on a small bench, where our route turns right (northwest). This moderate ascent fords the aforementioned stream and arrives at aptly named Summit Lake (10,160'). Like Peeler Lake to the north, Summit Lake contributes water to both sides of the Sierra. It sits atop the crest in a **V**'d notch between the dark rock of Camiaca Peak and a lighter ridge extending north from Excelsior Mountain.

The trail skirts the north side of Summit Lake to the Sierra crest and then switchbacks steeply down the west slope. Looking back toward Summit Lake, we can see clearly that the glaciers that had their beginnings below Camiaca Peak on both the east and the west sides met at the present site of Summit Lake. Across the cirque basin of upper Virginia Canyon, the rounded eminence of Grey Butte and the sharply nippled tops of Virginia Peak and Stanton Peak dominate the views to the west. The descent levels out before it fords Return Creek and continues down-canyon. Recent avalanches have made obvious incursions into the sparse forest cover of lodgepole, aspen and occasional red fir and hemlock, and have left broken stubs on every hand.

The trail then fords several tributary streams as it keeps to the west side of Return Creek on a long, moderate descent to a junction with the Pacific Crest Trail. At this junction our route turns left, fords Return Creek, and arrives at some good campsites (8600') in the granite ledge system on the east side of the creek. Fishing for eastern brook and rainbow is fair to good.

3rd Hiking Day (**Lower Virginia Canyon** to **Glen Aulin**, 8 miles): The trail from the campsites near the ford continues southwest along the banks of Return Creek and fords McCabe Creek before beginning the steep ascent of the canyon wall. This gentle descent along Return Creek passes the stream's beautiful bedrock-granite cascades. Dropping into deep, clear potholes, the creek has carved and sculpted the bedrock into smooth, mollescent lines that invite the traveler to run his hands across them. Columbine clustered amid lupine and whorled penstemon add color to the green mats of swamp onion and gooseberry near the ford. (In late season fill your canteen at McCabe Creek, for there is no more water until Glen Aulin.)

Beyond this ford the trail begins long switchbacks across a slope moderately forested with fine specimens of silver pine, lodgepole and occasional red fir. These rocky switchbacks terminate at the McCabe Lake Trail junction, where our route turns right and descends gently over a duff surface. Birdlife abounds through the moderate-to-dense forest cover of red fir, lodgepole and silver pine, and the hiker is very likely to see chicadees, juncos, warblers, flycatchers, woodpeckers, bluebirds, robins and evening grosbeaks in these precincts.

A short ¾ mile beyond the last junction, close under Point 9186, you may find water even in late season. Then your route declines gently through cool, moist forest to a fairly large meadow east of Elbow Hill. After threading a course through a few stands of pines, you emerge in an even larger meadow—about 2 miles long, although the trail does not trace all 2 miles of it. At a stream fork shortly beyond a *very* large boulder to your west, you may find water even in late season. Then the trail climbs over a saddle in a low, forested ridge and gently descends for about ½ mile. Over the next mile, always near Cold Canyon Creek, the level, rutted path passes many possible campsites in pleasant meadowy areas studded with small lodgepole pines.

From this camping region a series of easy switchbacks accomplish about half the descent to the Tuolumne River, and where the trail re-reaches the creek there is another good campsite. On the final rocky downhill mile to the river, you catch glimpses of Tuolumne Falls and White Cascade, and their roar carries all the way across the canyon.

Finally, you reach "civilization" at the Glen Aulin High Sierra Camp. Within sight of the camp you pass the Tuolumne River Trail westbound, and in 15 yards come to the little spur trail that crosses Conness Creek on a bridge to the camp. Very meager supplies are sometimes available here. The backpacker campsites just upstream from the "lodge" are very popular with bears, and you would be less likely to have ursine visitors at one of the campsites a mile or two before you reach Glen Aulin—though it would be no guarantee.

4th Hiking Day (**Glen Aulin** to **Tuolumne Meadows**, 5.7 miles): From Glen Aulin the trail crosses the Tuolumne River on a low steel bridge, from which one has excellent views of White Cascade and the deep green pool below it. In a few minutes we reach the May Lake Trail, ascending west, and continue our steep climb to gain the height of White Cascade and Tuolumne Falls. The trail passes a fine viewpoint below the falls, and if the light is right, you'll get a great photograph. Above the falls, the river flows down a series of sparkling rapids separated by large pools and wide sheets of clear water spread out over slightly inclined granite slopes.

Soon the trail crosses the river for the last time, on a boulders-and-steel bridge, and then climbs a little way above the gorge the river has cut here. Across the stream one can easily make out basaltic "Little Devils Postpile," the only volcanic formation anywhere around here. Then we descend to larger, polished slabs near the river, and follow a somewhat ducked route across them for about a mile beside the beckoning waters. When trail tread resumes, we soon cross the three branches of Dingley Creek, which may be dry in late season, and stroll along a "levee" built to raise the trailbed above the flood level here. About ½ mile of almost level walking in cool forest brings the long-distance trekker to the Young Lakes Trail junction, and then he touches the northwest edge of his destination, Tuolumne Meadows. Soon after, we cross three branches of Delaney Creek, the last being the only one of consequence. Just beyond this ford, a trail veers left, bound for the Tuolumne Meadows Stables. We instead veer right and ascend a long, dry, sandy ridge. From the tiny reeded lakes on top of this ridge, the trail drops gently down through meadowed pockets and stands of lodgepole pine to Soda Springs, once a drive-in and then a walk-in campground, but since 1976 closed to camping.

From the effervescent springs, in their dilapidated enclosure, the trail follows a closed-off dirt road east above the north edge of Tuolumne Meadows, the largest subalpine meadow in the Sierra Nevada. The spiring summits of the Cathedral Range across the meadow provide challenging vistas as we stroll the last, level ¾ mile to a parking lot beside State Highway 120, the Tioga Road—unless our car is waiting a few hundred yards short of the highway on the road to the stables.

Looking east across the Hoover Lakes

Green Creek to Virginia Lakes **44**

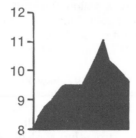

Distance   10 miles
Type   Shuttle trip
Best season   Mid or late
Topo maps   Matterhorn Peak
Grade (hiking days/recommended layover days)
　　Leisurely 2/1
　　Moderate 2/0
　　Strenuous ---
Trailhead   20, 21

HIGHLIGHTS This U-shaped trip circles around Kavanaugh Ridge and Dunderberg Peak, and in its passage touches 14 alpine and subalpine lakes. Scenery along this route is mostly of the open alpine variety, and the route is a fine sampling of the majestic Sierra crest. For the beginner or for the experienced back-country traveler, this trip is an excellent choice for a weekend excursion.

DESCRIPTION

1st Hiking Day: Follow Trip 42 to **East Lake**, 3.5 miles.

2nd Hiking Day (**East Lake** to **Virginia Lakes Campground**, 6.5 miles): Proceed to the Virginia Lakes Trail junction as described in the 2nd hiking day, Trip 43. At this junction our trail turns left (southeast) and climbs steeply up a series of switchbacks that overlook the Hoover Lakes in the valley of East Creek below. Beyond these zigzags we reach a sloping, willowed bowl surrounded by many snowbanks into late season. Then, under a small red cliff, the trail switchbacks up again, to cross the northern of the two streams in this two-headed canyon. Again the way steepens, and at frequent rest stops you can see the small white petals of Douglas phlox and the purple trumpetforms of Davidson's penstemon. There are even a few specimens of a yellow flower hardly ever found below 10,000 feet: alpine gold. Finally we cross the divide at 11,000 feet, where the red rocks of the crest on our right contrast with the somber dark grays of Black Mountain straight ahead.

The trail ahead has been altered slightly from that shown on the topo map, now being located farther south where it drops down the tundra steps of Frog Lakes. In Frog Lakes and in the willowed stream between them, anglers will find fair fishing for eastern brook and rainbow trout. Just north of Cooney Lake the new trail and that shown on the topo map once more coincide. This lake, with its willowed inlet and its precipitous outlet, contains thriving populations of eastern brook and rainbow.

Continuing the moderate descent over a rocky ledge system, the trail winds down through sparse clumps of whitebark pine past a mining claim, and then fords the willowed outlet stream of Moat Lake. In the wetter stretches here, wildflower fanciers will delight in the lush clumps of columbine, swamp onion and shooting star. Under the steep, avalanche-scarred south face of Dunderberg Peak, the second-highest peak in the North Boundary Country, the trail slopes down on a rocky traverse to the outlet of Blue Lake. The broken talus and scree to the north are a haven for marmots and conies, whose scats and hay harvests can be found on and between the rocks next to the trail. Like Cooney Lake, Blue Lake has a fishery of eastern brook and rainbow trout. Past Blue Lake the descending trail is within sight of one more tiny, unnamed lake. Soon the trail splits and ramifies, and even some roads appear, but route-finding is not a problem, because following any of them will in about ¼ mile bring you to Virginia Lakes Campground (9760').

Hetch Hetchy to Rancheria Creek **45**

Distance	13 miles
Type	Round trip
Best season	Early
Topo maps	**Hetch Hetchy Reservoir**

Grade (hiking days/recommended layover days)
  Leisurely 2/0
  Moderate ---
  Strenuous ---
Trailhead 16

HIGHLIGHTS Early season is the ideal time to view the falls along this route, and eager opening-day anglers will find the good fishing along Rancheria Creek a satisfying culmination to a fine trip.

DESCRIPTION

1st Hiking Day (**O'Shaughnessy Dam** to **Rancheria Creek**, 6.5 miles): From the trailhead at the south end of the dam, the thunder from the discharge pipe accompanies the traveler as he crosses this 600-foot-long piece of concrete. Although 8 miles of the Grand Canyon of the Tuolumne River were put under a reservoir for the sake of San Francisco's water supply, the actual intake for the aqueduct is 17 miles downstream in a relatively ordinary part of the canyon.

The first 0.7 mile of our route is on the service road (no longer used by vehicles, and badly deteriorated) to Lake Eleanor (part of San Francisco's water project). Once across the dam, the road passes through a long tunnel, beyond which it winds along the hillside above Hetch Hetchy's high-water mark. Views across the water include, from the left, Tueeulala Falls (seasonal), Wapama Falls, Hetch Hetchy Dome and Kolana Rock. Soon the road begins a gentle, shaded ascent through canyon live oak, incense-cedar, Douglas-fir, California bay, California grape, big-leaf maple and poison oak. As our route swings east and achieves a more southerly and drier position, trees become scarce. After we turn right onto the

signed trail to Rancheria Creek, there are Digger pines and live
oaks for shade. The trail winds along a sunny bench where
glacial polish and glacial erratics remind us that at times during
the Pleistocene Epoch glaciers up to 60 miles long—the longest
in the Sierra—flowed down this canyon.

After crossing seasonal Tueeulala Falls creek, we descend
to the bridges over Falls Creek. During high runoff this creek
can be impassable, as the bridges may be under water or
washed out. In early season Wapama Falls will cover these
bridges with spray. Beyond the creek our fly-infested trail
climbs onto a meadowy ledge system where we have an airy
view of the water below. In spring, wildflowers dot the
meadows here and you can see monkeyflower, paintbrush and
Sierra onion. This hike usually boasts a great variety of wildlife, and commonly seen animals include alligator lizard, Steller
jay and California ground squirrel.

Beyond the ledges our trail makes a long descent to
cascading Tiltill Creek, which we cross on a bridge. From here
we climb onto the low ridge separating Tiltill Creek and
Rancheria Creek. About ¾ mile beyond the bridge, the trail
enters a shaded flat where a spur trail (right) leads to
streamside campsites ¼ mile below Rancheria Falls. Please be
careful here as the area is heavily used and bears are persistent. Fishing in Rancheria Creek is poor-to-good for rainbow
trout (to 10").

2nd Hiking Day: Retrace your steps (6.5 miles).

Hikers near O'Shaughnessy Dam

Hetch Hetchy to Tiltill Valley   **46**

Distance	18.6 miles
Type	Round trip
Best season	Early
Topo maps	Lake Eleanor, **Hetch Hetchy Reservoir**

Grade (hiking days/recommended layover days)

    Leisurely 4/0
    Moderate 3/0
    Strenuous 2/0

Trailhead 16

HIGHLIGHTS Like the previous trip, this route tours the northern edge of Hetch Hetchy Reservoir. Across the lake the views of Kolana Rock and the sheer granite walls of the Grand Canyon of the Tuolumne provide a majestic accompaniment. The contrasting intimate serenity of Tiltill Valley is a pleasant terminus to this early-season trek.

DESCRIPTION (Leisurely trip)

1st Hiking Day: Follow Trip 45 to **Rancheria Creek**, 6.5 miles.

2nd Hiking Day (**Rancheria Creek** to **Tiltill Valley**, 2.8 miles): From the junction of the Pate Valley/Tiltill Valley trails above the campsites, the trail to Tiltill Valley climbs steeply for a full 1200 feet up to a timber-bottomed saddle. As the trail descends on the north side of the saddle, it traverses a pine forest with a sprinkling of incense-cedar and black oak. When this duff trail emerges at the east end of Tiltill Valley, it meets a trail to Tilden Canyon and Benson Lake. The valley is a long meadow which in early spring is usually quite wet and boggy at the east end. Lodgepole pine fringes the meadow, and the valley is flanked by polished outcroppings of granite and by brush-covered slopes. The trail crosses to the north side of the meadow and winds west to the excellent campsites just south of the Tiltill Creek ford (5600'). These camping places, located in an isolated stand of lodgepole and sugar pine, afford excellent views in both directions down the meadows. Campers have an uninterrupted vantage point from which to watch the large variety of wildlife that make this meadow their home. Fishing on Tiltill Creek for rainbow (to 10″) is excellent in early season.

3rd and 4th Hiking Days: Retrace your steps, 9.3 miles.

Rancheria Falls

Saddlebag Lake to McCabe Lakes **47**

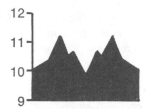

Distance	11 miles
Type	Round trip; part cross-country
Best season	Mid or late
Topo maps	**Tuolumne Meadows**

Grade (hiking days/recommended layover days)

Leisurely	3/0
Moderate	2/1
Strenuous	---
Trailhead	22

HIGHLIGHTS Alpine from beginning to end, this trip crosses the Sierra crest between the east end of Shepherd Crest and North Peak. High tundra meadows, sparkling clear-water lakes and weathered whitebark pines are hallmarks of this loftily routed excursion. Although the route is not marked as a trail on the topo map, there is sometimes a well-worn trace and sometimes adequate duck-on-the rock markings to delineate the route. This is a trip for intermediate and advanced backpackers.

DESCRIPTION

1st Hiking Day (**Saddlebag Lake** to **Lower McCabe Lake**, 5.5 miles): Saddlebag Lake (10,087'), caught in the barren subalpine basin between the Tioga Crest and the main Sierra divide, is one of the largest lakes of the North Boundary Country. About 340 acres in area, it is a long lake to walk around, and hikers may elect to use the boat-taxi that runs the length of the lake from Saddlebag Lake Resort. Rates are reasonable, and the service convenient. Those who wish to walk should take the mining road that leaves from the east end of the resort area, rounds the south end of the lake, and then skirts the rocky, open northeast side. At various times dating back to the 1880s, it provided access for the numerous mining ventures that occupied the basin above Saddlebag Lake and nearby Lundy Canyon.

To the east, the gently rounded summits of the Tioga Crest dip to Dore Pass, and hikers with a little imagination can see and hear the struggling men and animals of the winter of 1882 as they "snaked" and hauled 16,000 pounds of mining machinery across this pass on balky skid sleds. Bound for Bennettville, the sleds were lowered to the edge of Saddlebag Lake and run across on the thick midwinter ice.

Near the northwest end of the lake, the mining road meets a short trail leading up from the boat-taxi dock, and through a sparse forest cover of stunted lodgepole pine it continues west to the north shore of Greenstone Lake. This rocky lake is back-grounded by the glacier-footed crest of Mt. Conness, and its cold waters hold cutthroat and eastern brook trout. The road then winds gently up through swales in the buckling fields of glacially smoothed granite and past several small tarns to Wasco Lake. The wonderful variety of alpine flora along this gentle ascent includes primrose, heather, paintbrush (several varieties), wallflower, monkey flower, penstemon, corn lily, Douglas phlox, alpine columbine and aster.

The road then descends along the gullied stream flowing into Steelhead Lake, and at the south end of Steelhead Lake the cross-country route we will follow branches left around the west side of Steelhead Lake. Crossing granite ledges, the route fords Mill Creek, and then veers west around the small, unnamed lake to the northwest. At this point, anglers may wish to sample the golden trout fishing at Cascade Lake before going on. The steep ascent of the crest begins as our route turns north-west beside a flower-lined inlet stream. The course of this tiny rill bends northward, and our route follows it to the small, unnamed lake it drains, locally called Secret Lake.

Pausing at Secret Lake to survey your route up the head-wall, you have three choices. Adept mountaineers can attack the wall directly, preferably keeping just to the right of the black, lichen-stained vertical streak on the headwall. Once on top, they will walk to the low point on the divide, from where a route descends the west side of the ridge. Hikers who want to put out some extra effort to achieve certainty and lack of steep exposure can arduously pick their way up the scree north of Secret Lake to the lip of what looks like—but isn't—a lake basin. From there, they will traverse slightly upward to their left, under the solid face of the east end of Shepherd Crest, to the low point on the headwall divide. Probably most people choose the third way: From the south side of Secret Lake walk directly up the increasingly steep headwall until, about halfway up, you come to a long ledge that slopes slightly up to the south. About 200 yards south up this ledge, you leave it and climb almost directly up to the ridgecrest. Once on it, follow it north to the low point of the divide to find a route descending on the west side of the ridgecrest.

NOTE: Many hikers have reported to us an inability to find a route over the ridge that contains no Class 3 segments. Such routes exist, as we have written, but it's possible you'll end up crossing some very steep places.

Excellent views northwest from the ridgecrest include Tower Peak and Saurian Crest. Descending from this ridge, a steep, eroded trail follows the gully northeast of upper McCabe Lake. This section levels out near some small tarns, and our route continues to the north shore of upper McCabe Lake. (One could camp here in a small stand of whitebark pines.) Turning west along the shore, we ford the outlet and then strike out for the low, rock-cairned saddle due west of the outlet. Beyond this saddle, the best route drops past snowmelt tarns not shown on the topo map and then winds down through a dense forest cover of lodgepole and whitebark pine and hemlock to the east shore of beautiful lower McCabe Lake (9850'). The best campsites on the lake are near the outlet. Fishing for eastern brook (to 12") is excellent.

2nd Hiking Day: Retrace your steps, 5.5 miles.

Saddlebag Lake to Tuolumne Meadows

48

Distance	20.4 miles
Type	Shuttle trip; part cross-country
Best season	Mid or late
Topo maps	**Tuolumne Meadows**

Grade (hiking days/recommended layover days)
>   *Leisurely* 4/1
>   *Moderate* 3/1
>   *Strenuous* 3/0

Trailhead   22, 23

HIGHLIGHTS Some hikers may choose this trip for its easy shuttle, but the country that this route tours should be adequate reason in itself. The variety of a trip that is part cross country, part on trail and part over water should appeal to the most jaded mountaineer's appetite. This route does that and more. Crossing the Sierra crest above upper McCabe Lake, the trip traverses the long meadows of Cold Canyon, and finishes by touring the splashing cascades and roaring falls of the Tuolumne River.

DESCRIPTION (Moderate trip)

1st Hiking Day: Follow Trip 47 to **Lower McCabe Lake**, 5.5 miles.

2nd Hiking Day (**Lower McCabe Lake** to **Glen Aulin**, 9.2 miles): From the campsites at the outlet of lower McCabe Lake the trail descends along the west side of the stream through a moderate-to-dense forest cover of hemlock, lodgepole, whitebark and silver pine and occasional red fir. The trail between lower McCabe Lake and the place where it veers west is usually very wet and swampy, a soggy condition hospitable to the fields of corn lily that line the way. As the trail veers west it becomes drier, and most of the timber near the trail is lodgepole pine. Flowers indigenous to better-drained soils are found along this section of trail, including wallflower, Douglas phlox, lupine, buckwheat, aster and pussy paws. The descent becomes gentle as the trail passes through a "ghost forest" caused by the needleminer moth and crosses an unnamed tributary of McCabe Creek before reaching the junction with the Virginia Canyon Trail. At this junction our route turns left (west) and continues to Glen Aulin as described in the third hiking day, Trip 43.

3rd Hiking Day: Follow the 4th hiking day, Trip 43, 5.7 miles.

White Cascade near Glen Aulin *National Park Service*

49   Saddlebag Lake to Twin Lakes

Distance   34.5 miles
Type   Shuttle trip; part cross-country
Best season Mid or late
Topo maps   **Tuolumne Meadows**, Matterhorn Peak
Grade (hiking days/recommended layover days)
  Leisurely 7/2
  Moderate 5/2
  Strenuous 4/2
Trailhead   22, 19

HIGHLIGHTS Of the many crestal routes throughout the
                Sierra, this is one of the most exciting. The
scenery is wild and rugged, the six watersheds visited provide
excellent fishing, and the route touches some of the most
remote country of Yosemite National Park. Most of the campsites mentioned below are situated in central locations that
invite side trips, and the visitor is advised to allow enough
layover days for such trips.

DESCRIPTION (Moderate trip)

  1st Hiking Day: Follow Trip 47 to **Lower McCabe Lake**,
5.5 miles.
  2nd Hiking Day (**Lower McCabe Lake** to **Matterhorn
Canyon**, 9 miles): This is the longest hiking day of the trip, and
the prudent hiker will get an early start. From the outlet of
Lower McCabe Lake the trail descends to the Virginia Canyon
Trail junction as described in the 2nd hiking day, Trip 48. At
this junction our route turns right and descends down the steep

switchbacks into Virginia Canyon. The trail along these switchbacks is T-blazed, and the deep layers of bark that have built up around these blazes give the passerby an indication of this trail's age. Blazed by the U.S. Cavalry under the acting superintendency of Captain Abram Epperson Wood in the 1890s, this trail was once used for access to the more remote portions of the North Boundary Country. As the intimidated sheepmen who had been encroaching on Park lands moved their herds northward, it became necessary for the Army caretakers to widen the area of their patrols. The traveler of today, like the mounted cavalryman of yesterday, may pause in wonder at the magnificent specimens of red fir and silver pine along this descent.

The trail descends nearly to Return Creek before turning northeast to ford McCabe Creek. Near the ford are magnificent examples of water-sculpting on the granite bedrock of Return Creek, and this bedrock is bordered with colorful patches of columbine, tiger lily and shooting star.

A short way beyond the ford of McCabe Creek the trail passes a packer campsite and there fords to the north side of Return Creek (difficult in early season), where it meets the Summit Pass Trail. Our route turns left (southwest) and ascends moderately across the easy juniper-crowned divide to Spiller Canyon. One's first views of Spiller Creek are those of open granite bedrock, over which Spiller Creek splashes in a series of lovely chutes and miniature falls. The trail ascends along the creek for about ¼ mile and then fords it.

Through a moderate forest cover that now includes hemlock, the trail then climbs by steady switchbacks. At the hairpin turns one has fine views up Spiller Canyon all the way to the sky-parlor meadows at its headwall, and south across Return Creek to North Peak and Mt. Conness. The trail descends briefly through a long, dry, sandy meadow, and then ascends again over a grassy saddle. From the saddle, the trail dips gently to beautiful Miller Lake. Foregrounded by a large green meadow, the sparkling waters of this small lake tempt the traveler to stop and rest, but drama lies right around the bend.

From Miller Lake the rutted trail bends north, up a grassy swale to a timbered saddle. The views from this saddle burst upon the traveler as he is suddenly confronted with the chasm of Matterhorn Canyon and the distant teeth of the Sawtooth Ridge. This viewpoint marks the beginning of a long, switchbacking descent into Matterhorn Canyon, until finally the rocky trail levels off in the sand of the meadowed junction with the Matterhorn Canyon Trail (8480'). There are good campsites in the meadow and more just upstream. Fishing for eastern brook (to 12") is good in Matterhorn Canyon Creek, and the granite potholes upstream from the junction provide fine swimming in late season.

3rd, 4th and 5th Hiking Days: Follow the 6th, 7th and 8th hiking days of Trip 41, 20 miles.

Ragged Peak over Young Lake

Tuolumne Meadows to Young Lakes **50**

Distance	15.1 miles
Type	Semiloop trip
Best season	Mid or late
Topo maps	**Tuolumne Meadows**

Grade (hiking days/recommended layover days)

   Leisurely ---
   Moderate 2/1
   Strenuous 2/0

Trailhead   23

HIGHLIGHTS The three Young Lakes, cupped under soaring Ragged Peak, offer a large selection of campsites, some in heavy woods and some at timberline. These camps provide a base for exciting excursions into the headwaters of Conness Creek and for climbing Mt. Conness itself.

DESCRIPTION

1st Hiking Day (**Glen Aulin Trailhead** to **Young Lakes**, 8.2 miles): The first part of this trip follows the Glen Aulin "highway," a heavily traveled path from Tuolumne Meadows to the High Sierra Camp down the Tuolumne River. From the parking area west of State Highway 120 we stroll down a dirt road, pass a locked gate that bars autos, and continue west along the lodgepole-dotted flank of Tuolumne Meadows, with fine views south across the meadows of Unicorn Peak, Cathedral Peak and some of the Echo Peaks. Approaching a boulder-rimmed old parking loop, we veer right and climb slightly to the now-closed Soda Springs Campground. Once this campground was the private holding of John Lembert, namesake of Lembert Dome. His brothers, who survived him, sold it to the Sierra Club in 1912, and for 60 years Club members enjoyed a private campground in this marvelous subalpine meadow. But in 1972 the Club deeded the property to the National Park Service so that everyone could use it.

From the Soda Springs the sandy trail undulates through a forest of sparse, small lodgepole pines, and then descends to a boulder ford of Delaney Creek. Immediately beyond the ford we hop a branch of Delaney Creek, then hop another in 300 yards. Soon our trail almost touches the southwest arm of Tuolumne Meadows before ascending to the signed Young Lakes Trail. From the junction we ascend slightly and cross a broad expanse of boulder-strewn, grass-pocketed sheet granite. An open spot affords a look south across broad Tuolumne Meadows to the line of peaks from Fairview Dome to the steeplelike spires of the Cathedral Range.

After crossing the open granite, our trail climbs a tree-clothed slope to a ridge and turns up the ridge for several hundred yards before veering down into the meadowy, bouldery, shallow valley of Dingley Creek, an easy ford except in early season. In the first mile beyond this small creek, we jump across its north fork and wind gently upward in shady pine forest carpeted with a fine flower display even into late season. Groundsel, daisies, lupine, squawroot and gooseberries all are colorful, but one's admiration for floral beauty concentrates on the delicate cream flower cups of Mariposa lily, with one rich brown spot in the throat of each petal. Near the ridgetop, breaks in the lodgepole forest allow us glimpses of the whole Cathedral Range.

On the other side of the ridge a new panoply of peaks appears in the north—majestic Tower Peak, Doghead and Quarry Peaks, the Finger Peaks, Matterhorn Peak, Sheep Peak, Mt. Conness, and the Shepherd Crest. From this viewpoint a moderate descent leads to a ford of a tributary of Conness Creek, where more varieties of flowers decorate the green banks of this icy, dashing stream. Soon our downwinding trail reaches the Dog Lake Trail junction, where we veer left and descend into thickening hemlock forest. On a level stretch of trail we cross another branch of Conness Creek, and then switchback ¼ mile up to a plateau from where the view is fine of the steep north face of Ragged Peak.

After passing a meadow which was the fourth Young Lake before it filled in with stream sediments, we descend to the west shore of lower Young Lake (9850′). There are both primitive and well-developed campsites along the north shore of this lake. More secluded campsites may be found on middle Young Lake by following the trail east from the ford of the lower lake, and forking right at a junction 400 yards beyond. From the middle lake you can go up the inlet to the upper lake (10,200'), which is the most attractive but also the most exposed. Fishing on the Young Lakes is fair-to-good for brook trout (to 12").

2nd Hiking Day (**Young Lakes** to **Glen Aulin Trailhead**, 6.9 miles): After retracing our steps to the Dog Lake Trail junction, we turn left onto the southwest spur of Ragged Peak and ascend a sandy, boulder-scattered slope under a moderate lodgepole-and-hemlock forest cover. From the shoulder of Ragged Peak the trail descends through a very large, gently sloping meadow. This broad, well-watered expanse is a wild-flower garden in season, laced with meandering brooks. Paint-brush, lupine and monkey flower in the foreground set off the great views of the entire Cathedral Range, strung out on the southern horizon.

Near the lower edge of the meadow we cross the head-waters of Dingley Creek, and then descend, steeply at times, some 300 feet through a moderately dense forest of lodgepoles and a few hemlocks. Then the trail levels off and veers east on a gently rolling course through more lodgepole forest where the sandy soil sprouts thousands of prostrate little lupine plants. Beyond is a very large level meadow where the reddish peaks of Mts. Dana and Gibbs loom in the east, Delaney Creek meanders lazily through the grass, and Belding ground squirrels pipe away. The Delaney Creek ford is difficult in early season; shallower fords may be found upstream. Beyond the creek, you will find the trail about 20 yards upstream from the main ford.

After crossing a little ridge, our route drops once more toward Tuolumne Meadows. Lembert Dome, the "first ascent" of so many visitors to Tuolumne Meadows, can be glimpsed through the trees along this stretch of trail. The trail levels slightly before it meets the 0.1 mile lateral to Dog Lake. Then it passes a junction with a trail that leads east along the north side of Lembert Dome, and fords Dog Lake's outlet. The 560-foot descent from here is terribly dusty as it switchbacks down close under the steep west face of Lembert Dome. At the bottom of the deep dust, the trail splits into three paths. The right one leads to the stables, the left one to the parking area where we started.

51 Horse Meadow to Gibbs Lake

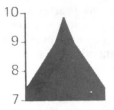

Distance   8 miles
Type   Round trip
Best season   Mid or late
Topo maps   Mono Craters
Grade (hiking days/recommended layover days)
   Leisurely 2/0
   Moderate ---
   Strenuous ---
Trailhead   24

HIGHLIGHTS The destination of this trip is a little-known lake in Ansel Adams Wilderness on the dramatic east slope of the Sierra east of Yosemite Park. It's a great place to find peace and quiet, and for serious anglers there is a chance to catch some beautiful golden trout.

DESCRIPTION

1st Hiking Day (**Horse Meadow** to **Gibbs Lake**, 4 miles): Ordinary cars will have to park 2.1 miles up the dirt road from U.S. 395 in a little meadow that has a grove of aspen trees and a stream that runs until August. More mountain-worthy cars can ascend another mile to upper Horse Meadow.

We leave the lower meadow and climb steeply, leveling off at a fork where we go right. Soon we pass upper Horse Meadow on our right, which is bounded on the north by the gigantic right lateral moraine of Lee Vining Canyon.

Past the upper meadow the road forks, and 0.1 mile up the left fork is a small parking area below a locked USFS gate. Beyond the gate we climb steeply up an old road on a north-trending ridge, to an overlook of Lee Vining Canyon, far below. Continuing the steep climb, we walk through mixed forest eligible for cutting and pass a road leading left (east). Just beyond a deer hunter's camp we come to a water ditch and then a sign heralding the wilderness ahead. From the ditch, the road ascends gently for ¼ mile and then mercifully ends. From the roadend, a trail takes off up a dry ravine that lies over a little ridge east from Gibbs Canyon creek. Then it crosses the ridge and dips down near the stream, where recent blazes mark the trail. We ascend through a cool forest of lodgepole, whitebark and silver pine, with an occasional mountain hemlock and with much Labrador tea along the creek, to the signed border of Ansel Adams Wilderness. Here, perhaps, one will feel a distinct relief that autos and the rest of civilization are locked out beyond the invisible gate Congress erected here in 1963.

The remaining gentle climb to Gibbs Lake proceeds through moderate-to-dense forest near Gibbs Canyon creek, as we catch glimpses through the trees of the majestic Sierra crest dead ahead. There are fair-to-good campsites south of the outlet and west of the inlet of emerald-green Gibbs Lake (9500'). For the adventurous camper, an easy if steep route to Kidney Lake goes up the forested south side of the stream, and the expansive views of Mono Lake and the mountains around it are worth the climb. Most of the shore of this lake is barren, but some whitebark pines at the east end provide shelter for a primitive camp.

2nd Hiking Day: Retrace your steps, 4 miles.

Gibbs Lake

52   Tenaya Lake to Sunrise Camp

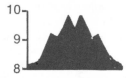

Distance	11.4 miles
Type	Round trip
Best season	Mid or late
Topo maps	**Tuolumne Meadows**

Grade (hiking days/recommended layover days)
    Leisurely 2/1
    Moderate 2/0
    Strenuous ---
Trailhead   28

HIGHLIGHTS Although this route is very popular, being within the Yosemite High Sierra Camp network, the superb, unusual scenery of the high country makes this trip a must. The spectacular topography of the Tenaya canyon and of the serrated northwestern end of the Cathedral Range combine to overcome the most strident objections of the solitude-seeker.

DESCRIPTION

1st Hiking Day (**Tenaya Lake Walk-in Campground** to **Sunrise Camp**, 5.7 miles): From the campground parking lot (8149′) the trail crosses the outlet of Tenaya Lake and skirts the meadowy edge of the walk-in campground. For a mile the trail winds south through moderate forest cover interrupted by small meadows where the quiet early-morning hiker will probably see browsing mule deer. The first part of this trail is lush with wildflowers as late as July, and one can expect to see blooming lupine, aster, larkspur, brodiaea and buttercup. Just past the stream from Lower Sunrise Lake the ascent begins to steepen, and soon it becomes a long series of rocky switchbacks up a slope clothed with pine and hemlock. From these switchbacks one can see the highway and can hear passing autos, but these are infinitesimal compared to the polished granite expanses of Tenaya Canyon. The Indian name for Tenaya Creek, Py-wi-ack

("Stream of the Shining Rocks"), was quite apt, for this canyon exhibits the largest exposed granite area in Yosemite, and its shining surfaces are barren except for sporadic clumps of hardy conifers that have found root in broken talus pockets.

Where the trail begins to rise, the long, gradual slope falling from the promontory called Clouds Rest comes into view in the south. This slope is a 4500-foot drop, one of the largest continuous rock slopes in the world. The traveler who feels sated by the panorama will find a different world to wonder at, right at his own boot-clad feet, for these slopes grow dozens of wildflower species, among them pussy paws, penstemon, paintbrush, lupine, streptanthus, aster, larkspur, brodiaea and buttercup. Finally the switchbacks end and the trail levels as it arrives at a junction with the lateral trail to Sunrise camp. Turning left (east), we stroll on a nearly level path under a sparse forest cover of pine and fir until the trail dips for about ¼ mile to the first Sunrise Lake.

After passing the west side of the lake on a trail fringed with red mountain heather, we cross the outlet and ascend gradually northeast. Then the trail levels off and wanders roughly north through a sparse lodgepole forest. The second Sunrise Lake comes into view on the left, but we veer east and climb away from it, paralleling its inlet some distance from the cascading water. The few trees here are not enough to block our views of granite domes all around. Then our trail skirts the south side of the meadow-fringed highest Sunrise Lake and begins a gradual ascent by crossing the lake's inlet stream.

Continuing southeast, we cross a little saddle and descend gradually almost straight south from the upper lake. After passing most of the hogback lying east of us, we swing northeast and switchback down to a bench overlooking spacious Long Meadow. There are fair campsites or, if advance reservations have been made, one may enjoy the luxury of a hot shower, a hot meal and a made-up bed at the High Sierra Camp (9320') nearby.

2nd Hiking Day: Retrace your steps, 5.7 miles. Alternatively, you could retrace the steps of Trip 54, 9.2 miles.

53 Tioga Road to Lower Cathedral Lake

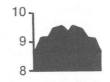

Distance	7.8 miles
Type	Round trip
Best season	Mid or late
Topo maps	**Tuolumne Meadows**

Grade (hiking days/recommended layover days)
   Leisurely 2/0
   Moderate ---
   Strenuous ---
Trailhead 27

HIGHLIGHTS Used since the time of the Indians, this trail offers some of the finest views of the Tuolumne Meadows region. Two large granite domes, Fairview and Medlicott, and the foremost landmark of the area, Cathedral Peak, line this route. Because of the relatively short mileage and the high-country scenery, this round trip is an excellent beginner's selection.

DESCRIPTION

1st Hiking Day (**Trailhead on Tioga Road** to **Cathedral Lake**, 3.9 miles): From the parking area (8560') on the Tioga Road, we follow a gently ascending trail that is quite objectionably dusty except after rainy sprinkles. But after this initial section the trail itself is not bad at all, and the panoramic views more than make up for the early unpleasantness. A few steps from the trailhead our route crosses the Tenaya Lake/ Tuolumne Meadows Trail and then begins to climb more steeply. After ½ mile of ascent under a welcome forest cover, the trail levels off and descends to a small meadow that is boggy in early season. From here we can see the dramatically shaped tops of Unicorn Peak and the Cockscomb, and the apparent granite dome in the south is in reality the north ridge of Cathedral Peak, whose steeples are out of sight over the "dome's" horizon.

The trail cruises gently up and down through more little meadows set in hemlock forest and then dips near a tinkling stream whose source, we discover after further walking, is a robust spring on a shady set of switchbacks. Beyond this climb our tread levels off on the west slope of Cathedral Peak and makes a long, gentle, sparsely forested descent on sandy underfooting to a junction with the spur trail to lower Cathedral Lake, where our route turns right. Periodically the traveler has westward views of another granite sentry left by the glacial ice, Medlicott Dome, and one can easily discern the difference between the rounded, polished tops of the domes and the jagged crest of Cathedral Peak. The domes were completely covered by the ice, whereas the top few hundred feet of Cathedral Peak stood above the grinding glacier, and hence was not rounded and smoothed by the ice.

From the junction, a ⅔-mile stroll across stream-braided meadows leads to the shores of lower Cathedral Lake (9320′). Fishing is poor for rainbow and brook (to 9″) but swimming is good. The views more than make up for the shortcomings, however, for from here Polly Dome, Cathedral Peak, Echo Peaks, Medlicott Dome and Unicorn Peak provide a rugged glacial setting.

2nd Hiking Day: Retrace your steps, 3.9 miles.

Tuolumne Meadows *National Park Service*

54   Tioga Road to Sunrise Camp

Distance   18.4 miles
Type   Round trip
Best season   Mid or late
Topo maps   **Tuolumne Meadows**
Grade (hiking days/recommended layover days)
   Leisurely 4/1
   Moderate 3/1
   Strenuous 2/1
Trailhead   27

HIGHLIGHTS The Sunrise Trail, of which this is the first leg, is a justly famous and popular route. Superlative views confront the traveler at every summit and oftentimes in between—views of whole ranges in the distance as well as spectacular peaks nearby.

DESCRIPTION (Leisurely trip)

1st Hiking Day: Follow Trip 53 to **Cathedral Lake**, 3.9 miles.

2nd Hiking Day (**Cathedral Lake** to **Sunrise High Sierra Camp**, 5.3 miles): First retrace the steps of the 1st hiking day to the Sunrise Trail at the foot of Cathedral Peak. Here our route turns right (south) and ascends gently to upper Cathedral Lake, a few yards to the right of the trail. Though camping is prohibited here, one may enjoy a stop for a snack and a swim. Our trail then skirts the east side of the lake and ascends to Cathedral Pass, where the excellent views include Cathedral Peak, Tresidder Peak, Echo Peaks, Matthes Crest, the Clark Range farther south and Matterhorn Peak far to the north. Beyond the pass is a long, beautiful swale, the headwaters of Echo Creek, where the midseason flower show is alone worth the trip.

Our path traverses up the east flank of Tresidder Peak on a gentle climb to the actual high point of this trail, at a marvelous viewpoint overlooking most of southern Yosemite Park. The inspiring panorama includes the peaks around Vogelsang High Sierra Camp in the southeast, the whole Clark Range in the south, and the peaks on the Park border in both directions farther away. Then our high trail switchbacks quickly down to the head of the upper lobe of Long Meadow, levels off, and leads down a gradually sloping valley dotted with little lodge-pole pines to the head of the second, lower lobe of l-o-n-g Long Meadow. Passing a junction with the trail down Echo Creek, this route continues its meadowy descent to the fair campsites along the stream at the south end of the meadow, past Sunrise High Sierra Camp, which is near the south end of the meadow, almost out of sight on a bench above and west of the trail. There are other well-used campsites south of the High Sierra Camp on the bench west of the meadow.

3rd and 4th Hiking Days: Retrace your steps, 9.2 miles. Alternatively, you could retrace the steps of Trip 52, 5.7 miles.

Upper Cathedral Lake, Cathedral Peak

55   Tioga Road to Merced Lake

Distance	34.2 miles
Type	Shuttle trip
Best season	Mid or late
Topo maps	**Tuolumne Meadows, Merced Peak**

Grade (hiking days/recommended layover days)

   Leisurely 6/1
   Moderate 5/1
   Strenuous 3/1

Trailhead   27, 26

HIGHLIGHTS This looping excursion out of Tuolumne Meadows samples everything the Cathedral Range has to offer, from sweeping vistas at 10,000-foot passes to the deeply glaciated Merced River canyon to forested side streams with secluded campsites. For anglers there are lakes large and small, meadowed creeks, and huge river pools.

DESCRIPTION (Moderate trip)

1st Hiking Day: Follow Trip 53 to **Cathedral Lake**, 3.9 miles.

2nd Hiking Day (**Cathedral Lake** to **Echo Creek Crossing**, 9 miles.): First, follow Trip 54 to the trail junction in Long Meadow. Here we turn left (east) on the signed Echo Creek Trail and ford the Long Meadow stream on boulders. The trail quickly switchbacks up to the top of the ridge that separates this stream from Echo Creek and then descends through dense hemlock-and-lodgepole forest toward the Cathedral Fork of Echo Creek. Where our route approaches this stream, we have fine views of the creek's water gliding down a series of granite slabs, and then the trail veers away from the creek and descends gently above it for more than a mile. Even in late season this shady hillside is watered by numerous rills that are bordered by still-blooming flowers. On this downgrade the trail crosses the Long Meadow stream, which has found an escape from that meadow through a gap between two large domes high above our trail.

Then our route levels out in a mile-long flat section of this valley where the wet ground yields a plus of wildflowers all summer but a minus of many mosquitoes in early season. Beyond this flat "park," the trail descends a more open hillside, and where it passes the confluence of the two forks of Echo Creek, we can see across the valley the steep course of the east fork plunging down to its rendezvous with the west fork. Finally the trail levels off and reaches the good campsites just before a metal bridge over Echo Creek (8100'). Fishing in the creek is good for rainbow and golden trout to 10".

3rd Hiking Day (**Echo Creek Crossing** to **Merced Lake**, 4.9 miles): After crossing the bridge over Echo Creek, our trail leads down the forested valley and easily fords a tributary stream, staying well above the main creek. This pleasant, shaded descent encounters fibrous-barked juniper trees and then tall, brittle red firs as it drops to another metal bridge 1 mile from the last one. Beyond this sturdy span, the trail rises slightly and the creek drops precipitously, so that we are soon far above it. Then our sandy tread swings west away from Echo Creek and traverses down a hillside where views are excellent of Echo Valley, a wide place in the great Merced River canyon below. Our trail passes a junction with the High Trail, which leads west to the Sunrise Trail, and then descends south to a green-floored forest of mixed conifers threaded by a tinkling all-year stream.

Then a last series of switchbacks span the descent to the floor of Echo Valley, where we meet and turn left (east) on the Merced River Trail. After crossing several forks of Echo Creek on wooden bridges, we pass a burn area where a 1966 fire killed most of the mature trees. But new, small lodgepoles grow by the hundreds, and the grassy valley floor is extensively decorated with the blue flowers of lupine and the white blossoms of yarrow and yampah. Leaving Echo Valley, the trail leads up immense granite slabs.

At the hairpin angle of a set of switchbacks, the trail comes very close to the cascading Merced River, and a breather stop here will allow the traveler to drink in the sights and sounds of this dramatic part of the river—a long series of chutes, cascades, falls, cataracts and pools that are all due to the glacier that roughened up the formerly smooth bed of the Merced River. Above this turbulent stretch, the trail levels off beside the now-quiet river and arrives at the outlet of Merced Lake (7216'). This large lake has a High Sierra Camp at its east end, where the only presently legal campsites are. You can buy a few provisions at the small store, or even rent a rowboat to try your luck for rainbow and brown trout to 9". Be sure to bear-proof your food.

4th Hiking Day (**Merced Lake** to **Emeric Lake**, 5.6 miles): The first short mile of this day's hike follows an almost level, wide, sandy path under a green forest canopy of fir and pine, juniper and aspen. Immediately beyond a bridge over roaring Lewis Creek we arrive at the Merced Lake Ranger Station (emergency services available in summer) and beside it find the Lewis Creek Trail, leading north. Quickly the ascent up this cobbled trail becomes steep, and it remains so for a panting half-mile-plus. Fortunately, Sierra junipers and Jeffrey pines cast plenty of morning shade. The trail levels momentarily as we pass a fine viewpoint for taking pictures of Merced Lake, far below, and Half Dome, due west. One more cobbled, steep climb leads to a junction with the Fletcher Creek Trail, and we turn left onto this path.

Several switchbacks then descend to a wooden bridge over Lewis Creek. From here the trail enters more open hillside as it climbs moderately on a cobbled path bordered by proliferating bushes of mountain whitethorn and huckleberry oak. Just past a tributary ½ mile from Lewis Creek, we have fine views of cataracts and waterfalls on Fletcher Creek where it rushes down open granite slopes dotted with lodgepole pines. The trail then passes very close to the creek before veering south and climbing, steeply at times, on the now-familiar cobbling placed by trail crews. Here one has more good views of Fletcher Creek chuting and cascading down from the notch at the base of a granite dome before it leaps off a ledge in free fall. The few solitary pine trees on this otherwise blank dome testify to nature's extraordinary persistence.

At the notch, our trail levels off near some nice but illegal campsites, and then soon passes a side trail to small Babcock Lake. From this junction the sandy trail ascends steadily through a moderate forest cover just east of Fletcher Creek. After a mile this route breaks out into the open and begins to rise more steeply via rocky switchbacks. From these zigzags one can see nearby in the north the outlet stream of Emeric Lake—though not the lake itself, which is behind a dome just to the right of the outlet's notch. Leaving the trail, we cross Fletcher Creek, follow up this outlet and stroll along the northwest shore of Emeric Lake (9370') to the excellent campsites midway along this shore. Fishing is often good for rainbow trout to 12″. Sometimes windy, this lake was nevertheless so still one night that one could see the Milky Way clearly reflected in it.

5th Hiking Day (**Emeric Lake** to **Tuolumne Meadows**, 10.8 miles): This is the longest hiking day on this trip, but the ascent is not too severe and it comes at the beginning: from Tuolumne Pass at the crest of the Cathedral Range, the rest is downhill. After circling the head of Emeric Lake and crossing the inlet stream without benefit of trail, we find a trail at the northeast corner of the lake, at the base of a granite knoll. This trail leads east-northeast for 0.6 mile to an **X** junction in the valley of Fletcher Creek. Taking the left branch up the valley, we follow a rocky-dusty trail through the forest fringe of the long meadow that straddles Fletcher Creek. This trail climbs farther from the meadow and passes northwest of a bald prominence that sits in the center of the upper valley of Fletcher and Emeric creeks, separating the two. Topping a minor summit, the trail descends slightly and then winds levelly past a long series of lovely ponds that are interconnected in early season. Just beyond it, the old trail veers sharply right, and our rutted meadow trail, going left, ascends to the top of a little swale with another good swimming pond and reaches an overlook above Boothe Lake. Our trail contours along this meadowy hillside about 50 vertical feet above the lake, passing a junction with a rutted use trail down to the lake. About ¼ mile farther we reach west Tuolumne Pass and a junction with the trail to Vogelsang High Sierra Camp, from where we retrace most of the steps of Trip 61.

56   Tioga Road to Tenaya Lake

Distance	25.6 miles
Type	Shuttle trip
Best season	Mid or late
Topo maps	**Tuolumne Meadows, Merced Peak**

Grade (hiking days/recommended layover days)
    Leisurely 4/1
    Moderate 4/0
    Strenuous 3/0
Trailhead   27, 28

HIGHLIGHTS The first and last parts of this trip are along favorite and well-used trails, but in the middle we follow a little-used stretch of trail in the heart of Yosemite's spectacular glaciated highlands. Views of the immense domes and deep-cut canyons will impress the traveler's eye forever.

DESCRIPTION (Leisurely trip)

1st and 2nd Hiking Days: Follow Trip 55 to the **Echo Creek Crossing**, 12.9 miles.

3rd Hiking Day (**Echo Creek Crossing** to **Sunrise Creek**, 5.1 miles): First follow the third hiking day, Trip 55, to the junction of the Echo Creek and High trails above the Merced River. Here our route turns right (west) and climbs rockily several hundred feet before leveling off above the immense Merced River canyon. This trail segment was part of the route from Yosemite Valley to Merced Lake until a path up the canyon was constructed in 1931. Before that, the steep canyon walls coming right down to the river near Bunnell Point, the great dome to our southwest, had made passage impossible. Finally a trail was built that bypasses the narrowest part of the canyon by climbing high on the south wall, and the trail we are now on fell into relative disuse.

With fine views of obelisk-like Mt. Clark in the south, we descend gradually for ½ mile over open granite in a setting that is sure to give you a feeling of being above almost everything. Then the trail passes a stagnant lakelet and ascends to even better viewpoints for appreciating the grandeur of the glaciated granitic wonder of nature spread out before you. It takes time to grasp the immensity of Mt. Clark, Clouds Rest, Half Dome, Mt. Starr King, Bunnell Point, and the great unnamed dome across the canyon west of it. Our continuing ascent then rounds a ridge and veers north into a forest of handsome Jeffrey pines. Here the trail levels off, and it remains level for a mile of exhilarating walking through Jeffreys, lodgepoles and red firs which shade patch after patch of vivid green ferns and a complement of multihued floral displays. Still in forest, we descend slightly to meet the John Muir Trail, go right on it for 150 yards to the Forsyth Trail, and then go left up it 150 yards to the fair campsites on Sunrise Creek (8080'). Fishing in this enticing stream for small rainbow and brook trout is fair at best.

4th Hiking Day: Reverse the steps of the 1st hiking day, Trip 58, 7.6 miles.

Looking up the Merced River Canyon

57   Tioga Road to Yosemite Valley

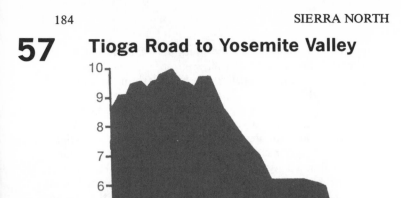

Distance	21.8 miles
Type	Shuttle trip
Best season	Mid or late
Topo maps	**Tuolumne Meadows, Merced Peak, Yosemite**

Grade (hiking days/recommended layover days)
   Leisurely 4/0
   Moderate 3/0
   Strenuous 2/0
Trailhead   27, 29

HIGHLIGHTS The Sunrise Trail route from the Meadows to the Valley is one of the Park's most famous and most used backpack routes. Its reputation is an honest one, for these miles contain a magnificent range of flora and fauna, and the trail surveys some of the Park's best-known landmarks. This is a fine trip for the beginning backpacker who has a couple of shorter trips under his (or her) belt, and wants more.

DESCRIPTION (Leisurely trip)

1st and 2nd Hiking Days: Follow Trip 54 to **Sunrise High Sierra Camp**, 9.3 miles.

3rd Hiking Day (**Sunrise High Sierra Camp** to **Sunrise Creek**, 5.1 miles): The trail from Sunrise High Sierra Camp continues south through Long Meadow, undulating gently below the eastern crest of Sunrise Mountain. After climbing to a forested saddle over a mile past the meadows, the trail parallels the headwaters of Sunrise Creek, descending steeply by switchbacks down a rocky moraine.

This moraine is the largest of a series of ridgelike glacial deposits in this area, and the gigantic granite boulders along their sides testify to the power of the *mer-de-glace* that once filled Little Yosemite Valley and its tributaries. One such "erratic," about the size of a compact car, was found poised on the side of Moraine Dome to the southwest, and geologists have determined that it came from the slopes of the peaks at the northwest end of the Cathedral Range. At the foot of the morainal descent, the trail crosses Sunrise Creek, and then descends on a westward course to the fair campsites on Sunrise Creek (8080′) 150 yards up the Forsyth Trail from our trail's junction with it. Fishing on Sunrise Creek is poor-to-fair for rainbow and brook (fry).

4th Hiking Day (**Sunrise Creek** to **Yosemite Valley**, 7.5 miles): First retrace your steps 150 yards south to the first junction. Back on the John Muir Trail, our route continues southwest on a gradual descent, passing the High Trail to Merced Lake. Our trail is bounded on the north by the Pinnacles (the south face of the Clouds Rest eminence) and on the south by Moraine Dome. Francois Matthes, in an interesting "detective story" written in the form of a geological essay (Professional Paper 160), discusses Moraine Dome extensively. He deduced, using three examples (one was the "erratic" cited above), that the moraines around the dome were the product of at least *two* glacial ages—a notion contrary to the thinking of the time. The morainal till of the last glacial age characterizes the underfooting of our descent into Little Yosemite Valley. A mile from the last junction is a ford of Sunrise Creek in a red-fir forest whose stillness is broken by the creek's gurgling and by the occasional screams of Steller jays. In another mile we pass the trail to Clouds Rest, and about ½ mile from there, the lateral to Half Dome (about 4 miles round trip). From this junction our shady path switchbacks down through a changing forest cover.

There are improved campsites on Sunrise Creek at the foot of the descent, and more numerous ones along the Merced River south of the river trail. A summer ranger is on duty near the trail junction. This is prime bear territory, so be sure to secure your food.

From here, reverse the steps of the 1st hiking day, Trip 66, to Yosemite Valley.

58   Tenaya Lake to Yosemite Valley

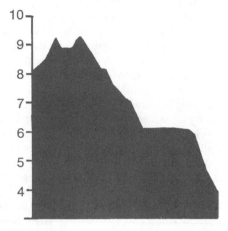

Distance   15.1 miles
Type   Shuttle trip
Best season   Mid or late
Topo maps   **Tuolumne Meadows, Merced Peak,
                  Yosemite**
Grade (hiking days/recommended layover days)
   Leisurely 2/1
   Moderate 2/0
   Strenuous ---
Trailhead   28, 29

HIGHLIGHTS Through an elevation change of over 5000 feet
                (mostly down hill) this route covers most of
Yosemite's spectrum of life zones. Views from various points
above Tenaya Canyon are breath-taking in their panoramic
scope. By contrast, a different kind of appreciation is evoked
when walking alongside the serene waters of the Merced River
as it serpentines across the floor of Little Yosemite Valley. The
ever-changing nature of a river is a high point of this trip—
slides, cascades, and earth-shaking waterfalls add exclamation
points.

DESCRIPTION

1st Hiking Day (**Tenaya Lake Walk-In Campground** to **Sunrise Creek**, 7.6 miles): First, follow Trip 52 to the junction of the trail going east to Sunrise Camp. From the junction, our trail makes a 320-foot descent on switchbacks, rises over a talus-swollen little ridge, and drops beside a pleasant-looking lakelet. The lightly forested hillside ahead leads up to three unnamed streams that we cross in quick succession. This watery slope is boggy till midseason, and the plentiful groundwater nourishes rank gardens of wildflowers throughout the summer. Leveling off beyond the streams, our trail meets the 2-mile trail to the summit of Clouds Rest. Hikers with plenty of energy may take this short lateral to this lofty prominence. Views from Clouds Rest are among the most spectacular in the Sierra, including a 4500-foot continuous granite slope stretching all the way down to Tenaya Creek and rising on the other side—the largest exposed granite area in the Park.

From the Clouds Rest junction, the trail meanders over sandy, level terrain for ½ mile, detouring around many fallen trees, before it starts its plunge down toward Sunrise Creek. This switchbacking descent is a little tough on the knees but in repayment the green fir-and-pine forest is a classic of its kind, and occasional views down into the Merced River Canyon are sweeping in their range. Finally our trail approaches a stream, parallels it for almost ½ mile, fords it and then fords Sunrise Creek to the fair campsites on the creek (8080'). Fishing for rainbow and brook (fry) is poor-to-fair.

2nd Hiking Day: Follow the 4th hiking day, Trip 57, 7.5 miles.

59 Tuolumne Meadows to Nelson Lake

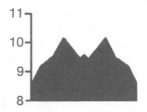

Distance	11.8 miles
Type	Round trip
Best season	Mid or late
Topo maps	**Tuolumne Meadows**

Grade (hiking days/recommended layover days)
    Leisurely ---
    Moderate 2/1
    Strenuous ---
Trailhead   25

HIGHLIGHTS This interesting and varied route visits the scenic Elizabeth Lake basin and then crosses the serrated Cathedral Range to Nelson Lake. No trail route offers finer views of those geologic wonders called Unicorn Peak and the Cockscomb. Open, meadow-fringed Nelson Lake makes a pleasantly fitting end to this exciting trip, and anglers can look forward to good brook-trout fishing on the placid waters of this subalpine gem.

DESCRIPTION

1st Hiking Day (**Tuolumne Meadows Campground** to **Nelson Lake**, 5.9 miles): To reach the trailhead, walk to the Group Camping Section of the Tuolumne Meadows campground, where the signed trail begins across from a masonry building. In a few hundred feet we cross the Tenaya Lake/Lyell Canyon Trail and then continue a steady southward ascent. The shade-giving forest cover is almost entirely lodgepole pine as the trail crosses several runoff streams that dry up by late summer. More than a mile from the start, our route veers close to Unicorn Creek, and the music of this dashing, gurgling, cold-water stream makes the climb easier. When the ascent finally ends, the hiker emerges at the foot of a long meadow containing Elizabeth Lake, at the foot of striking Unicorn Peak.

Past Elizabeth Lake, the meadow gives way to a moderately dense forest cover of lodgepole interspersed with mountain hemlock, and the trail climbs, steeply, then moderately, and steeply again. A few hundred feet before you reach the ridgecrest, you come to a late-lingering snowbank where the trail splits. If you go left, you will pass through a narrow gully between granite walls. If you go right, you will walk up a bare granite-sand slope. We recommend that if you have a full pack, you take the right trail going to Nelson Lake and the left one returning, because of some steep places on the left trail just beyond the crest.

Because of the close proximity of the Cockscomb, about 1 mile due west, the hiker has excellent views of that knifelike spire from just beyond the left pass. Well-named by Francois Matthes, this slender crest bears clear marks of the highest level reached by the ice of the last glacial episode. Its lower shoulders reveal the rounded, well-polished surfaces that betray glacial action, while its jagged, sharply etched crest shows no such markings. Further evidence of glacial action may be clearly seen on the steep descent into the head of long, typically U-shaped Echo Creek valley. The shearing and polishing action of the ice mass that shaped this rounded valley is evident on the cliffs on the west side.

About ⅓ mile from where the trail split, and several hundred yards beyond the crest, the forks come together again on a steep, tree-dotted, ravined hillside. As our route descends along winding, clear, meadowed Echo Creek for about 2 miles, the valley floor is lush with wildflower growth. During midseason the passerby can expect to see Davidson's penstemon, Douglas phlox, groundsel, red heather, lupine and swamp whiteheads. At the end of the second large meadow in this canyon, our trail leaves Echo Creek and veers east up a low, rocky ridge, undulating through sparse forest. One is almost at Nelson Lake (9636') before he can see his destination, meadow-fringed at the foot of imposing granite Peak 11282. Good campsites may be found on the southeast and southwest sides. Anglers will find the lake's waters good fishing for brook trout (7–11").

2nd Hiking Day: Reverse your steps, 5.9 miles.

60 Tuolumne Meadows to Lyell Canyon

Distance	17.4 miles
Type	Round trip
Best season	Early, mid or late
Topo maps	**Tuolumne Meadows**

Grade (hiking days/recommended layover days)
    Leisurely 2/1
    Moderate ---
    Strenuous ---

Trailhead 26

HIGHLIGHTS Alpine meadows have a fascination that claims the trail traveler, whether he be novice or hoariest veteran. Campers' descriptions of favorite camping places invariably favor the forested western fringe of a remote meadow (your camp gets the first warming sunlight there). The meadows of Lyell Canyon are the stuff of which such memories are built. Idyllic from beginning to end, this long, gentle grassland with its serpentining river is a delight to travel.

DESCRIPTION

1st Hiking Day (**Tuolumne Meadows Lodge** to **Lyell Base Camp**, 8.7 miles): The trailhead is beside the Tuolumne Meadows Lodge parking lot, southwest of the office-dining room. The route goes about 100 yards to the Dana Fork of the river, and crosses it on a bridge. Then this segment of the John Muir Trail leads over a slight rise and descends to the Lyell Fork, where there is a substantial double bridge. The meadows above this bridge are among the most delightful in all the Sierra, and anytime you happen to be staying all night at the lodge or nearby, they are a wonderful place to spend the last hour before dinner. Mts. Dana and Gibbs fill the eastern horizon, catching the late sun, and the river has good fishing for brown trout.

About 50 yards past the bridge we meet the trail that comes up the river from the campground, turn left (east) onto it, and skirt a long, lovely section of the meadow. This re-routed trail is relatively new, established because of extensive trail wear and subsequent erosion of the old route. Re-routing is one of several far-sighted Park Service policies that have been adopted to allow areas in the wilderness a "breather"—a chance to recover from overuse. Going through a dense forest cover of lodgepole pine, our route passes the trail that ascends south to Tuolumne Pass and Vogelsang High Sierra Camp, and then fords Rafferty Creek. This ford may be difficult in early season, but you may find a log 200 yards downstream.

From this point on, the trail traverses alternating meadowed and forested sections as it veers southward, and the silent walker may come upon grazing deer in the meadows and an occasional marmot that has ventured from the rocky hillside on the right. Fields of wildflowers color the grasslands from early to late season, but the best time of the year for seeing this color is generally early-to-mid season. From the more open parts of the trail, one has excellent views of the Kuna Crest as it slopes up to the southeast and the river itself has delighted generations of mountain photographers.

Our route then passes a trail branching southwest to Evelyn Lake and Tuolumne Pass. There are fair campsites around this junction. Beyond this junction the trail fords Ireland Creek (difficult in early season), passes below Potter Point, and ascends gently for almost 3 miles to the fair campsites at Lyell Base Camp (9040'). Fishing is fair for brook trout. This base camp, surrounded on three sides by steep canyon walls, marks the end of the meadowed sections of Lyell Canyon, and is the traditional first-night stopping place for those touring the John Muir Trail beginning at Tuolumne Meadows.

2nd Hiking Day: Retrace your steps, 8.7 miles.

Mt. Lyell above Lyell Canyon

61 Tuolumne Meadows to Vogelsang

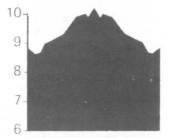

Distance   15.4 miles
Type   Round trip
Best season   Mid or late
Topo maps   **Tuolumne Meadows**
Grade (hiking days/recommended layover days)
  Leisurely 2/1
  Moderate   2/0
  Strenuous ---
Trailhead   26

HIGHLIGHTS Vogelsang Camp has the most dramatic setting of all the famous High Sierra Camps. Located right under the somber north face of Fletcher Peak, it has an authentic alpine atmosphere. Many nearby lakes offer exciting side-trip possibilities for anglers, swimmers and picnickers.

DESCRIPTION

1st Hiking Day (**Tuolumne Lodge** to **Vogelsang High Sierra Camp**, 7.7 miles): First, follow Trip 60 to the John Muir Trail-Rafferty Creek Trail junction. Here our route turns right and immediately begins the toughest climb of this entire trip. Even so, the grade is moderate as often as it is steep, the trail is fairly well shaded by lodgepole pines, and the length of the climb is well under a mile. Then, as the ascent decreases to a gentle grade, we pass through high, boulder-strewn meadows that offer good views eastward of reddish-brown Mts. Dana and Gibbs, and gray-white Mammoth Peak. Soon the trail dips close to Rafferty Creek, and since this stream flows all year you can count on refreshment here. Then the nearly level trail passes above an orange snowcourse marker in a large meadow below and continues its long, gentle ascent through a sparse forest of lodgepole pines unmixed with a single tree of any other species. About ⅓ mile beyond a stream that dries up in late summer, we ford another that also does in some years and immediately veer right at a junction where the abandoned old trail up the long meadow veers left. Our relocated trail up a cobbly hillside was built to allow the damaged meadow below to recover from the pounding of too many feet.

Finally the exclusive lodgepole pines allow a few whitebark pines to join their company, and these trees diminish the force of the winds that often sweep through Tuolumne Pass. Through breaks in this forest one has intermittent views of cliff-bound, dark-banded Fletcher Peak and Peak 11799 in the south. Then our path leaves the green-floored forest and leads out into an area of bouldery granite outcroppings dotted with a few trees. Around this granite and past these trees we wind down to the west side of saucer-shaped Tuolumne Pass, a major gap in the Cathedral Range. Taking the signed trail to Vogelsang here, we follow a rocky-dusty path up a moderately steep hillside below which Boothe Lake and its surrounding meadows lie serene in the west. Finally, our trail reaches the top of this climb, and suddenly we see the tents of Vogelsang High Sierra Camp (10,180') spread out before us. A few snacks may be bought here, or dinner or breakfast if you make a reservation. There are good campsites by Fletcher Creek just beyond the camp, but remember the bears that live here are always interested in your food.

2nd Hiking Day: Retrace your steps, 7.7 miles.

Looking north from Tuolumne Pass

62 Tuolumne Meadows to Emeric Lake

Distance   28.8 miles
Type   Semiloop trip
Best season Mid or late
Topo maps   **Tuolumne Meadows, Merced Peak**
Grade (hiking days/recommended layover days)
    Leisurely 5/1
    Moderate 4/0
    Strenuous 2/0
Trailhead   26

HIGHLIGHTS With Tuolumne Pass as the neck of the noose,
                this trip "lassos" Vogelsang Peak by dashing
down the valley of Lewis Creek and then cruising back up the
valley of Fletcher Creek. In addition to the spectrum of views
of this fine peak, the traveler will constantly have good vistas of
many parts of the Cathedral Range, and for anglers there is
good fishing in both creeks and at Emeric Lake.

DESCRIPTION (Moderate trip)

1st Hiking Day: Follow Trip 61 to **Vogelsang High Sierra
Camp**, 7.7 miles.

2nd Hiking Day (**Vogelsang High Sierra Camp** to
Florence Creek, 4.3 miles): Taking the Vogelsang Pass Trail
from the camp, we descend slightly to ford Fletcher Creek on
boulders and then begin a 550-foot ascent to the pass. The
panting hiker is rewarded, as always in the Sierra, with increasingly good views. Fletcher Peak rises grandly on the left, far
north is Mt.Conness, and Clouds Rest and then Half Dome
come into view in the west-southwest. The trail skirts above the

west shore of Vogelsang Lake as we look down on the turfy shores and the large rock island of this timberline lake. Nearer the pass, views to the north are occluded somewhat, but expansive new views appear in the south: from left to right are Parsons Peak, Simmons Peak, Mt. Maclure, the tip of Mt. Lyell behind Maclure, Mt. Florence and, in the south, the entire Clark Range, from Triple Divide Peak on the left to Mt. Clark on the right.

From the windswept pass the trail rises briefly northeast before it follows steep switchbacks down into sparse lodgepole forest where many small streams provide moisture for thousands of lupine plants, with their light blue, pea-family flowers. The singing of the unnamed outlet stream from Gallison Lake becomes clear as the trail begins to level off, and then we reach a flat meadow through which the stream slowly meanders. There is a fine campsite beside this meadow, though wood fires are illegal here.

Proceeding down a rutted, grassy trail for several hundred yards, we come to a brief, steep descent on a rocky path that swoops down to the meadowed valley of multi-braided Lewis Creek. In this little valley in quick succession we boulderhop the Gallison Lake outlet and then cross Lewis Creek on a log. In a few minutes we pass the steep ½ mile lateral to Bernice Lake. The shady trail winds gently down east of the creek under a moderate overhead canopy of lodgepole pine mixed with some hemlock, crossing a little stream about ½ mile from the last ford. Then, after almost touching the creek opposite a steep, rusty west canyon wall, the trail veers away and crosses another small tributary stream as it winds through dense hemlock forest to the good campsites beside Florence Creek (9200'). This year-round creek cascades down to the camping area over steep granite sheets, and the water sounds are a fine sleeping potion at bedtime. Fishing in Florence and Lewis creeks is good for brook trout to 12".

3rd Hiking Day (**Florence Creek** to **Emeric Lake**, 6.0 miles): Leaving the densely shaded hemlock forest floor, our trail descends a series of lodgepole-dotted granite slabs, and Lewis Creek makes pleasant noises in a string of chutes not far away on the right. Then, where the creek's channel narrows, the traveler will find on his left a lesson in exfoliation: granite layers peeling like an onion. One is more used to seeing this

kind of peeling on Yosemite's domes, but this fine example is
located on a canyon slope. As the bed of Lewis Creek steepens
to deliver the stream's water to the Merced River far below, so
does the trail steepen, and our descent to middle altitudes
reaches the zone of red firs and silver pines. After dipping
beside the creek, the trail climbs away from it to a junction with
the High Trail, which leads south along the rim of the Merced
River canyon.

From this junction the Lewis Creek Trail, now out of
earshot of the creek, switchbacks down moderately, sometimes steeply, under a sparse cover of red fir, juniper, and
lodgepole and silver pine for 1 mile to a junction with the
Fletcher Creek Trail. We turn right onto this trail and follow the
latter part of the 4th hiking day, Trip 55, to Emeric Lake.

4th Hiking Day: Follow the 5th hiking day, Trip 58, to
Tuolumne Meadows, 10.8 miles.

Mt. Clark above Emeric Lake

Tuolumne Meadows to Lyell Fork **63**

Distance	40.3 miles
Type	Semiloop trip
Best season	Mid or late
Topo maps	**Tuolumne Meadows, Merced Peak**

Grade (hiking days/recommended layover days)

Leisurely	7/1
Moderate	6/1
Strenuous	4/0

Trailhead   26

HIGHLIGHTS Every beginning backpacker sooner or later wants to try his newfound skills on a challenging trip of some length. This excursion in Yosemite Park is made to order for him: long mileage but not too long; tough climbs, but manageable ones; lonely stretches, but two popular campsites in between. And it's all wrapped up in some of the best scenery in Yosemite National Park.

DESCRIPTION (Moderate trip)

1st and 2nd Hiking Days: Follow Trip 62 to **Florence Creek**, 12.0 miles.

3rd Hiking Day (**Florence Creek** to **Lyell Fork**, 7.4 miles): First, follow the 3rd hiking day, Trip 62, to the junction of the High Trail and the Lewis Creek Trail, and turn left. The ascent from here is a tough, unrelieved 1000 vertical feet, but fortunately most of it is in shady forest of red fir and silver and lodgepole pine. Near the top, where the grade is a little less steep, the panting hiker is also shaded by altitude-preferring whitebark pines. At about 9000 feet, views to the west and north grow expansive, and one can make out Half Dome, Clouds Rest, the Cockscomb and Unicorn Peak. After crossing a ridge, our sandy path descends into a meadow long since invaded by lodgepole trees and reaches an all-year stream where you can refill your body's cooling system depleted by the long climb.

Beyond this easy ford the High Trail lives up to its name as it traverses a broad bench about 10,000 feet above sea level. A second all-year stream, larger than the last, can present slight fording problems in early season. Then the trail climbs again, away from the lip of the main canyon, until it veers south back to the lip at a spectacular viewpoint for studying the headwaters of the Lyell Fork (in the east) and the Merced Peak Fork (in the south) of the Merced River. One could spend many days in these vast, trailless headwaters without seeing another human being.

From this overlook the trail descends a bit steeply in places to a third all-year stream, an easy boulderhop, and then continues down to the cascading, chuting Lyell Fork (9080'). The last segment of trail before the stream, over granite slabs, is a little hard to follow, but the route leads where you would expect it to. The campsites at the ford are poor, but good ones lie 150 yards downstream, where the chutes and rapids flowing over the sculpted granite bedrock are fine visual attractions and provide good music to sleep by. There are also good campsites ½ mile upstream, a better base if you are going to explore the remote lake basins at the headwaters of the Lyell Fork. Fishing in the Lyell Fork is good for brook trout to 11".

4th Hiking Day (**Lyell Fork** to **Babcock Lake**, 9.1 miles): First, retrace your steps to the Lewis Creek Trail and turn left (south). From this junction the Lewis Creek Trail, now out of earshot of the creek, switchbacks down moderately, sometimes steeply, under a sparse cover of red fir, juniper, and lodgepole and silver pine for 1 mile to a junction with a trail that comes steeply up from the main canyon floor. We turn right on this trail and follow several switchbacks down to a bridge over tree-shaded Lewis Creek. From here the rocky trail enters more open hillside as it climbs moderately on a cobbled path bordered by clumps of mountain whitethorn and huckleberry oak. Just past a tributary ½ mile from Lewis Creek we have fine views of cataracts and waterfalls on Fletcher Creek where it rushes down open granite slopes dotted with lodgepole pines. The trail then passes very close to the splashing creek before veering northeast and climbing, steeply at times, on the now-familiar cobbling placed by trail crews. Here one has more good views of Fletcher Creek chuting and cascading down from the notch at the base of a granite dome before it leaps off a ledge in free fall. The few solitary pine trees on this otherwise blank dome are mute testimony to nature's extraordinary persistence.

At the notch our trail levels off near some nice but illegal campsites and soon we arrive at the trail to Babcock Lake. Turning left (north) we ford Fletcher Creek (difficult in early season) and follow a winding trail ⅓ mile west to narrow, granite-bound Babcock Lake (8983'). There are fine campsites all around this forested lake, and fishing is good for brook trout to 10".

5th Hiking Day (**Babcock Lake** to **Boothe Lake**, 4.4 miles): After retracing our steps to the Fletcher Creek Trail, we turn left (north). From this junction the sandy trail ascends steadily through a moderate forest cover just east of the verdant banks of rollicking Fletcher Creek. After a mile, the trail breaks out into the open and begins to rise more steeply via rocky but shaded switchbacks. These zigzags lead to another notch between two granite domes, and upon reaching this notch the slogging traveler suddenly achieves a wonderful panorama. A long, barely sloping, lush meadow stretches several miles ahead, and it is flanked on both sides by soaring, snow-streaked peaks. Down this meadow flows Fletcher Creek, meandering from pool to trout-holding pool. Here one has the feeling of being in truly high country, and the distance passes easily as we stroll to an **X** junction with trails to Emeric Lake and Vogelsang. From this junction follow part of the 5th hiking day, Trip 55, to the overlook of Boothe Lake (9900') and then leave the trail to find the good campsites on the south side of the lake.

6th Hiking Day (**Boothe Lake** to **Tuolumne Lodge**, 7.4 miles): First, hike briefly cross country back to the trail you left at the end of the previous hiking day. From that point, near broad Tuolumne Pass, hike up to the junction in the pass, and then retrace most of the steps of Trip 61.

Tuolumne Meadows to Triple Peak Fork

64

Distance   51 miles
Type   Semiloop trip
Best season Mid or late
Topo maps   **Tuolumne Meadows, Merced Peak**
Grade (hiking days/recommended layover days)
   Leisurely 8/1
   Moderate   7/0
   Strenuous 4/0
Trailhead   26

HIGHLIGHTS The headwaters of the Triple Peak Fork of the
                Merced River are about as far as one can get
from civilization, so this is a trip for those who feel they
encounter too many people on most of their hikes. Their opportunity to view most of the High Sierra from the southern border
of Yosemite is won by a long walk through grand high country.

DESCRIPTION (Moderate trip)

1st, 2nd and 3rd Hiking Days: Follow Trip 63 to the **Lyell
Fork of the Merced River**, 19.1 miles.

4th Hiking Day (**Lyell Fork** to **Triple Peak Fork
Meadows**, 6.9 miles): This day's hike starts off strenuously up
switchbacks on the south wall of the Lyell Fork canyon. As we
progress slowly up the rocky path, views open up to reward us
for our struggle. In the northeast, on the Sierra crest, are Mt.
Maclure and Mt. Lyell, highest point in Yosemite Park. After
Lyell passes from view, Rodger Peak, second highest in the
Park, appears as the dark triangle beyond the right flank of
Peak 12132. Other towering peaks in view this side of the crest
don't even have names, but in the company of lesser summits
they surely would have. Where our trail extends close to the lip
of the Merced River canyon, we can step off the path to an

overlook for viewing most of the Clark Range in the southwest, and Clouds Rest in the northwest.

Beyond the top of the ascent, the route winds among large boulders on "grus"—granite sand—which is the result of the breakup of just such boulders by the fierce erosional forces at work in these alpine climates. After crossing a seasonal stream, the trail ascends to a second broad ridge, from which views through the whitebark-pine trees continue to be excellent. About ½ mile beyond this ridge a trail to Foerster Lake (not named on the topo map) veers off to the left. This unsigned trail is indicated by parallel rock borders and occasional flame-shaped blazes on trees. Secluded Foerster Lake has no fish, but swimming and camping there are excellent.

From this spur trail our route makes a long descent, paralleling Foerster Lake's outlet part of the way, to a boulder ford of Foerster Creek. The well-shaded trail then undulates past a number of pocket meadows to another small stream, and yet another not shown on the map. A gentle traverse downward extends almost a mile to a small creek that winds through a flat area densely forested with hemlock and lodgepole pine. From this flat the High Trail begins a climb that doesn't end until it reaches the Yosemite border at Isberg Pass. Very soon the trail fords the outlet of the unnamed lake north of Isberg Peak, and in another 200 yards it reaches a large cairn which marks the junction with a trail down to the Triple Peak Fork. All hikers who arrive here with any surplus energy will greatly enjoy a 4-mile round trip to Isberg Pass before heading down to camp on the Triple Peak Fork.

The trail to Isberg Pass first climbs moderately for ¼ mile up a beautiful hillside covered with whitish broken granite in whose cracks a dozen species of alpine wildflowers grow. Looking west and north from this slope, one can see all the peaks of the Clark Range and most of the peaks of the Cathedral Range. Using your **Tuolumne Meadows** map, you can probably make out Tenaya Peak, Tressider Peak, Cathedral Peak, Echo Peaks, Matthes Crest and the Cockscomb. At the top of this little climb a truly marvelous sight comes into view, for here we enter a large, high bowl nearly encircled by great peaks which has in it an enormous meadow and two sparkling lakes. Here and there, clumps of whitebark and lodgepole pines help give scale to the vast amphitheater, and the delicateness of the meadow flowers is a perfect counterpoint to the massiveness of the encircling summits. The setting is absolutely euphoric.

On the far side of the bowl, the trail begins to rise toward the crest and soon comes to a junction where the right fork leads to Post Peak Pass and the left to Isberg Pass, ¾ mile away. The left fork ascends moderately a short way to reach the height of the pass, and then contours over to it. The best views—other than those we have already been enjoying for the last several miles—are to be had from a point on the ridgeline a few hundred yards beyond the sign-marked pass. You can see most of the High Sierra, from the Ritter Range close in the east, to peaks around Mt. Goddard southwest of Bishop.

Back at the cairned junction, our route turns west and starts straight downhill, then veers southwest and switchbacks down into deep hemlock forest, turning north for the last ¾ mile down to the river. There are good campsites around the junction of our trail and the trail to Red Peak Pass, which begins just across the placid Triple Peak Fork (9100'). Fishing is good for brook and rainbow trout to 9".

5th hiking Day (**Triple Peak Fork Meadow** to **Washburn Lake**, 6.9 miles): Reverse the 4th and part of the 3rd hiking day, Trip 72, to the good campsites at the head of Washburn Lake.

6th Hiking Day (**Washburn Lake** to **Emeric Lake**, 7.3 miles): The sandy trail along the east side of Washburn Lake leads over slopes dotted with white fir, aspen, juniper, lodgepole pine and Jeffrey pine, and from these slopes on a typical morning, the still water makes a fine mirror for the soaring granite cliffs across the lake. Beyond this lake, our descending trail stays near the singing river in open forest, fording a small stream every quarter mile or so as it descends on a moderate grade. Then the canyon floor begins to widen, and the trail proceeds levelly under a canopy of imposing Jeffrey pines and other tall conifers to a junction with the Lewis Creek Trail beside the Merced Lake Ranger Station. Here we turn right and follow the latter part of the 4th hiking day, Trip 55, to Emeric Lake.

7th Hiking Day (**Emeric Lake** to **Tuolumne Lodge**, 10.8 miles): Follow the 5th hiking day, Trip 55.

Tuolumne Meadows to Agnew Meadows

65

Distance	28.2 miles
Type	Shuttle trip
Best season	Mid or late
Topo maps	**Tuolumne Meadows, Devil's Postpile**

Grade (hiking days/recommended layover days)
    Leisurely 5/1
    Moderate 4/1
    Strenuous 4/0
Trailhead   26, 36

HIGHLIGHTS "Sky parlor" meadows, alpine lakes, clear, icy streams, magnificent peaks—this trip has them all. Except for the last 4 miles, this route follows the well-known John Muir Trail as it tours Lyell Canyon and the view-filled eastern slopes of the Ritter Range. Because of its fame, this trail sees a lot of use, but the incomparable scenery en route more than compensates for the lack of solitude.

DESCRIPTION (Moderate trip)

1st Hiking Day: Follow Trip 60 to **Lyell Base Camp**, 9 miles.

2nd Hiking Day (**Lyell Base Camp** to **Rush Creek**, 7 miles): From Lyell Base Camp the trail ascends the steep, southern terminal wall of Lyell Canyon above the west side of the Lyell Fork. There is no water here in late season. Just before the confluence of the Maclure Creek tributary of the Lyell Fork, our route crosses a bridge to the east side and then switchbacks up to some very used campsites just before another crossing (wet in early season). The rocky underfooting above here is pleasantly relieved by superb alpine meadows.

Along the first 3 miles of this day's ascent, views of the glaciers on the north faces of Mt. Maclure and Mt. Lyell are superlative.

From this ford our trail climbs steeply up rocky going to Donohue Pass (11,056') at the crest of the Sierra. This pass, lying between Donohue Peak (northeast) and Mt. Lyell (southwest), affords majestic views of the Sierra crest, the Cathedral Range and the Ritter Range—not right at the pass, but just before and just after. From Donohue Pass the trail descends by rocky switchbacks to sparse timber cover at the headwaters of Rush Creek, passing a lateral to Marie Lakes. As the trail levels out somewhat, it meets and then parallels a small, unnamed tributary of Rush Creek descending to join the main stream. In the Rush Creek watershed the forest cover of lodgepole and hemlock becomes denser, and the trail fords two tributaries to the "Improved" campsites on Rush Creek (9600'), where our route meets the Rush Creek Trail. Fishing is good for brook and rainbow (to 10").

3rd Hiking Day (**Rush Creek** to **Shadow Creek**, 8.0 miles): Through a continuing forest cover of lodgepole and mountain hemlock, our route ascends steadily beyond the junction with a trail to Davis Lakes, climbing southeast to the low saddle known as Island Pass (10,200'). Just south of this pass the trail passes two small lakes and then veers eastward.

The trail emerges from the lodgepole-and-hemlock ground cover to a metamorphic slope above the outlet at the east end of Thousand Island Lake. Views from this rocky slope are sweeping, and the hiker immediately notices the difference between the predominantly darker rock of the Ritter Range and the lighter granite of the Sierra crest's alpine peaks. Geologically, the Ritter Range is made up of somewhat older rocks originally volcanic in nature, and the spectacularly jagged skyline from Banner Peak southward attests to the strength of this rock, which resisted the massive glaciers that gnawed at the range. As the trail switchbacks down to the outlet of Thousand Island Lake, there are classic views across the island-studded waters to the imposing east facades of Banner Peak and Mt. Ritter.

From Thousand Island Lake, proceed to Shadow Creek by reversing the 2nd hiking day of Trip 76.

4th Hiking Day (**Shadow Creek** to **Agnew Meadows**, 4.2 miles): Reverse the 1st hiking day of Trip 74.

Yosemite Valley to Merced Lake 66

Distance	27.8 miles
Type	Round trip
Best season	Early
Topo maps	**Yosemite, Merced Peak**

Grade (hiking days/recommended layover days)

    Leisurely 4/1
    Moderate 3/1
    Strenuous 2/1

Trailhead 29

HIGHLIGHTS An early-season trip (low altitude, early snowmelt), this route offers all the scenic grandeur of the Valley attractions, plus the intimate knowledge of the back country that only the backpacker can have. Fishing is good during early season on the Merced River and at Merced Lake. Swimming is poor during the early season, owing to the chilly waters, but photographers and naturalists will find an exciting area of geologic spectacle and history.

DESCRIPTION (Leisurely trip)

1st Hiking Day (**Yosemite Valley** to **Little Yosemite Valley**, 4.7 miles): Though this trip is graded leisurely, the first hiking day is rigorous, with over 2000 feet of climbing, but the route is so spectacular that the hiker can easily forget his aches and pains. This trip starts at the beginning of the John Muir Trail, across the Merced River from the Happy Isles Trail Center. Ascending steeply south, we leave the wide, level canyon of the Merced River.

The John Muir Trail—which is more like a road here—climbs steeply under canyon live oak and California bay. Where the trail rounds Sierra Point we can look back at

Yosemite Falls, while below us are the river and the intake and reservoir for the Valley's water supply. Soon we arrive at the Vernal Fall bridge, and several hundred feet beyond we meet the Mist Trail. Ascending from here to the top of Nevada Fall, most people use the less steep John Muir Trail, but if you have not been up the Mist Trail, it is recommended. Returning via the John Muir Trail is both easier and safer. Both routes will be described here.

If you ascend the Mist Trail you will usually get wet. Climbing toward Vernal Fall, the trail soon becomes extremely steep as it ascends large, rocky steps where the mist can be a driving rainstorm in spring. As we rise above the base of the 320-foot fall, we pass through a hole, and then reach the base of a large, dripping overhang. Then we turn left on a ledge that exits onto slabs above Vernal Fall. From the railing by the fall proceed up past Emerald Pool to a junction with a lateral leading to the right to the Muir Trail. Here we turn left, then cross the river and ascend to a level area below Nevada Fall. Then the last section of the Mist Trail switchbacks up a steep, rocky gully several hundred yards north of Nevada Fall.

If you take the John Muir Trail up from the Vernal Fall bridge to the top of Nevada Fall, you start by ascending a long series of switchbacks. After passing a junction with a lateral to the Mist Trail, we climb more switchbacks and get very good views of Half Dome, Mt. Broderick and Liberty Cap. These last two, though rounded like Half Dome, were overridden by glaciers while Half Dome was not. Our trail then passes a junction with the Panorama Trail and arrives at the top of Nevada Fall. While admiring the view of Glacier Point you may notice patches of shiny, smooth bedrock at your feet—glacial polish— indicating that a glacier has been here recently. There is very little glacial polish below this point, which marks the farthest extent of a glacier that was here about 13,000 years ago.

The John Muir Trail meets the Mist Trail several hundred yards northwest of Nevada Fall. From the junction it is a short ascent and then a gentle descent into Little Yosemite Valley. Our trail passes a cutoff that later rejoins the Muir Trail, and ½ mile farther we leave the Muir Trail at a junction near the well-used camping area by the summer ranger station.

2nd Hiking Day (**Little Yosemite Valley** to **Merced Lake**, 9.2 miles): From the well-used, misused and abused camping area, our shaded route heads toward the east end of Little Yosemite Valley. The trail—40 feet wide in places—swings away from the complacent river and stretches along the flat valley floor under Jeffrey pines and white firs. As an indication of how thick glaciers were here, look up at Moraine Dome to the east: ice filled the valley almost to its summit 750,000 years ago. Since then glaciers have repeatedly entered this valley, but none that thick.

At the east end of Little Yosemite Valley the trail swings close to the river again. Here the lofty canyon walls converge and the grade steepens as we pass another camping area. The next section of our route is through a short, narrow gorge leading to Lost Valley.

Soon we arrive in wide, level Lost Valley, where the vertical walls reflect the vertical jointing in the bedrock. At the east end of Lost Valley we enter yet another short, narrow section of canyon, which leads to yet a smaller valley, on the north side of exfoliating Bunnell Point. Before the canyon narrows again, the trail crosses one branch of the river via an island, and a second branch on a new wood bridge. The lumber for this bridge was hewn in 1984 from a 175-year-old sugar pine that stood just below the trail.

From the bridge our rocky trail stays near the river until we begin the steep stretch up to Echo Valley. The trail avoids the gorge bottom by climbing 400 feet south and traversing over open slabs where glacial erratics have been rearranged to mark the trail. Our route then descends to cross the river on a bridge at the west end of Echo Valley. Following the river, then turning north, the trail arrives at a junction and a multibridged crossing of Echo Creek. We continue east through a very dense young forest of lodgepole pines.

Soon our route winds up slabs, and where the river is confined in yet another gorge we walk right above the fast-moving water. The grade eases once again as we arrive at yet another wide, flat valley, this one containing Merced Lake. Following the north shore, the trail passes a drift fence and arrives at the camping area at the lake's east end. Bears are plentiful. The lake contains a population of brook and rainbow trout. A High Sierra camp with tents, showers and meals—if you have a reservation—is here.

3rd and 4th Hiking Days: Retrace your steps, 13.9 miles.

67 Bridalveil Creek to Royal Arch Lake

Distance   26 miles
Type   Round trip
Best season   Early or mid
Topo maps   **Yosemite**
Grade (hiking days/recommended layover days)
  Leisurely 4/1
  Moderate   3/0
  Strenuous 2/0
Trailhead   31

HIGHLIGHTS In early season this trip route is lush with wild-flowers of every variety, and color film is a must for the photographer. Anglers will find few lakes within the Park to rival the fishing at Royal Arch Lake. The easy grade of the topography makes this an excellent early-season choice.

DESCRIPTION (Leisurely trip)

1st Hiking Day (**Bridalveil Campground** to **Turner Meadows**, 6.3 miles): From the trailhead at the southeast end of the campground, the trail begins winding southeastward along meandering Bridalveil Creek. The grade is gentle as the trail winds through the dense lodgepole forest. Periodically, the thick undergrowth gives way to intimate, mountain-bluebell-filled meadows. Beyond a left-leading trail to the Glacier Point Road, near Lost Bear Meadow, the trail veers south beside one of the larger tributaries of Bridalveil Creek. It crosses this tributary, passes a lateral to the Ostrander Lake trail, and in ½ mile crosses the tributary again, and each fording is heralded by banks covered with lavender shooting stars.

The second crossing marks the beginning of an easy 400-foot climb over the ridge that separates the Bridalveil Creek and Alder Creek watersheds. In early and mid season this ridge is colorfully decked out in lush pink and white fields of pussy paws, brodiaea, mat lupine and Douglas phlox. From the top of this ridge, the trail drops to the Deer Camp Trail junction, climbs over Turner Ridge and then offers a short walk to Turner Meadows and the campsites at the northern end. The cabin site at the head of the meadows (indicated by the rock fireplace) is all that remains of Bill Turner's pioneer abode. He occupied these grasslands while running cattle around the turn of the 20th century. There is stream water except in late season.

2nd Hiking Day (**Turner Meadows** to **Royal Arch Lake**, 6.7 miles): Before leaving Turner Meadows, one should take the opportunity to study the wildlife that frequents the meadows, particularly in the early morning. On the trail you will pass many little rills supporting colorful wildflower gardens before you reach, in ½ mile, the Wawona Trail, which branches south, and ¾ mile farther, the Chilnualna Lakes Trail, branching east. These trails were used by U.S. Cavalry patrols at the turn of the century. Their purpose was to facilitate administration of the Park.

Just after the last junction you ford swirling Chilnualna Creek (difficult in early season), and then climb on switch-backs over an eastward-rising ridge to a junction with a second lateral trail to Wawona, leading right. South of the ridgecrest, where views to the south open up, we turn east up the valley of Grouse Lake's little outlet stream and ascend gently for 2 miles. You can leave the trail where it veers a bit northward away from the creek and follow that stream to Grouse Lake, should that be your goal, or you can stay on the trail for another ¼ mile to find a spur trail leading to the right to the lake.

From the spur-trail junction your trail provides an easy, shaded walk over a small rise and thence down to cross the inlet of shallow Crescent Lake, just out of sight in the south. Another mile of level walking into increasing mosquito-infested forest brings us to Johnson Lake, with its good fishing for brook and rainbow (9–13"). Johnson Lake and its perimeter were one of the last acquisitions of private property within the Park's boundaries, and two crumbling cabins remain to remind us of our homesteading era.

The next ¾ mile, to a junction with the Royal Arch Lake Trail, is a 250-foot ascent up a lodgepole-covered slope. Here our route leaves the Buck Camp Trail and turns north for a small climb through dense forest that gives way to open hill-side as we approach dramatic Royal Arch Lake (8700'). This lake is small but it is deep, and it supports an excellent, self-sustaining fishery of brook and rainbow (8–14"). Its regal name derives from the blackened granite streaks that rainbow across the steep eastern face of the lake basin. There are numerous good campsites not far from a seasonal lakelet beside the west shore, which is perfect for bathing when it has warmed up by mid-season.

3rd and 4th Hiking Days: Retrace your steps, 13 miles.

Royal Arch Lake   *National Park Service*

Bridalveil Creek to Glacier Point 68

Distance   29.1 miles
Type   Shuttle trip
Best season   Early or mid
Topo maps   **Yosemite**
Grade (hiking days/recommended layover days)
   Leisurely 5/1
   Moderate 4/1
   Strenuous 3/0
Trailhead   31, 30

DESCRIPTION (Moderate trip)

1st and 2nd Hiking Days: Follow Trip 67 to **Royal Arch Lake**, 13 miles.

3rd Hiking Day (**Royal Arch Lake** to **Buena Vista Creek Tributary**, 11 miles): Today's hike is long but it's mostly downhill. It's also unusual as it crosses several areas that are in the early stages of fire succession. We gain most of our elevation today by climbing 2 miles from Royal Arch Lake to Buena Vista summit. This easy ascent winds past delightful meadows that are drained by a small creek. From the pass (9300') it is an easy ¾-mile climb to the top of aptly named Buena Vista Peak (9709'). Being the highest point for miles around, this peak offers some of the most expansive views in the Sierra.

After a short descent past the north shore of Buena Vista Lake, we meet the signed Chilnualna Lakes Trail on a ridge. Turning right, we descend steeply past two ponds into Buena Vista Creek canyon. After crossing the creek several times and then the outlet from Hart Lakes, we climb over a large moraine. Beyond, our descent is steady for 2 miles through dry forest until we cross the seasonal outlet from Edson Lake between two wet meadows. Turning northeast, the grade soon steepens and we descend over indistinct glacial moraines. Presently, the forest of white fir and Jeffrey pine shows sign of a fire that occurred in 1981.

As we near some-years-seasonal Buena Vista Creek, we see many living trees whose trunks were barely touched by flames, indicating that the fire here was not very hot and burned slowly along the ground. This type of low-intensity fire is a normal event of natural coniferous forests. Such fires prevent a large buildup of dead wood, which in turn prevents fires from reaching severe intensity. But always, there are variations in nature, and after we climb over a low ridge we descend to cross two small creeks where stands of lodgepole pine have been completely killed. Lodgepoles, like most pines, burn easily, and having thin bark also, they often die in a fire. The logical counterpart to this property is that lodgepole pines produce a dense crop of fast-growing seedlings. The new generation thrives in bright light and dry soil, and out-competes other trees in newly opened parts of a forest.

After crossing another low ridge we descend along the margins of a flowery meadow to ford a larger creek, beside which we find a good campsite in a stand of unburned pine and fir.

4th Hiking Day (**Buena Vista Creek Tributary** to **Glacier Point**, 5.1 miles): Descending northwest, we see more signs of fire, as well as massive Mt. Starr King looming in the northeast. Our route passes several giant sugar pines, survivors of many fires over the centuries. After 1⅓ miles we reach a signed junction near Illilouette Creek, on the right. (A short distance toward the creek is an overused campsite, but there are better ones upstream). We go left and in 50 yards reach a signed junction with a trail west to Mono Meadow. Our trail veers right and soon steepens, and in ⅓ mile we cross the creek from Mono Meadow on rocks or logs.

From here, we descend parallel to Illilouette Creek as it winds through a gorge for almost a mile. Beyond the gorge we begin the challenging 1200' ascent to Glacier Point. Soon we leave the shade of huge white firs and enter an area that burned in 1987. The ascent here is gentle, and we see fire succession in the form of black oaks that have regrown from the crown of their roots. A small creek provides a lush rest stop before we meet the Panorama Trail, coming up from Illilouette Fall.

On this famous trail, on a clear day, one can look across the vast chasm of the Merced River canyon and with the aid of binoculars see hikers on the summit of Half Dome. Nearer at hand, we can see the work of avalanches that have thundered down from the heights, carrying rocks, trees and soil across the trail. The fine views from just below Washburn Point include Nevada Fall, Vernal Fall, Half Dome, Mt. Starr King, and many high peaks of eastern Yosemite, marching off to the southeast horizon. The last half mile to Glacier Point (7214') is accomplished by switchbacks that rise to the parking area near this famous overlook.

Half Dome from Glacier Point

69 Bridalveil Creek to Yosemite Valley

Distance   32.7 miles
Type   Shuttle trip
Best season   Early or mid
Topo maps   **Yosemite, Merced Peak**
Grade (hiking days/recommended layover days)
    Leisurely 5/1
    Moderate   4/1
    Strenuous 3/0
Trailhead   31, 29

HIGHLIGHTS This route traverses some of the finer forest
                 stands in Yosemite, crosses the Buena Vista
Crest, and concludes via the famous Panorama and Nevada
Fall trails into the Valley.

DESCRIPTION (Leisurely trip)

1st and 2nd Hiking Days: Follow Trip 67 to **Royal Arch
Lake**, 13 miles (20.9 km).

3rd Hiking Day: Follow the 3rd hiking day of Trip 68 to
Buena Vista Creek Tributary, 11.0 miles.

4th Hiking Day: (**Buena Vista Creek tributary** to
Yosemite Valley, 8.7 miles via the John Muir Trail, or 8.0
miles via the Mist Trail): From the unburned area by the creek
we reenter recently burned forest. Descending northwest, we
pass several centuries-old sugar pines, the survivors of more
than one fire. In 1.3 miles we reach a signed junction with the
trail up Illilouette Creek. We turn right on it and descend past

an overused campsite. A short ascent then brings us to a small clearing on red ground. Ford Illilouette Creek here, toward a leaning Jeffrey pine on the north bank (difficult in high runoff). A short ascent on deeply weathered glacial deposits brings us to a dry flat and a signed junction with the Merced Pass Trail. Here we go left and descend through trees to cross a lovely little creek. There is a good campsite shortly before the creek.

Ascending steeply now, and then moderately through Jeffrey pine, white fir and bracken fern, we come to a seasonal creek. Here the soil thins, as does the forest cover, and the grade steepens. This sunny slope gets hot and we can rest while taking in the view of the burn across the canyon. There we can see one reason forests vary in both tree age and species composition. This typical mosaic pattern results when a fire kills some trees entirely while barely touching others nearby.

From this slope we climb through more shady environs and reach a signed junction where we turn left and cross a low ridge to join the aptly named Panorama Trail. Turning right, we begin a paved descent into the immense, glacially polished canyon of the Merced River. Half Dome falls behind Liberty Cap as we drop 600' to the John Muir Trail. To descend this famous trail to the Valley, reverse the first part of the 1st hiking day, Trip 66.

Nevada Fall from above *Dick Beach*

70 Bridalveil Creek to Royal Arch Lake

Distance   27.7 miles
Type   Semiloop trip
Best season   Early or mid
Topo maps   **Yosemite**
Grade (hiking days/recommended layover days)
   Leisurely 5/1
   Moderate 4/1
   Strenuous 3/0
Trailhead   31

HIGHLIGHTS For the first-timer, exploring Yosemite's South Boundary Country is a memorable experience, and this loop trip provides an exciting route. Angling on the many lakes around Buena Vista Peak is excellent, particularly in early season, and the easy access and return recommend this trip as an early-season "warm up."

DESCRIPTION (Leisurely trip)

1st Hiking Day: Follow Trip 67 to **Turner Meadows**, 6.3 miles.

2nd Hiking Day: (**Turner Meadows** to **Upper Chilnualna Lake**, 4.9 miles): From Turner Meadows the trail continues southeast. One half mile from the campsites at the south end of the meadow our route passes the Wawona Trail, and ¾ mile later it turns east along Chilnualna Creek. This junction marks the beginning of a long, easy ascent that is pleasantly accompanied by the creek. Fishing along this cascading stream is fair (small brook and rainbow); most anglers will keep their lines dry until they reach Chilnualna Lakes (8480'). Here, all except the lowest lake provide excellent fishing for brook and rainbow (7–12"). Small (7-acre) upper Chilnualna Lake, alongside the trail, has several good campsites on its north side, but the best and most secluded Chilnualna Lake is the southernmost one.

3rd Hiking Day (**Upper Chilnualna Lake** to **Royal Arch Lake**, 3.5 miles): From the north side of the lake, the trail climbs steeply up the 480-foot, densely forested slope to a junction with the Buena Vista Trail. Our route turns right (southeast) and climbs the ridge to beautiful Buena Vista Lake (9080'). On this high lake fishing is good for rainbow and brook (9–13") and anglers may wish to tarry. It is a 300-foot hike up to the pass (and another 400 feet east up Buena Vista Peak, if you choose). The remaining 2 miles to Royal Arch Lake are an easy descent past lovely patches of meadow between granite slabs.

Royal Arch Lake (8700') is a fine fishing lake (excellent angling for brook and rainbow to 14"), and there are numerous good-to-excellent campsites on the west shore. The lake's name is well-suited, deriving from the blackened granite streaks that rainbow across the sheer eastern facade of the lake basin.

4th and 5th Hiking Days: Reverse the steps of the 1st two hiking days, Trip 67, 13 miles.

Mts. Dana and Gibbs, Dana Fork of the Tuolumne River

71   Glacier Point to Merced Lake

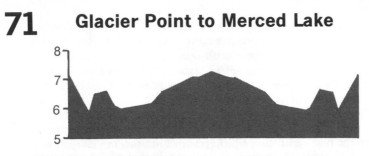

Distance   31.8 miles
Type   Round trip
Best season   Early
Topo maps   **Yosemite, Merced Peak**
Grade (hiking days/recommended layover days)
    Leisurely 4/1
    Moderate 4/0
    Strenuous 2/1
Trailhead   30

HIGHLIGHTS This early-season excursion has all the scenic
advantages of the Yosemite-Valley-to-Merced-
Lake trip (Trip 66) without the 2000-foot climb from Happy
Isles to Nevada Fall. Beginning high above the Merced River
canyon, one gets an airy view that provides a better feeling for
the glacial history of the area. Mild elevation change and solid
mileage make this route a fine choice for the hiker who wants to
shake winter's kinks out of early-season muscles.

DESCRIPTION (Leisurely trip)

1st Hiking Day (**Glacier Point** to **Little Yosemite Valley**,
6.7 miles): This trip begins near the snack bar east of the
parking-lot restrooms. If you haven't seen the views from the
actual point, you should walk 200 yards north to the fenced-in-
overlook. Views are very impressive of the east end of Yosemite
Valley, Half Dome, Vernal and Nevada falls, and domelike Mt.
Starr King in the southeast. From the picnic area by the snack
bar our route climbs a short distance south to a signed junction
where we turn left onto the big, wide Panorama Trail. The trail
begins a moderate-to-steep descent, and makes one switchback before angling south toward Illilouette Creek. Views of
Half Dome and the sound of the falls filter through a forest
cover that includes white fir, sugar pine, Jeffrey pine and black

oak. Under them, manzanita, huckleberry oak and deer brush form most of the ground cover.

After 1⅔ miles we find a junction with the Buena Vista Trail, leading up-canyon. We turn left here and switchback down to seasonally raging Illilouette Creek. Just before the bridge a short spur trail leads down to an airy overlook of Illilouette Fall. Beyond the large steel, rock and concrete bridge, the now-less-used trail begins an 800-foot ascent to the top of Panorama Cliff. On this ascent, at about 6500 feet, we see some Douglas-firs. This is an unusually high elevation for this species. Warm air flowing up the Merced River canyon rises up Panorama Cliff, creating an unusually warm and favorable microclimate here.

Our route traverses along the top of aptly named Panorama Cliff to a junction with the Mono Meadow Trail (leading right), and then our now-paved trail begins the 800-foot descent to Nevada Fall. Via a long series of switchbacks the trail descends through a dense forest of tall, water-loving Douglas-firs and incense-cedars. Then our route joins the John Muir Trail and soon arrives at the slabs above Nevada Fall. On these slabs you may notice large patches of smooth, shiny rock—glacial polish. All these slabs were polished by glaciers of the Tioga glaciation—the last time glaciers were here—at the end of the Pleistocene epoch, about 12,000 years ago. There is much, much less glacial polish below this point, indicating that no glaciers may have entered the Yosemite Valley from the Merced River canyon during the late Pleistocene. In fact, the last time glaciers flowed through the Valley was probably 750,000 years ago.

Beyond Nevada Fall the trail ascends past a junction with the Mist Trail and switchbacks over a low bedrock ridge under Liberty Cap. After ½ mile we pass a John Muir Trail cutoff and soon reach a junction where the John Muir Trail itself turns left (north). Here is the main, heavily used camping area, where there are outhouses, a ranger station and bear boxes. If this area doesn't suit you, you could continue for about 2 level miles to the less crowded sites at the east end of Little Yosemite Valley.

2nd Hiking Day: Follow the 2nd hiking day, Trip 66, to **Merced Lake**, 9.2 miles.

3rd and 4th Hiking Days: Retrace your steps, 15.4 miles.

72 Glacier Point to Rutherford Lake

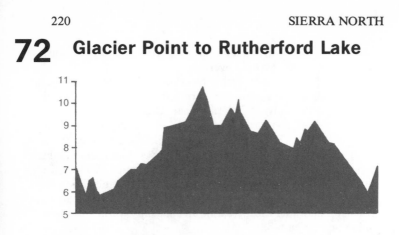

Distance   69.5 miles
Type   Loop trip
Best season   Mid or late
Topo maps   **Yosemite, Merced Peak**
Grade (hiking days/recommended layover days)
  Leisurely 12/2
  Moderate 10/1
  Strenuous 6/0
Trailhead   30

HIGHLIGHTS Designed for the experienced backpacker, this trip offers a combination of excellent fishing and superlative vistas. Almost a dozen angling lakes, most of them in high-country settings, also provide swimming to alleviate the trail dust. Three major passes challenge the most ambitious hiker, and the wide variations in plants and wildlife will satisfy the most discriminating naturalist.

DESCRIPTION (Moderate trip)

1st Hiking Day: Follow Trip 71 to **Little Yosemite Valley**, 6.7 miles.

2nd Hiking Day: Follow the 2nd hiking day, Trip 66, to **Merced Lake**, 9.2 miles.

3rd Hiking Day: (**Merced Lake** to **Lyell Fork, Merced River**, 5.8 miles): From Merced Lake High Sierra Camp the trail ascends slabs to a drift fence and enters an area much used by livestock. A shaded ¾-mile stroll brings us to an engineered ford of multibranched Lewis Creek, a junction with the Lewis Creek Trail, and the Merced Lake Ranger Station. From the station we continue our level stroll to a riverside drift fence. Staying closer to the river now, our trail soon begins a moderate ascent along the east canyon wall, crossing several small creeks before traversing above the outlet of Washburn Lake (7600').

The outlets of Merced and Washburn lakes are similar, as both lakes are dammed by similar bedrock ribs. Skirting the east shore of the lake, we cross a small creek and pass the shaded campsites at the head of the lake, near a fine sandy beach for swimming. Beyond the lake our trail ascends a dry slope and then swings over to riverside by a lovely waterfall. The gentle ascent continues as the trail passes through very large stands of bracken fern under a beautiful, tall forest of huge white firs and Jeffrey pines, with smaller lodgepole pines and aspens. An emerald-green, placid Merced River flows near the trail in places along this idyllic setting. Where the Lyell Fork comes down on the left we meet the main river, and good campsites can be found in the vicinity of the bridge. Fishing in the river is fair-to-good for rainbow trout (to 9").

4th Hiking Day (**Lyell Fork, Merced River**, to **Triple Peak Fork Meadow**, 4.2 miles): Beyond the sturdy wood bridge spanning the Merced River, our trail soon begins to climb south into the great granite **V** carved by the lower stretches of the Merced Peak Fork of the river. This ascent steepens as it enters the zone of red fir and juniper, and then the path levels momentarily where it crosses the Merced Peak Fork on another wooden bridge, which spans a short section of quiet water between roaring cascades above and below. Our trail leaves the riverside and climbs by long switchbacks up the north side of the bowl, leading to excellent viewpoints for visual enjoyment of the huge granite slabs, the aspen grove and the pockets of conifers below.

Another overlook at a switchback turn is close beneath a cascade and a waterfall on the Triple Peak Fork, whose upper reaches our trail is searching out. It was in these upper reaches of the river that the Merced glacier began, and the polished granite on every hand is a constant reminder of its presence. Above the switchbacks our trail ascends gently to a verdant flat where the green Triple Peak Fork slowly winds among the tall trees. After one more steep—but short—climb, the trail ascends gradually near the river under a moderate forest cover of lodgepoles for 2 miles to the foot of long Triple Peak Fork Meadow. The river curves in a lovely fashion through this mile-long grassland, past many campsites made illegal by the prohibition against camping within 100 feet of streams. Side pools out of the main current warm up enough to provide pleasant swimming in midsummer. The best campsites are at the south end of the meadow, near the junction with the Red Peak Pass Trail (9100′). Fishing is good for brook and rainbow trout (to 9″).

5th Hiking Day (**Triple Peak Fork Meadow** to **Post Creek**, 7.2 miles): This hiking day begins with a gradually increasing climb for a long mile southward away from the Triple Peak Fork, out of lodgepole forest into dense hemlock. Then the duff trail turns northeast and climbs almost a mile on a traverse interrupted by two short switchbacks, to arrive at the rock monument at the junction with the high trail that goes along the top of the east wall of the Merced River canyon.

Here our route turns right (south) and quickly ascends a beautiful hillside with broken, light-colored granite close on the left and the soaring Clark Range across the canyon on the right. The trail then levels off in a spectacular high bowl, encircled by Triple Divide Peak, Isberg Peak and some unnamed peaks between. The feeling of spaciousness here is worth the four days' hike to get to this Shangri-la, and in midseason the green grass and many-hued flowers add enough stimulation to surfeit the senses. After fording the unmapped, unnamed outlet of the unnamed but mapped lakes in this bowl, our trail dips into a bowl-within-the-bowl and there crosses another clear stream.

Finally we ascend out of the huge meadow and cross another stream before arriving at a hillside junction with the Isberg Pass Trail, where we turn right (south). Our Post Peak Pass Trail climbs to the ridgeline north of Post Peak, then follows this ridge south to the actual pass (10,700′). This ascent is not without compensation, for the views from the trail are among the most outstanding in the South Boundary Country. From this divide between the Merced and the San Joaquin rivers the traveler has views of the Clark Range to the west, the Cathedral Range to the north and the tops of Banner Peak, Mt. Ritter and the Minarets to the east.

At this point our route leaves Yosemite, later to recross the boundary at Fernandez Pass—6 miles away. The trail descends 600 feet to little Porphyry Lake (10,100'), where fishing is fair for brook and rainbow. Below the lake, the trail improves slightly in the stretch to Isberg Meadow, then becomes fairly good. Conies and marmots may appear on the rocky parts of this trail, and deer, grouse and quail in the meadowy parts. After going almost level for ½ mile through several meadows, we enter lodgepole forest and descend moderately to the good campsites at Post Creek (9040'). Fishing along the creek is good for brook trout (to 8").

6th Hiking Day (**Post Creek** to **Rutherford Lake**, 3.9 miles): From Post Creek the trail crosses a small rise, passes two small, unnamed lakelets (no fish), and fords West Fork Granite Creek. Shortly beyond, the trail fords Fernandez Creek and strikes the Fernandez Pass Trail. Here our route turns right (west) along a gently ascending, densely timbered stretch that offers fine views across Fernandez Creek. After a long ½ mile the trail switchbacks moderately up a morainal slope, trending northwest, to a junction with the Rutherford Lake lateral. Here our route turns right (north) and climbs steeply to the cirque nestling 28-acre Rutherford Lake (9800'). There are fair-to-good campsites on the west side of the lake south of the outlet. Views from these sites are excellent, and fishing is fair for brook and golden (to 16").

7th Hiking Day: Reverse the steps of the 2nd hiking day, Trip 83, to **Middle Chain Lake**, 7.7 miles.

8th Hiking Day: Follow the 2nd hiking day, Trip 84, to **Royal Arch Lake**, 9 miles.

9th and 10th Hiking Days: Follow the 3rd and 4th hiking days, Trip 68, 16.1 miles.

73   Glacier Point to Granite Creek

Distance   41.5 miles
Type   Shuttle trip
Best season   Mid or late
Topo maps   **Yosemite, Merced Peak**
Grade (hiking days/recommended layover days)
  Leisurely 7/1
  Moderate 5/1
  Strenuous 3/1
Trailhead   30, 33

HIGHLIGHTS This route traverses the very heart of Yosemite's
                South Boundary Country, and crosses the
divide of the Merced and San Joaquin River watersheds at
Isberg Pass. Fishing on the lakes and streams is fair-to-
excellent, and the life zones range from Canadian to Arctic-
Alpine. Remoteness and panoramic vistas beckon the traveler
to choose this trip.

DESCRIPTION (Leisurely trip)

   1st Hiking Day: Follow Trip 71 to **Little Yosemite Valley**,
6.7 miles.

   2nd Hiking Day: Follow the 2nd hiking day, Trip 66, to
Merced Lake, 9.2 miles.

   3rd and 4th Hiking Days: Follow the 3rd and 4th hiking
days Trip 72 to **Triple Peak Fork Meadow**, 10 miles.

   5th Hiking Day (**Triple Peak Fork Meadow** to **Isberg
Lakes**, 4.9 miles): First, follow the 5th hiking day, Trip 72, to
the junction of the Post Peak Pass and Isberg Pass trails. From

this junction at timberline, our route turns left (northeast) and climbs steadily among large blocks of talus. The views north and west, which already have been excellent, become even better as our route switchbacks farther up the ridge, as high as the pass we are approaching. Then the tread goes more or less level to signed Isberg Pass (10,500′) and beyond it continues to weave sinuously along the crest. Finally it passes through a tiny defile between two stunted whitebark pines which frame a very dramatic view of the Ritter Range a few miles east. In the distance to the right of this dark range, most of the High Sierra is visible, and hikers who have rambled among its summits will spy some of their favorite monuments. From this pass between the Merced River and the San Joaquin River watersheds, the trail descends by switchbacks to rocky upper Isberg Lake, and then more gradually to lower Isberg Lake (9800′). Fishing in these lakes is fair-to-good for brook and some rainbow (to 8″). There are a few fair campsites at lower Isberg.

6th and 7th Hiking Days: Follow the steps of the 4th and 5th hiking days, Trip 86, 10.3 miles.

Unnamed lake, Triple Divide Peak   *National Park Service*

Devils Postpile

This area of *Sierra North* hikes is reached through the popular winter-summer resort of Mammoth Lakes. From the town, one drives west over Minaret Summit, which is on the Sierra Nevada crest. The road to Devils Postpile is the only eastside road that surmounts the Sierra crest, and you could be misled into thinking you were still east of the crest because the Ritter Range, west of this summit and of the Postpile, is so imposing.

If you want to acclimate overnight before hiking, there are many places to stay in Mammoth Lakes, and a few cabins at Reds Meadow Resort at the end of the Postpile road.

In recent years no cars have been allowed beyond Minaret Summit during daytime hours unless the driver had a reservation at a campground up ahead or at Reds Meadow Resort. To find out the status of this requirement, write Mammoth Ranger District, Mammoth Lakes, CA 93546.

This is the gateway to 228,669-acre Ansel Adams Wilderness, created in 1984 by Congress when it enlarged the formerly named Minarets Wilderness.

One trailhead—Rush Creek—not reached via the Postpile road is included in this chapter because the destination of the trip from there is shared with trips from the Postpile road.

Silver Lake to 1000 Island Lake   **74**

Distance	21 miles
Type	Loop trip
Best season	Early-to-mid
Topo maps	Mono Craters, **Devils Postpile**

Grade (hiking days/recommended layover days)

Leisurely 4/1
Moderate 3/0
Strenuous 2/0

Trailhead   35

HIGHLIGHTS This loop trip visits many lakes, forested and alpine, manmade and natural. After joining the John Muir Trail, the route crosses a gently inclined pass amid several lakelets surrounded by wildflowers to reach 1000 Island Lake. The spectacular return descent looks out over Mono Lake more than 3000 feet below.

DESCRIPTION (Moderate trip)

1st Hiking Day (**Rush Creek Trailhead** to **Waugh Lake**, 7 miles): This excellent trail begins at the Rush Creek trailhead parking lot (7220′). Leaving the aspen cover along Alger Creek, you ascend somewhat steeply, and relentlessly, for 1300 feet. The first half of this climb is very exposed and hot, but affords glorious views of Silver Lake and the abstract marsh patterns at its south end. Colorful wildflowers abound: paintbrush and Bridges penstemon, stonecrop and wild buckwheat, blazing star and pennyroyal. Ahead, Rush Creek forms a several-hundred-foot-long waterfall ribbon, very full in early season. Giant, windshaped cedars provide patches of welcome shade. The trail switchbacks steeply to cross and then recross an active Southern Cal Edison funicular track, ascending stairs blasted out of the rock toward the dam at the outlet of Agnew Lake (8508'). If you wish to camp here, descend to and cross the outlet of Agnew Lake below the dam: campsites are very sparse but good.

To continue toward Gem Lake stay high and to the right of Agnew Lake: you quickly climb the 500 feet of switchbacks to Gem Lake (9052'). On the opposite side of Agnew Lake, you can see the steep trail to the Clark Lakes, your return route. Gem Lake richly deserves its name, despite the stark evidence of man's handiwork in the dam at its east end. As you skirt the lake's north side, the beauty of lake, the surrounding peaks, the stalwart lodgepoles and the breathtaking giant junipers compensate for the dusty, stock-used trail, which perversely reaches the top of every ridge and the bottom of every gully. About halfway around the north side of the lake there are several attractive campsites with privacy and superlative views, but they require a hike down for water.

At the northwest end of Gem Lake, you cross Crest Creek and immediately encounter the signed trail to Alger Lakes. There is extensive camping here—also intensive mosquitoes and extensive evidence of stock. Continuing around Gem Lake, the trail converges with an old mine road and, passing a cabin, ascends westward. A quick southward descent brings you past two lovely tiny lakes (the first is called Billy Lake; the second is unnamed) and beautiful Rush Meadow. The trail junction to Waugh Lake is very well marked, though it is hard to see on the maps, being at the border of two topo maps. Just beyond this junction, you can see the bridge over Rush Creek on the trail to Clark Lakes, but your route turns right (west) toward Waugh Lake. There are ample excellent campsites here. An easy 300-foot climb (the route still coincides with an old road) brings you to the dam at the outlet of Waugh Lake (9424'). There are only a few poor campsites at the outlet. To your left, a signed trail leads south to Weber Lakes. Your route ascends the rounded granite to your right and skirts the north side of Waugh Lake. In about ½ mile beyond the outlet you will find excellent campsites upslope from the trail, and there are many more toward the west end of the lake. Mt. Ritter and Banner Peak own the sky beyond the west end of the lake. A layover day here would permit you to visit Weber and Sullivan lakes.

2nd Hiking Day (**Waugh Lake** to **1000 Island Lake**, 6.5

miles): The trail along the northwest shore of Waugh Lake passes through beautiful lodgepole pines to an unmarked junction at the west end of the lake. The left fork leads to campsites; you keep right, climbing through large pines and over granite slabs. The indicated crossing over Rush Creek is underwater; fifty feet upstream is a considerably drier log. Shortly you reach a signed trail junction with the John Muir and Pacific Crest trails, which coincide from here to 1000 Island Lake. At this junction turn left. You soon make several stream crossings. Less than a mile upstream you pass the signed trail to Davis Lakes. Your trail then ascends gently through lodgepoles and across meadows with grand views back toward the north of the rugged backs of Koip and Parker peaks.

As you near Island Pass (10200') you traverse a very lush ridge, covered with wildflowers, and pass two small, very beautiful lakes. Near these lakes you have remarkable views of Banner and Ritter and their snow fields, and good but exposed camping. At the last saddle before beginning your descent to 1000 Island Lake, you pass an unmarked trail on the right and continue left, descending gradually toward the lake, visible below. This is one of the best locations from which to count the islands, if you feel the need. Your trail reaches 1000 Island Lake (9834') at the northeast end. No camping is permitted at this end of the lake, but if you follow the unsigned trail west (right) at the edge of the lake, you will find excellent campsites, more isolated and less hardened the farther westward you explore.

If you spend a layover day here, you can enjoy a beautiful and nonstrenuous loop trip overland to Garnet Lake. Continue around to the south end of 1000 Island Lake, cross the obvious low point in the ridge to the southeast, and follow the watercourse down to Garnet Lake. Return on the John Muir Trail past Ruby and Emerald lakes.

3rd Hiking Day (**1000 Island Lake** to **Silver Lake**, 7.5 miles): Follow the 3rd hiking day of Trip 72 to the signed junction where the High Trail branches right toward Badger Lakes. You turn left toward Clark Lakes. Ascending steeply through lodgepoles, you cross the Sierra Crest at an unmarked pass. Looking back, you view the San Joaquin River canyon, with the Minarets crowning the far ridge, and Ritter and Banner closer on your right. Directly below you can see the Badger Lakes.

Gently descending, you pass three small Clark Lakes, one of which is guarded by a sheer and beautiful rock wall. Your descent continues along the west side of the largest Clark Lake, where windswept grass and wild onion border the west end of this lake.

At the outflow is a three-way signed junction: the left branch descends to Gem Lake; the right one skirts the lake on its east and leads up over Agnew Pass to the High Trail and thence to Agnew Meadows. Your route is the middle branch, which ascends gently past a tarn and then descends through meadows full of senecio, lupine and shooting stars. Pause here to view Mono Lake nearly 20 miles away and 3000 feet below, before the trail switchbacks steeply down to Spooky Meadow. After descending along a stream garnished with monkey-flowers, you then switchback steeply down the 1000-foot south wall of Agnew Lake's basin. The trail, not maintained here and mostly over talus, has been obliterated by rockslides. At the west ends of the switchback legs you find solid turf and welcome shade under immense red firs. Crossing the outflow of Agnew Lake on a footbridge, you meet the funicular tracks and then the Rush Creek Trail. Now retrace the first part of the first hiking day.

Peaceful Waugh Lake

Agnew Meadows to Shadow Creek **75**

Distance	8.4 miles
Type	Round trip
Best season	Mid or late
Topo maps	**Devils Postpile**

Grade (hiking days/recommended layover days)
    Leisurely 2/0
    Moderate ---
    Strenuous ---
Trailhead 36

HIGHLIGHTS Shadow Lake has been subject to very heavy use, and in consequence the Forest Service no longer allows camping there, but there are fine campsites up the inlet stream. This short trip is a good one for beginning backpackers.

DESCRIPTION

1st Hiking Day (**Agnew Meadows** to **Shadow Creek**, 4.2 miles): From the trailhead west of the pack station (8335') your route skirts a flowery meadow before crossing a small ridge covered with red fir and lodgepole pine. Just under a mile from the start, beyond a long gully, you meet a trail from Agnew Meadows Campground, coming in on the right. In 80 yards the Pacific Crest Trail, on which you have been hiking, branches left to switchback down toward Devils Postpile. Here you leave the Pacific Crest Trail and continue straight ahead on the River Trail. Your route descends steadily west toward the river. The first part of this downslope shows many of the ground-cover changes typical of the Mammoth Lakes region. One moment you are in dense pine-and-fir forest, and the next you are walking on an exposed slope of pumice, with low-growing manzanita and vivid clumps of yellow buckwheat and red and orange paintbrush.

You re-enter forest cover at the canyon bottom and skirt the east side of shallow, lily-padded Olaine Lake. Just beyond it

you leave the River Trail and head west to the Middle Fork San
Joaquin River. The river crossing is easy if you continue 50
yards past the stock crossing and use the sturdy wooden footbridge. Beyond the ford your trail winds steeply up a sage-
brush-and-juniper-dotted slope. This 700-foot climb can be
very warm in midsummer, but soon you swing over to
cascading Shadow Creek and arrive at the outlet of beautiful
Shadow Lake. Skirting the north shore, we pass several illegal
and abused campsites, and above the head of the lake we find
appropriate campsites beyond the junction with the John Muir
Trail.

2nd Hiking Day: Retrace your steps, 4.2 miles.

Shadow Lake   *Ron Felzer*

Agnew Meadows to Garnet Lake   **76**

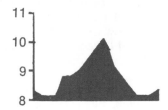

Distance	14.1 miles
Type	Loop trip
Best season	Mid or late
Topo maps	**Devils Postpile**

Grade (hiking days/recommended layover days)
    Leisurely 3/1
    Moderate 3/0
    Strenuous 2/0

Trailhead   36

HIGHLIGHTS Employing about a 4-mile stretch of the well-known John Muir Trail, this trip visits some of the northern Sierra's most dramatic country. In the region east of the jagged Ritter Range are some of the area's most vivid alpine lakes and spectacular landforms.

DESCRIPTION (Leisurely trip)

1st Hiking Day: Follow trip 75 to **Shadow Creek**, 4.2 miles.

2nd Hiking Day (**Shadow Creek** to **Garnet Lake**, 4.3 miles): On the John Muir Trail this route ascends west for ⅔ mile through Shadow Creek canyon before turning north. The trail suffers heavy use and is likely to be dusty, particularly in late season. The dust, however, settles as the trail emerges from pine forest and tops the 1100-foot climb from the Shadow Creek Trail junction to the rocky ridge above Garnet Lake. This is an excellent place from which to appreciate the view of the lake itself, Ritter and Banner, and Mt. Davis to the west. The traveler will also note the striking change in the countryside. In contrast to the heavily timbered slopes of Shadow Creek canyon, the landscape, except for scattered stands of stunted hemlock, lodgepole and whitebark, is now predominantly glacially polished rock. From this viewpoint the trail descends

500 feet to the outlet of Garnet Lake (9680'). Fair campsites may be found on the north side of the lake west of the "no camping" zone, and several hundred feet below the outlet. Fishing for brook and rainbow (to 10") is only fair.

3rd Hiking Day (**Garnet Lake** to **Agnew Meadows** via the River Trail, 5.6 miles): Two steep, converging trails lead to the River Trail. The easier one, shown on the topo map, leaves the main trail 50 feet south of the footbridge over Garnet Lake's outflow. After a brief climb, this route descends a 100-foot boulder chute to emerge in open terrain above a meadow, to which the trail, clearly visible here, descends on easy footing. The alternative route leaves the John Muir Trail just north of the footbridge and follows the waterfall course of the Garnet Lake outflow. This route, tricky with a backpack but worth it for the dramatic scenery, descends rock ledges on the south side of the water. The southern wall has been V'd by water; the northern side has been polished and V'd by a glacier. Your ledge becomes a vertical wall, so cross the stream and join the easier path from Garnet Lake.

Three-fourths mile northeast from Garnet Lake your route strikes the river, crosses on a log, and meets the River Trail, where you turn right (southeast). The River Trail from this junction is heavily timbered as you pass the Agnew Pass Trail lateral and wind down the canyon. The sound of cascading San Joaquin River is a pleasant part-time accompaniment to this dusty descent when the river is nearby. Fishing on the San Joaquin for rainbow and brook (to 9") is only fair, and swimming, even in late season, is likely to be somewhat chilly. This route meets the Shadow Lake Trail 2 miles from Agnew Meadows and retraces part of the 1st hiking day.

Routes between Agnew Meadows
and 1000 Island Lake

Three very different trails connect Agnew Meadows and 1000 Island Lake, offering the hiker a choice of several loop trips.

The River Trail (7.1 miles) is the shortest, most gradual and smoothest. This route descends to the San Joaquin River and follows it upward, often through forest. You are almost always within the sound of water, and the forest cover offers welcome shade on hot days. One wonderful section of this trail climbs polished rock slabs directly along the water, which falls in sheets over the smooth rock into deep pools. See the 3rd hiking day of Trip 76.

The Pacific Crest Trail (9.1 miles), also shown as the High Trail on the topo map, ascends 500 feet of switchbacks, then contours up the side of San Joaquin Mountain before turning westward to intersect the River Trail about 1 mile from Thousand Island Lake. This is the return route of Trip 78. The trail is exposed much of the way to sun and wind (the latter very welcome during mosquito season). The route offers panoramic views of the glaciers and the jagged peaks of the Ritter Range; it also traverses innumerable tributaries of the San Joaquin, banked by spectacular gardens of head-high delphinium, lupine, and corn lilies.

The John Muir Trail (10.5 miles) is the longest and most strenuous route. Trip 77 uses it. You descend to the San Joaquin on the River Trail, then climb upward 800 feet to Shadow Lake, to join the John Muir Trail. After turning northward and ascending 1300 dusty feet, the trail descends to round the eastern end of Garnet Lake. A brief 500-foot ascent and a stroll past Ruby and Emerald Lakes are sufficient to reach 1000 Island Lake. Shadow and Garnet lakes are almost impossibly beautiful yet they differ greatly, being located in different life zones: Shadow Lake is surrounded by tall trees; in contrast, Garnet Lake, 1000 feet higher, is stark and alpine. If you have the time and the fitness, this is the route of choice.

77 Agnew Meadows to 1000 Island Lake

Distance   17.6 miles
Type   Loop trip
Best season   Mid or late
Topo maps   **Devils Postpile**
Grade (hiking days/recommended layover days)
   Leisurely 3/1
   Moderate 3/0
   Strenuous 2/0
Trailhead   36

HIGHLIGHTS The climax of this trip is Garnet and 1000 Island lakes. Settings of alpine grandeur make these large lakes favorites of photographers and naturalists alike. Although this trip can be made in a weekend, the superlative scenery warrants a slower pace. Almost half of this route follows the scenic John Muir Trail.

DESCRIPTION (Leisurely trip)

1st Hiking Day: Follow Trip 75 to **Shadow Creek**, 4.2 miles.

2nd Hiking Day (**Shadow Creek** to **1000 Island Lake**, 6.3 miles): Follow the 2nd hiking day, Trip 76 to Garnet Lake. Beyond the outlet of Garnet Lake, the trail ascends 500 feet to the ridge that separates Garnet and 1000 Island lakes. En route, the trail circles the east shore of dramatic Ruby Lake and then drops down past colorful Emerald Lake, where there are a few campsites on the east side—far less populated than 1000 Island Lake. In less than ¼ mile you cross the outlet of that lake (9834') on a rickety log bridge. The very large, island-dotted lake often reflects the imposing facade of Banner Peak and the more sharply etched Mt. Ritter at sunset. During the day the lake is generally very windy—which is welcome, however bone-chilling, in early season when mosquitoes swarm. Several

exposed campsites (subject to a great deal of wind) may be
found on the north side of the lake, the better ones being a mile
or more west of the Muir Trail and back from the water. Hang
your food carefully; bears have discovered this splendid spot,
too. Fishing for rainbow and brook (7–13″) is particularly good
in early and late season. Camping is also possible at the lakelet
about ¼ mile east down the River Trail.

3rd Hiking Day (**1000 Island Lake** to **Agnew Meadow**,
7.1 miles): This route leaves the John Muir Trail at the
meadowy outlet of 1000 Island Lake, and proceeds northeast
past several small snowmelt tarns. The alpine setting is soon
left behind as the trail re-enters forest cover. Your route then
veers southeast, passing several unsigned laterals, to a signed
junction with the High Trail, branches right at this junction, and
slants down through dense lodgepole and fir to the Garnet Lake
lateral, whence it proceeds as described in the 3rd hiking day,
Trip 76.

78 Agnew Meadows to 1000 Island Lake

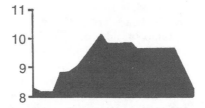

Distance	19.6 miles
Type	Loop trip
Best season	Mid or late
Topo maps	**Devils Postpile**

Grade (hiking days/recommended layover days)

    Leisurely 3/1
    Moderate 3/0
    Strenuous 2/0

Trailhead 36

HIGHLIGHTS The San Joaquin River drainage offers different views and different experiences of two parallel but very different mountain crests. Trip 77 to 1000 Island Lake traverses Ritter Range forests in terrain fed by ample snowmelt, with views of the gentle, pastel-toned Sierra Crest east across the canyon. Upon your return on this trip, you have spectacular, unbroken views of the snowcapped, rugged Ritter Range while traversing those pastel slopes just below the Sierra Crest. A first assessment would indicate that this hillside was a scrubby, arid stretch, but it is not. Many streams interrupt the trail, even in late season, and wildflowers line the route.

DESCRIPTION (Leisurely trip)

1st and 2nd Hiking Days: Follow Trip 77 to **1000 Island Lake**, 10.5 miles.

3rd Hiking Day (**1000 Island Lake** to **Agnew Meadows**, via the High Trail, 9.1 miles): Reverse the last part of the 3rd hiking day, Trip 76, to the signed High Trail junction. The High Trail here is part of the Pacific Crest Trail. On it you ascend past a left-branching trail to Clark Lakes through lodgepole pine and past mosquito-heaven Badger Lakes.

On this first slope the trail emerges from the dense forest cover, and then it winds up and down through a ground cover that, except for a few scattered stands of pine, is sagebrush, bitterbrush, willow, and some mountain alder. The trail then contours along the side of San Joaquin Mountain. The dry sage slopes are slashed by streams lined with wildflowers as far up as you can see: larkspur, lupine, shooting star, columbine, penstemon, monkey flower, scarlet gilia and tiger lily. For a while views are excellent of the Ritter Range to the west; particularly impressive is the **V**'d view of Shadow Lake directly across the San Joaquin River canyon about 2¾ miles from the trailhead. The trail then descends through a forest of pine and fir. Five hundred feet of well-graded switchbacks bring you to the parking lot north of the pack station.

1000 Island Lake and Banner Peak

79 Agnew Meadows to Ediza Lake

Distance	14 miles
Type	Round trip
Best season	Mid or late
Topo maps	**Devils Postpile**

Grade (hiking days/recommended layover days)
    Leisurely 2/1
    Moderate 2/0
    Strenuous ---

Trailhead   36

HIGHLIGHTS This is one of the finest routes in the Mammoth Lakes region for viewing the spectacular Ritter Range, including Banner Peak, Mt. Ritter and the Minarets. The alpine beauty of Ediza Lake is almost legendary. In the shadow of the breathtaking Minarets, one can appreciate the grand processes that formed this very striking landscape.

DESCRIPTION

1st Hiking Day (**Agnew Meadows** to **Ediza Lake**, 7.0 miles): First follow trip 75 to **Shadow Creek**, 4.2 miles. The ascent from Shadow Creek to the outlet of Ediza Lake is gradual and very beautiful, with fine campsites all along the way. Following the John Muir Trail for about ⅔ mile, we wind in and out of tall firs, some slashed down by 1986 avalanches, passing some lovely waterfalls and pools along the creek. After the Muir Trail turns north away from our route, we cross several meadows, and then rock hop or chance unstable logs to cross the lovely, shaded outlet from Nydiver Lakes. Continuing up Shadow Creek you will have several choices of trail but you should have no trouble getting to the outlet of Ediza Lake (9300′). To get to the legal campsites on the west end of the lake, you can go around the south side, but the north-side route is shorter. The delicate environs of this lake are heavily used, so please be careful. Ediza Lake makes a fine base for exploring the basin above.

2nd Hiking Day: Retrace your steps, 7.0 miles.

Agnew Meadows to Devils Postpile **80**

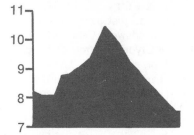

Distance	16.2 miles
Type	Shuttle trip
Best season	Mid or late
Topo maps	Devils Postpile

Grade (hiking days/recommended layover days)
  Leisurely ---
  Moderate 3/0
  Strenuous ---
Trailhead 36, 37

HIGHLIGHTS For those travelers who enjoy spectacular alpine landscapes this trip is excellent. The route, however, is difficult, and is recommended for highly experienced backpackers only. Climbers use this route to reach the base of the jagged Minarets.

DESCRIPTION (Moderate trip)

1st Hiking Day: Follow Trip 79 to **Ediza Lake**, 7.0 miles.

2nd Hiking Day (**Ediza Lake** to **Minaret Lake**, 3.0 miles): From the south side of Ediza Lake the trail steeply and unevenly climbs the south wall over scree and through dense willows in streambeds. There are several routes: the best switches against the east wall (to your left). A beautiful meadow of red and white heather, penstemon and rockfringe leads to Iceberg Lake (9800'). There are a few campsites on the northeast side of the lake.

Looking up to the south one can see the outlet from Cecile Lake pouring over the lip of its basin. You want to climb to that point. The trail circles and gradually ascends on the east side of Iceberg Lake, then disappears in boulders in the large talus slope above the lake, where there is usually a large snowbank, which may be icy. The last 60 vertical feet are just east of the waterfall from Cecile—and just as precipitous. At the top of this 500 foot ascent is windswept Cecile Lake (10,280'), right at the base of towering Clyde Minaret. The trip around Cecile Lake is a boulderwalk on either side. The east side is shorter; the west a bit easier. (There are several campsites in the whitebarks at the northwest end of the lake, and one wonderful site at the southeast end.)

The route to Minaret Lake begins in the left end of the moraine that forms the southeast side of Cecile Lake. Cross this moraine and descend to a turn. Then go to the whitebarks at the far end. The trail goes over the lip of a steep wall at the extreme left, against the mountainside. The first few steps demand both hands—they are difficult with a backpack. From here head south and pass between two rock outcrops. The trail descends steeply down a scree slope that offers few firm footholds. It then turns south and follows the contours of the rockface. After a few switchbacks it reaches an inlet of Minaret Lake, below. The trail then descends to the north shore of the lake, passes a small lake on the left and rounds the eastern lobe of Minaret Lake (9800') to the outlet. There are many lovely campsites around this lake (campfires illegal), and the trout-filled waters often reflect the Minarets at sunset.

3rd Hiking Day (**Minaret Lake** to **Devils Postpile Campground**, 6.2 miles): From the outlet of Minaret Lake one gets a last view of the spectacular Minarets over the lake before descending steeply to a forested flat along Minaret Creek. Our trail then crosses a tributary and steepens again to temporarily join the old road from Minaret Mine. We pass through a meadow along the creek with 6'–10' stumps whose tops were sliced off by 1986 avalanches. Their different heights show the different depth of the snow when the avalanches occurred. Now you descend an outcrop of red rock down which the creek cascades in a spray of white. After about two miles of gentle and then moderate descent in dense fir forest, we arrive at a junction with the John Muir Trail beside Johnston Meadow. You can see Johnston Lake just past the junction.

Here we leave the Ansel Adams Wilderness. The log crossing over Minaret Creek is not well marked. If you miss it, you will wade the stream farther down at the stock crossing. On the south side, a fisherman's trail leads back to Johnston Lake, but your route is unmistakable; you follow the well-built trail heading southeast on the south side of the creek. In 500 feet you pass a signed junction with the trail to Beck Lakes and begin a steep, dusty descent to Devils Postpile National Monument. Near the forested canyon floor we leave the John Muir Trail at a junction with the Pacific Crest Trail. Following signs, we cross the Middle Fork San Joaquin River on a bridge and arrive at the geological wonder called Devils Postpile. A short walk north brings us to the parking lot at Devils Postpile Campground.

Ritter Range over upper Lost Lake

81 Agnew Meadows to Devils Postpile

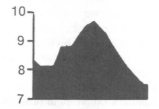

Distance	12.2 miles
Type	Shuttle trip
Best season	Mid or late
Topo maps	Devils Postpile

Grade (hiking days/recommended layover days)

> *Leisurely* ---
> *Moderate* 2/0
> *Strenuous* ---

Trailhead   36, 37

HIGHLIGHTS After crossing the Middle Fork San Joaquin, this route ascends to picturesque Shadow Lake. Then, doubling back, it traverses the long, narrow, lake-dotted bench that breaks the slope from Volcanic Ridge to the river. Dense fir forests, intimate lakes, and good fishing make this an excellent beginner's weekend trip.

DESCRIPTION

1st Hiking Day (**Agnew Meadows** to **Rosalie Lake**, 5.4 miles): Follow the 1st hiking day, Trip 75, to Shadow Lake. Just past a small rise, about 200 feet beyond the inlet to beautiful Shadow Lake, this route joins the John Muir Trail and crosses Shadow Creek on a large log bridge. The eastbound trail rounds the south side of the lake, and begins a series of 22 switchbacks up a densely forested slope. Breather stops along this 650-foot climb afford colorful views of the deep blues and greens of Shadow Lake, and the crest of the ridge is soon topped at a rocky saddle with a meadowy bottom. This saddle leads to a good campsite by the outlet of charming Rosalie Lake (9350'). Fishing is good for rainbow and brook (to 9").

2nd Hiking Day (**Rosalie Lake** to **Devils Postpile Campground**, 6.8 miles): The trail soon climbs over the southeast ridge that flanks Rosalie Lake. From the outlet of Gladys Lake one has views out over the San Joaquin River canyon. To the west, the black, recrystallized volcanic rocks of Volcanic Ridge are on the skyline, and to the east the rock drops away into the San Joaquin and rises on the far side to red-topped San Joaquin Mountain and the distinctive Two Teats. From here the route drops 200 feet down into the Trinity Lakes basin. Access to Castle and Emily lakes is via a short, steep foot trail that takes off from the west side of our trail, and fishing at these lakes is fair-to-good for rainbow and brook (to 8"). From the lowest of the Trinity Lakes, the trail descends steeply via dusty under-footing to Johnston Meadow, where it meets the trail from Minaret Lake. From here we proceed as described in the 3rd hiking day, Trip 80.

An alternative descent follows a trail of use along Minaret Creek. Leave the John Muir Trail at the Beck Lake Trail junction, south of the creek, and turn back north, directly toward Minaret Creek. Your route runs along the south side of the creek, descending quickly to the top of Minaret Falls. Rock climbers can descend next to the falls; acrophobes make a detour to the south and return to the falls at their base. From the base, follow the Pacific Crest Trail south until it intersects the John Muir Trail, and continue to Devil's Postpile Campground, as described in the last two sentences of Trip 76.

South of Yosemite

South of Yosemite there are no roads across the Sierra crest until one is well south of Mt. Whitney. Hence there are a number of shorter access roads for the trips in this chapter, some on the east side and some on the west.

Most of the trips in this chapter go into the 584,478-acre John Muir Wilderness, the largest in any California national forest, which stretches along the east Sierra slope from Mammoth Lakes south to beyond Mt. Whitney, and also curls around the northwest side of Kings Canyon National Park.

For acclimating the night before your hike, there are many places in Mammoth Lakes, several at Rock Creek Lake, and one—Vermilion Resort—at Lake Edison. There are also campgrounds very near all the trailheads in this chapter.

Two trailheads in this chapter—Rock Creek (Mosquito Flat) and Lake Edison—are also used for some trips in *Sierra South*, which you might like to consult.

Finally, five trips in this variegated chapter have trailheads along the Beasore Road, just south of Yosemite, and several of them actually enter the Park. There are no resorts along that road, but there are several campgrounds.

Chiquito Creek to Chain Lakes   **82**

Distance	14.6 miles
Type	Round trip
Best season	Mid
Topo maps	**Merced Peak**

Grade (hiking days/recommended layover days)
    Leisurely 2/1
    Moderate 2/0
    Strenuous ---
Trailhead   32

HIGHLIGHTS Chain Lakes are a traditional and attractive destination for a moderate weekend trip. Though not difficult, this hike is long enough and varied enough to provide the hiker with the feeling of a substantial trip. Fishing is often good at Chain Lakes.

DESCRIPTION

1st Hiking Day (**Chiquito Creek Trailhead** to **Middle Chain Lake**, 7.3 miles): From the trailhead parking lot (7320′) the signed Chiquito Lake Trail heads northwest through mixed forest. Although it is designated a hiker trail only, horses use this trail, and even motor vehicles travel the first ¼ mile. After the first ¼ mile, the dusty trail steepens and climbs a hot, sunny hillside; then it levels off to pass the old trail coming in on the left. Soon we cross a small creek and climb another hot hillside before swinging into shade to come within earshot of Chiquito Creek.

The trail continues on a moderate ascent until it fords the creek just below Chiquito Lake. From the lake's south shore we head briefly west and then pass a junction with a trail to the Sky Ranch Road. Then we traverse north to the Yosemite Park boundary. Leaving the cows behind, we go through a barbed-wire fence to another junction. Turning right here, we stroll to a sharp-crested moraine, cross it, and descend gently for ½ mile to ford the seasonally wide outlet of Spotted Lakes. From the ford our trail ascends moderately through red fir up a large moraine to a small meadow. This meadow marks the top of the moraine, and the remainder of this 500-foot climb takes us past a few bedrock outcrops. Past the top of the ridge, we descend gently through mixed forest to ford Chain Lakes creek. On the other side of the creek is a junction; here we turn right (east) and then ascend steeply to lower Chain Lake, signed CHAIN LAKES. From here the trail swings around the north side of the lake, turns south, crosses a seasonal stream and makes a rocky, 150-foot ascent to the middle lake, also signed CHAIN LAKES. Camping is best on the south side of this lake.

Those wishing to visit the upper lake can reach it from the abused campsite near the middle lake's outlet. From here the trail to the upper lake climbs steeply above the north shore of the middle lake onto a rocky ridge. The trail then passes a tarn, turns left around a small lake and crosses the creek. From here a short ascent leads to the timbered west side of beautiful Upper Chain Lake. All three lakes contain rainbow or brook trout, or both.

2nd Hiking Day: Reverse your steps, 7.3 miles.

Middle Chain Lake

Chiquito Creek to Rutherford Lake **83**

Distance	25.4 miles
Type	Shuttle trip
Best season	Mid or late
Topo maps	**Merced Peak**

Grade (hiking days/recommended layover days)
>   *Leisurely* 4/1
>   *Moderate* 3/1
>   *Strenuous* 3/0

Trailhead 32, 34

HIGHLIGHTS On this trip the hiker will encounter a great variety of terrain and scenery, going from dense red-fir forests to alpine lakes and back again. Fishing on both sides of Fernandez Pass is good-to-excellent.

DESCRIPTION (Moderate trip)

1st Hiking Day: Follow Trip 82 to **Middle Chain Lake**, 7.3 miles).

2nd Hiking Day (**Middle Chain Lake** to **Rutherford Lake**, 9.4 miles): This hiking day takes one through a wide variety of landscape features: forests, meadows, streams, lakes and passes. After we retrace our steps to the junction by the outlet of Chain Lakes, we turn right to continue the steep descent beside the creek. The grade soon eases where there is a newly formed clearing along the creek. Here are downed trees and a jumble of boulders—the remains of a debris flow. A debris flow is something like a combination flood and landslide—a thick, slow-moving, water-saturated mixture of rock, soil, trees and anything else lying around.

Turning north away from the creek, we soon pass a signed junction with a trail to Buck Camp. Continuing north, our trail winds among glacial erratics and over bedrock outcrops under a partial forest cover, climbs steeply over a low ridge, and passes a glacial tarn. The trail then descends along a small watercourse to a lodgepole-pine-covered flat where a zealous CCC and Park Service crew has dug trenches in order to lower the water table. The excavated soil has been used to build a causeway nearby. From here a very short ascent brings us past a packer campsite on the left, and then to the Merced River in Moraine Meadows. Beyond the ford (wet in early season) the trail passes more campsites and arrives at a signed junction with another trail to Buck Camp.

Here we turn right and then ascend gently under lodgepole pine over a very maintained trail. After an easy mile the trail turns south and fords the flower-lined Merced River (wet in early season). The grade soon steepens as we begin a two-stage climb to Fernandez Pass. For 400 vertical feet the shaded trail winds up to a shallow, meadow-fringed lake, crossing a seasonal stream en route. Here the grade eases, and in another ¾ mile we reach a signed junction with the trail south to Breeze Lake. This trail leads past a small lake, then becomes faint, and the last stretch is a ducked route over slabs to the hemlock-lined north shore of large, scenic Breeze Lake.

From the junction we begin the second stage of the climb to Fernandez Pass, and immediately the trail becomes very steep and rocky. Our route ascends through lodgepole and silver pine over weathered granite for 600 feet to signed Fernandez Pass (10,175'). Here we leave the Park and then ascend a bit more before descending past another tree-dotted saddle. The trail now winds down ledges into the headwaters of Fernandez Creek, and we get good views of the Ritter Range to the east. The grade eases temporarily where we cross a small meadow, and steepens again before we arrive at a signed junction with a trail to Rutherford Lake (9800'). This eroded trail begins in a small forested flat and climbs very steeply for ¼ mile to the small dam at the south end of this well-used alpine lake. Campsites can be found on the lake's east side. Fishing is fair for brook and golden to 16".

3rd Hiking Day (**Rutherford Lake** to **Fernandez Trailhead**, 8.7 miles): From the small dam at the south end of Rutherford Lake we descend the steep trail ¼ mile back to the Fernandez Trail and turn left onto it. This rocky trail switchbacks down the sunny canyon wall to the gentler descent under tall red firs. About 1½ miles from Rutherford Lake we ford Fernandez Creek (wet in early season) and arrive at a junction with the Post Peak Pass Trail. Keeping to the right on the Fernandez Trail, we traverse past a low exfoliation dome. Soon we pass over a low ridge, descend a wooded gully, and arrive at the signed trail to Rainbow Lake. From here it is an easy 1½ miles down gentle slabs through open lodgepole and juniper to the northern junction with the Lillian Lake Loop. From this junction our trail heads east and begins a long descent to Madera Creek.

Initially, the trail descends gently, enters a forested gully, and crosses a small creek. Continuing southeast under red fir, lodgepole pine and occasional Jeffrey pine and juniper, our trail gains the crest of a moraine where we get views east through the trees. The trail then becomes steep, completes two sets of switchbacks and passes a junction with the Timber Creek Trail. After some more dusty switchbacks we arrive at a shaded flat alongside peaceful Madera Creek. Proceeding across this flat, we pass a signed junction with the Walton Trail, left, and some good campsites, and then ford wide Madera Creek (wet in early season). The trail climbs steeply up the south bank and then continues on a moderate ascent through lodgepole pine and red fir. Along the ascent you notice a mixture of light and dark rocks on the ground. Many times during the Pleistocene Epoch glaciers originating near Madera Peak flowed over this area, and the darker, metamorphic rocks came from the vicinity of Madera Peak while the lighter, granitic rocks came from farther east, perhaps around Staniford Lakes.

Forest cover thins and views improve until we reach the southern end of the Lillian Lake Loop. Here, atop a broad ridge, we leave Ansel Adams Wilderness and begin the 2-mile descent southeast to the Fernandez trailhead. This section of trail, which passes two laterals to the Norris Creek trailhead, is described (in reverse) in the first day of Trip 85.

84 Chiquito Creek to Bridalveil Creek

Distance	29.4 miles
Type	Shuttle trip
Best season	Mid or late
Topo maps	**Merced Peak**

Grade (hiking days/recommended layover days)
    Leisurely 4/2
    Moderate 4/0
    Strenuous 3/0
Trailhead 32, 31

HIGHLIGHTS This shuttle trip crosses some of the more scenic southern Yosemite Park boundary country. Some of the finest fishing in the Park is found along this route at Chain and Royal Arch lakes, and bonus angling spots can be explored on layover days at Breeze, Spotted, Johnson and Crescent lakes. The gigantic, sweeping effects of glacial action are seen throughout this trip. The resulting cirques, **U**-shaped valleys, jagged crests, and polished granite are a constant source of awe and delight to the traveler.

DESCRIPTION (Leisurely trip)

1st Hiking Day: Follow Trip 82 to **Middle Chain Lake** (7.3 miles)

2nd Hiking Day (**Upper Chain Lake** to **Royal Arch Lake**, 9 miles): First, retrace your steps to yesterday's junction, and then continue downstream. In ⅓ miles the trail veers north to a junction, where we turn left (west) and parallel the outlet creek from Chain Lakes as it falls to rendezvous with the South Fork Merced. Just before the South Fork a signed lateral trail leads south ¼ mile to good camping at Soda Springs. Our route fords the South Fork and swings southwest over a lodgepole-covered slope. The depth of the **U**-shaped, glacially formed slopes gives a good account of the forces that were at work when the ice flow originating in the Clark Range to the north was in its heyday.

After fording Givens Creek the trail passes a southbound trail to Chiquito Pass. Just 60 yards farther we choose a well-used left fork over a little-used right fork and then continue ½ mile to meet the Buck Camp/Merced Pass Trail on a ridgetop. Turning southwest, we descend through red-fir forest and then climb northwest to the meadowy precincts of Buck Camp. At Buck Camp, Yosemite National Park has a summer ranger station, and emergency services may be obtained.

From Buck Camp the trail ascends a tough 750 feet via switchbacks, then drops 350 feet to a junction with the Royal Arch Lake Trail. From this point it is but ¾ mile to Royal Arch Lake (8700′). Large, black, rainbow-arched striations across the eastern wall of polished granite gave this picturesque lake its name. These distinctive markings are the result of water discoloration due to centuries of seepage. They make a magnificent backdrop to the excellent fishing for brook and rainbow (8–14″) and anglers may well regard this relatively small lake as the high point of the trip. Numerous good campsites are on the west shore, and this lake makes an excellent base camp for scenic and angling excursions to nearby Buena Vista, Johnson and Crescent lakes. Swimming is good in late season.

3rd and 4th Hiking Days: Reverse the steps of the 2nd and 1st hiking days, Trip 67, 13 miles.

85   Granite Creek to Rutherford Lake

Distance   20.7 miles
Type   Semiloop trip
Best season Mid or late
Topo maps   **Merced Peak**
Grade (hiking days/recommended layover days)
    Leisurely 3/1
    Moderate   3/0
    Strenuous 2/0
Trailhead   34

HIGHLIGHTS The lake-filled area east of Gale and Sing peaks
                provides a choice trip for the angler. Except for
a midsummer slack period, these lakes are good producers of
brook, rainbow, and even golden trout. Add to this benefit the
dramatic peaks that lie to the west, and the 35-mile views to the
south, and every hiker will find cause for visiting this country.
This trip is the answer for the hiker with a short time for travel
who wishes to get into the spectacular South Boundary Country.

DESCRIPTION (Leisurely trip)

1st Hiking Day (**Fernandez Trailhead** to **Vandeburg
Lake** 4.5 miles): From the west side of the turnaround loop at
the end of the road, the signed Fernandez Trail begins a gentle
ascent through a forest of white fir, Jeffrey pine and lodgepole
pine. In ⅓ mile our route arrives at a signed junction with a
lateral to the Norris Creek trailhead. Here we turn right and
soon begin a moderate ascent to another signed junction with a
trail to the Norris Creek trailhead. From here we gain an open
ridgetop, where we meet a signed junction with the Lillian Lake
loop. With grand views over our shoulder, we turn west onto
the loop and enter Ansel Adams Wilderness. In a mixed forest
of red fir, mountain hemlock, and lodgepole and silver pine, we

pass two cow-infested meadows on the left, and then swing north and climb steeply up a rocky ridge. From the ridgetop we descend for a short distance through hemlock forest to ford the outlet of Vandeburg Lake. A little uphill to the west are the well-used campsites on the north side of this attractive lake.

2nd Hiking Day (**Vandeburg Lake** to **Rutherford Lake**, 7.5 miles): From the northwest side of Vandeburg Lake our trail ascends west up slabs to a signed junction with a trail to Lady Lake, at the edge of a lodgepole-pine-covered flat. A moderate ¾-mile ascent up this trail would bring one to the shady campsites on the northeast side of Lady Lake.

From the Lady Lake junction the main route continues up more slabs dotted with lodgepole pines. Where the trail tops a low ridge, we can pause to take in the expansive views of the Ritter Range to the northeast. After a short descent to the north we arrive at the first of the trout-filled Staniford Lakes. Then our scenic trail passes above the largest Staniford Lake and boulder-hops Shirley Creek. Continuing north across slabs our trail crosses several seasonal creeks before swinging west to ford the shaded outlet of Lillian Lake.

Instead of proceeding to the well-used campsites on the northeast side of this large lake, our route turns east and descends moderately under lodgepole pine and hemlock for about a mile. Then the grade levels off, we ford the creek from Rainbow and Flat lakes, and after an easy ¼ mile arrive at a junction with the Fernandez Trail. We turn left on it and ascend gently over juniper-and-lodgepole-pine-covered slabs for over a mile to a junction with a trail to Rainbow Lake. (If you want to visit this lovely lake, this trail will take you there in 1½ miles. Follow the trail across the creek and ascend southwest through timber and slabs for ¾ mile. The ducked trail then turns northwest and descends to cross the same creek above Flat Lake. A short ascent leads to the wooded east side of fishless Rainbow Lake, where overnight camping is prohibited.)

From the Rainbow Lake trail junction, the Fernandez Trail heads north and climbs up a shaded ravine onto a flat ridge. For another mile the route is a gentle stroll through open lodgepole-pine forest to a junction with the Post Peak Pass Trail. Here turn left and ford Fernandez Creek. The Fernandez Trail then swings west and ascends moderately under tall red firs for about ½ mile. Then the trail begins a series of switchbacks up the rocky, sun-drenched north canyon wall. This ascent passes through sections of red metavolcanic rock, and views to the south and east are good reasons to pause and rest in the shade of a juniper or a silver pine. Our trail re-enters timber at a small flat where we arrive at a junction with the short trail to Rutherford Lake. This very steep and badly eroded trail ascends ¼ mile to the small dam on the south side of well-used Rutherford Lake (9800′). The shores of this scenic lake have been abused, so camp well away from the water This deep lake contains a number of large golden and brook trout.

3rd Hiking Day: Follow the 3rd hiking day, Trip 77, 8.7 miles.

Granite Creek Road to Isberg Lakes **86**

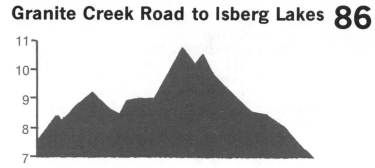

Distance   28.7 miles
Type   Shuttle trip
Best season   Mid or late
Topo maps   **Merced Peak**
Grade (hiking days/recommended layover days)
    Leisurely 5/1
    Moderate 4/1
    Strenuous 3/1
Trailhead   34, 33

HIGHLIGHTS This is a challenging hike, with an altitude gain of over 3000 feet. Scenery varies from the cloisters of dense forests and the intimacy of small meadows to the overwhelming panoramas from two high passes. Fishing is best in early and late season, and ranges from fair to excellent.

DESCRIPTION (Leisurely trip)

1st Hiking Day: Follow Trip 85 to **Vandeburg Lake**, 4 miles.

2nd Hiking Day (**Vandeburg Lake** to **Post Peak Pass Trail**, 5.7 miles): Follow the 2nd hiking day, Trip 85, to the junction of the Fernandez Trail and the Rainbow Lake Trail, by a small marsh. From the junction turn right on the Fernandez Trail and climb a short, shaded ravine up to a low ridge. On the ridge the trail makes a northwest traverse through open lodge-pole-pine forest, passing a broken dome on the west. After a nearly level mile and then a short, gentle descent we arrive at a junction with the Post Peak Pass Trail going right. There is a good campsite just north of the junction, by Fernandez Creek, and more are to be found several hundred yards down the Post Peak Pass Trail to the east, near the confluence of Fernandez

Creek and the creek from Slab Lakes. Both of these small creeks contain brook trout.

3rd Hiking Day (**Post Peak Pass Trail** to **Lower Isberg Lake**, 7.8 miles): This hiking day takes one over two steep passes that have excellent views. Heading east from the Fernandez Trail, the Post Peak Pass Trail soon crosses Fernandez Creek on logs. A short distance beyond we ford the creek from Slab Lakes and pass a junction with a trail to the lakes. We continue northeast over a low, wooded ridge past two glacial tarns where one may sometimes see families of mallards.

Beyond the second tarn the trail descends to ford seasonal Post Creek (9040') and begins a steep, three-stage ascent to Post Peak Pass. The first stage takes us up a densely forested hillside to marshy Isberg Meadow. Beyond this meadow our route leaves timber and ascends on a washed-out trail along a flower-lined creek. Then the grade eases and the trail enters the extraordinary "beachball" landscape around Porphyry Lake (10,100'). The dark blotches in this bedrock are inclusions of quartz diorite in a lighter-colored granite.

The last stage of the climb to Post Peak Pass is a steep ascent over a rocky, washed-out trail under the western ramparts of Post Peak. The last several hundred feet of this climb may be snowbound into summer, but a sign marks obvious Post Peak Pass (10,750'). From the wind-swept pass, the trail actually climbs a little more as it skirts a low peak ¼ mile northwest of the pass, where one can have excellent views. Our trail stays near the ridge as we pass high above Ward Lakes before descending west into Yosemite Park. A ⅓-mile descent brings us to a junction with the Isberg Trail, which we turn onto and then ascend back up to the Park boundary. This rocky ascent brings us to a point above Isberg Pass, which is a short descent away over ledges to the north. At the pass (10,520') we again enter Ansel Adams Wilderness, and then descend towards Upper Isberg Lake. The trail makes a very long traverse to the northeast, and if there is a lot of snow when you're there, it may be more efficient to descend directly east to the north side of the lake. From this lake the trail crosses the outlet and swings near a viewpoint above McClure Lake, then veers north and descends to the meadowed north side of Lower Isberg Lake. Scenic campsites can be found in the trees on the low moraine on the southeast side of the lake.

4th Hiking Day (**Lower Isberg Lake** to **Middle Cora Lake**, 5.7 miles): After rejoining the Isberg Trail we head east into forest cover, cross a small creek and swing south. Soon our lodgepole-pine-shaded trail becomes steep as it winds down to the meadowed fringes of trout-filled Sadler Lake (9345'). Camping is legal only on the south and west sides of this popular lake. Rounding the east side of the lake brings us to the outlet, and then to a junction with the trail to McClure Lake.

From here our trail descends moderately under lodgepole pines, then through a stretch of avalanche-downed trees, before fording East Fork Granite Creek. Descending more gently now, the trail follows the orange bedrock channel for ½ mile before veering away from the creek and passing a junction with the Timber Creek Trail. Our trail continues to descend, crossing several small creeks before it levels off in the cow-infested environs of the East Fork. Then the trail crosses to the east side of the creek (wet in early season), skirts a number of meadows, and swings away from the creek to cross a low bedrock ridge. Over a mile from the ford we pass a junction with a lateral to the Stevenson Trail. From this junction it is an easy ½ mile over a low moraine down to the shaded east shore of middle Cora Lake. Camping is legal only on the southwest side of the lake.

5th Hiking Day (**Middle Cora Lake** to **Granite Creek Campground**, 4.6 miles): From the outlet on the southeast side of middle Cora Lake, our trail heads south through lodgepole forest, and in 1¼ miles we ford East Fork Granite Creek for the last time (wet in early season). The trail descends the west bank for ½ mile and then swings west and passes a wilderness boundary sign. Soon we turn south again and the descent steepens as the trail winds down a ravine under red fir, lodgepole pine and Jeffrey pine. The grade eases before the last, dusty descent brings us to a trailhead parking lot on the east side of West Fork Granite Creek. A bridge downstream takes us to the east end of Granite Creek Campground (7040').

87 Lake Edison to Graveyard Meadows

Distance	10.4 miles
Type	Round trip
Best season	Mid
Topo maps	Kaiser Peak, Mt. Abbot

Grade (hiking days/recommended layover days)
  Leisurely 2/0
  Moderate ---
  Strenuous ---
Trailhead   41

HIGHLIGHTS The grail at the end of this quest is a pretty, meadowed campsite within the boundaries of John Muir Wilderness. This route travels densely forested country abounding in wildlife, and tops a crest offering superlative views.

DESCRIPTION

1st Hiking Day (**Vermilion Campground** to **Graveyard Meadows**, 5.2 miles): To reach the trailhead, proceed beyond the turnoff to the campground and follow the dirt road 0.15 mile to a parking area, turn right, up the hill, and go past the turnoff to the packstation (on the left) to a parking area at a Forest Service sign. Park here under the tall Jeffrey pines. After a stroll of 0.3 mile we reach a signed junction with the trail to Quail Meadows, and we veer right onto it and down to the bridge across Cold Creek. Beyond the bridge, our route reaches a junction, where we take the Goodale Pass Trail, the left fork, and proceed under Jeffrey pines, white firs and junipers. We soon begin a long, dusty ascent under a dense cover of mostly Jeffrey pines. Our route passes a meadow on the lower part of this climb, but the ascent is fairly monotonous until very near the top, where we are rewarded with good views of Lake Edison and the peaks of the Mono Divide. From the crown of the climb it is but a short distance to Cold Creek, which we ford in order to join a jeep road for a short distance before we arrive at the signed boundary of John Muir Wilderness. Graveyard Meadows (8850′) are on the right, and secluded camping can be found at the head of the meadows. Or if one prefers, one can stay at the more-used sites near the ford. Fishing in Cold Creek is poor-to-fair for brook (to 8″).

2nd Hiking Day: Retrace your steps, 5.2 miles.

Looking south over Lake Edison

88 Lake Edison to Graveyard Lakes

Distance   16.8 miles
Type   Round trip
Best season   Mid or late
Topo maps   Kaiser Peak, Mt. Abbot
Grade (hiking days/recommended layover days)
   Leisurely 4/1
   Moderate 3/1
   Strenuous 2/1
Trailhead   41

HIGHLIGHTS The California Department of Fish and Game
has never been called overly creative, but it
named the lakes in the Graveyard Lakes chain well. Beneath
tombstone-granited Graveyard Peak lie lakes with DF&G
names like Vengeance, Murder, Phantom, Headstone, Spook
and Ghost. This country is worth investigating if for no other
reason than to satisfy one's curiosity about these names. The
truth is that this particular lake basin is one of the loveliest and
most regal in the Silver Divide country.

DESCRIPTION (Leisurely trip)

1st Hiking Day: Follow Trip 87 to **Graveyard Meadows**,
5.2 miles.

2nd Hiking Day (**Graveyard Meadows** to **Lower Graveyard Lake**, 3.2 miles): From the south end of Graveyard
Meadows, the trail enters the John Muir Wilderness and skirts
the north edge of the meadows under a dense cover of lodgepoles and red firs. Birdlovers should keep an eye out for the
Brewer blackbird, whitecrowned sparrow, Cassin finch, robin
and sparrow hawk that inhabit this mountain field. At the north
end of the meadow, the trail begins climbing moderately, and
soon we cross Cold Creek on rocks (difficult in early season).
This forested, duff trail ascends the narrowing Cold Creek

valley, fording the creek in two places at the south end of Upper Graveyard Meadow.

The trail continues its gentle-to-moderate ascent under lodgepoles to a junction with the trail to Graveyard Lakes. We turn left onto it and ford Cold Creek in Upper Graveyard Meadow. Beyond the ford, the trail enters a cover of lodgepole and hemlock and begins a steep, rocky climb to the basin above. The lodgepole pine and mountain hemlock at the top of this 600-foot ascent give way to lush meadows at the eastern fringes of beautiful lower Graveyard Lake (9950'). Good though heavily used campsites may be found in the lodgepole stands where the trail first meets the lake, or along the east side of the lake between this point and the inlet stream.

From any of these places, the camper has marvelous views of Graveyard Peak and the tumbled granite cirque wall that surrounds the entire Graveyard Lakes basin. It is easy to derive the logic behind the name, "Graveyard Peak." Tombstone-makers have for years shown a preference for this particular kind of salt-and-pepper granite. These campsites along the east side of lower Graveyard Lake make an excellent base camp from which to fish and explore the remaining five lakes in the basin. The three small lakes directly above offer pretty and cleaner camping, and they can be reached by following the trail around to the head of the lake and climbing the hill. Fishing is good on lower Graveyard Lake for brook trout (to 13") and fair-to-good on the upper lakes, due to poor spawning waters.

3rd and 4th Hiking Days: Retrace your steps, 8.4 miles.

89   Rock Creek to Gem Lakes

Distance   8 miles
Type   Round trip
Best season Mid or late
Topo maps   Mt. Tom, Mt. Abbot
Grade (hiking days/recommended layover days)
   Leisurely 2/0
   Moderate Day
   Strenuous ---
Trailhead   42

HIGHLIGHTS Majestic scenery dominates this short, popular trip. Because of its moderate terrain and high country "feel" this route through the Little Lakes Valley has been a long-time favorite of the beginning hiker, and the varied and good fishing for brook and rainbow makes it also an excellent angling choice.

DESCRIPTION

1st Hiking Day (**Mosquito Flat** to **Gem Lakes**, 4 miles): The magnificent Sierra crest confronts the traveler at the very outset of this trip. From the trailhead at Mosquito Flat (10,200′), the wide, rocky-sandy trail starts southwest toward the imposing skyline dominated by soaring Bear Creek Spire. In a few minutes we enter John Muir Wilderness and then reach a junction at which the Mono Pass Trail is the right fork and our trail, the Morgan Pass Trail, is the left fork. Soon our route tops a low, rocky ridge just west of Mack Lake, and from this ridge one has good views of green-clad Little Lakes Valley. Gazing out, one cannot help but feel a sense of satisfaction that this beautiful valley enjoys protection as part of John Muir Wilderness. Aside from some early, abortive mining ventures, this subalpine valley remains relatively unspoiled.

From the ridgetop viewpoint our trail descends to skirt a marsh that was the west arm of Marsh Lake before it filled in. Anglers may wish to try their luck for the good fishing for brown and brook trout in Marsh Lake and the nearby lagoon areas of Rock Creek. While fishing on the numerous lakes and streams of Little Lakes Valley, one has views into the long glacial trough to the south—a long-time favorite of lensmen. Flanked by Mt. Starr on the right and Mt. Morgan on the left, the valley terminates in the soaring heights of Mts. Mills, Abbot, Dade and Julius Ceasar, and Bear Creek Spire, all over 13,000 feet. Still-active glaciers on the slopes of these great peaks are reminders of the enormous forces that shaped this valley eons ago, and the visitor cannot help but feel contrasting reactions of exhilaration and humility.

From the meadowed fringes of Marsh and Heart lakes, the trail ascends gently past the west side of Box Lake to the east side of aptly named Long Lake. For the angler with a yearning to try different waters, the unnamed lakes on the bench just to the east offer good fishing for brook and rainbow. Beyond Long Lake the trail ascends through a moderately dense forest cover of whitebark pines past a spur trail branching left to Chicken-foot Lake. Then we dip to cross a seasonal stream, climb slightly, and dip again, to the outlet stream of the Gem Lakes. Ahead on the left we see the last switchback on the trail up Morgan Pass, through which the abandoned road that has been our trail once reached the tungsten mines in the Pine Creek drainage.

Just after a rockhop ford of the Gem Lakes outlet, we take the trail that leads 150 yards up beside this steam to the lowest of the three main Gem Lakes. Many campsites in clumps of whitebark pines are scattered around these emerald-green lakes, under the sheer north wall of peak 11654. Fishing is fair-to-good for brook and rainbow trout to 10". The Treasure Lakes, located in barren cirques above here, are traditional basecamp locations for climbers bound for the high peaks to the west.

2nd Hiking Day: Retrace your steps, 4 miles.

90   Rock Creek to Ruby Lake

Distance   5 miles
Type   Round trip
Best season   Mid or late
Topo maps   Mt. Tom, Mt. Abbot
Grade (hiking days/recommended layover days)
   Leisurely 2/0
   Moderate   Day
   Strenuous ---
Trailhead   42

HIGHLIGHTS From the Little Lakes Valley upward to the heights of the Ruby Lake cirque, the traveler gains an appreciation of glacially formed country. One can almost see the main trunk of the glacier flowing northeast through the valley and being joined by the feeder glacier from the cirque that now holds Ruby Lake. The terminus of this trip, Ruby Lake, lies amidst the barren peaks of the awe-inspiring Sierra Nevada crest.

DESCRIPTION

1st Hiking Day (**Mosquito Flat** to **Ruby Lake**, 2.5 miles): First follow Trip 89 to the junction of the Morgan Pass and Mono Pass trails. Here our route branches right (west) and ascends steeply over rocky switchbacks. In the course of this switchbacking ascent, the traveler will see the moderate-to-dense forest cover of whitebark and lodgepole diminish in density as we near timberline. Views during the climb include the glacier-fronted peaks named in Trip 89 and, midway up the ascent, Mt. Morgan. Immediately below to the east, the deep blue of Heart and Box lakes and some of the Hidden Lakes reflects the sky above, and the viewer looking at the panorama of the valley can readily trace the glacial history that left these "puddles" behind.

Near the meadowed edge of the outlet stream from Ruby Lake is a junction, where we turn left. It becomes apparent that a cirque basin is opening up, although one cannot see Ruby Lake, which completely fills the cirque bottom, until one is actually at water's edge (11,000'). This first breathtaking view of the lake and its towering cirque walls makes the climb worth the effort. Sheer granite makes up the upper walls of the cirque, and the crown is topped by a series of spectacular pinnacles, particularly to the west. To the north, also on the crest, a notch indicates Mono Pass, and close scrutiny will reveal the switch-backing trail that ascends the south ridge of Mt. Starr. The lower walls of the cirque are mostly made up of talus and scree that curve outward to the lake's edge, and it is over this jumbled rock that ambitious anglers must scramble to sample the fair fishing for brook, rainbow and brown (to 12"). Good camp-sites can be found below the outlet of the lake. Lakeside camp-sites are exposed and usually windy.

2nd Hiking Day: Retrace your steps, 2.5 miles.

Outlet of Ruby Lake

91 McGee Creek to Steelhead Lake

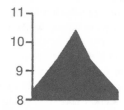

Distance	9 miles
Type	Round trip
Best season	Mid or late
Topo maps	Mt. Morrison, Mt. Abbot
Grade (hiking days/recommended layover days)	
Leisurely	2/1
Moderate	2/0
Strenuous	---
Trailhead	43

HIGHLIGHTS Travelers new to east-escarpment entry to the Sierra will find the ascent to Steelhead Lake fascinating because of the swirling patterns in the highly fractured red metamorphic rocks of the canyon wall. Though Steelhead Lake is relatively easy to reach, the hiker may find seclusion there.

DESCRIPTION

1st Hiking Day (**McGee Creek Roadend** to **Steelhead Lake**, 4.5 miles): From the parking area (8100′) the trail ascends a short distance to a Forest Service sign proclaiming the eastern boundary of John Muir Wilderness. The route, an old jeep road leading to the defunct Scheelore Mine, traverses the north and then the west side of McGee Creek canyon. The canyon is mostly sage- and rabbitbrush-covered except for an anomalous grove of aspen in an apparently dry area. Near the creek are more aspen, cottonwood, birch and willow. Soon our trail fords the steams emanating from the springs above Horsetail Falls, and the canyon narrows. As the trail passes close to the creek, the grade eases, and our route enters a lush area with a lovely floral display.

The gentle ascent continues to a ford of tree-lined McGee Creek, where there is sometimes a log (difficult in early season). Then the unshaded trail climbs more steeply until it passes a beaver dam. Above the dam, the creek wanders through a meadow, above which the trail fords the creek via logs and boards to the west bank. As the trail loops west, it becomes steeper and enters a moderately dense lodgepole forest. Then our route leaves the jeep road at a signed junction and continues its winding ascent to a junction with the Steelhead Lake lateral. (This junction is farther than indicated on the map; it is where the trail finally returns to creekside.)

Fording McGee Creek, this lateral climbs steeply by switchbacks along the north side of the outlet stream from Grass Lake. Fishing from the meadowed fringes of little Grass Lake is poor-to-fair for rainbow and brook. From Grass Lake the trail once more switchbacks up an abrupt, timbered slope, and ends at the good camping sites at the north end of fairly large (about 25 acres) Steelhead Lake (10,350′). Views from these campsites take in the granite grandeur of Mt. Stanford and Mt. Crocker to the south and west, and rust-and-buff-colored Mt. Baldwin to the north. Fishermen will find the angling for rainbow and brook excellent (best in early and late season). They will also find the name "Steelhead" Lake a misnomer, though an understandable error. Over the years, catches of rainbow trout from this lake have exhibited pale, faded markings, giving an appearance much like their silver cousins of coastal waters.

2nd Hiking Day: Retrace your steps, 4.5 miles.

Steelhead Lake

92   McGee Creek to McGee Lake

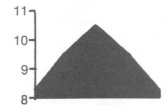

Distance   13 miles
Type   Round trip
Best season   Mid or late
Topo maps   Mt. Morrison, Mt. Abbot
Grade (hiking days/recommended layover days)
  Leisurely 2/1
  Moderate 2/0
  Strenuous ---
Trailhead   43

HIGHLIGHTS In an alpine setting close under the Sierra crest, Big McGee Lake shares a large granite basin with three other fishable lakes. This beautiful spot nestles under the sheer, colorful walls of Red and White Mountain, and close to impressive Mt. Crocker.

DESCRIPTION

1st Hiking Day (**McGee Creek Roadend** to **Big McGee Lake**, 6.5 miles): First, follow Trip 91 to the trail intersection with the Steelhead Lake lateral, where the trail continues south over a forested, rocky slope. The ascent eases as the trail passes a drift fence, and then we pass a tarn, climb above a meadow where there is a campsite, and emerge from timber into another meadow. The trail then undulates under a sparse cover of whitebark pine to join the creek briefly and skirt a smaller meadow from where an older section of trail heads back down-canyon. Soon the trail reaches the rocky, open slopes just north of Big McGee Lake (10,480'). Fair-to-good campsites may be found along the north shore. Fishermen will enjoy the fair-to-good fishing for rainbow and brook (to 13") on Big McGee Lake, and, if time and inclination allow, will want to explore the equally good fishing at nearby Little McGee Lake, Crocker Lake, or picture-book Golden Lake.

2nd Hiking Day: Retrace your steps, 6.5 miles.

McGee Creek to Lake Edison   **93**

Distance   33.6 miles
Type   Shuttle trip
Best season   Mid or late
Topo maps   Mt. Morrison, Mt. Abbot, Kaiser Peak
Grade (hiking days/recommended layover days)
   Leisurely 7/2
   Moderate 5/2
   Strenuous 4/2
Trailhead   43, 41

HIGHLIGHTS This trans-Sierra route is one of the finest in the northern Sierra. Two scenic passes, both over 11,000 feet, cross the Sierra crest and the Silver Divide. Between them the route visits alpine lakes and streams offering excellent fishing for rainbow, brook and golden trout.

DESCRIPTION (Leisurely trip)

1st Hiking Day: Follow Trip 92 to **Big McGee Lake**, 6.5 miles.

2nd Hiking Day (**Big McGee Lake** to **Tully Lake**, 5.5 miles): With the colorful and majestic heights of Red and White Mountain to the left (southwest) the route ascends steeply to Little McGee Lake, passing a signed junction with the route to Hopkins Pass. Fishing at this rockbound lake is fair for rainbow and brook. From Little McGee Lake our route swings northward and ascends a narrow, rocky canyon toward McGee Pass. The red rock walls of the canyon look very desolate, and the trail briefly disappears under snow until late season. The last few hundred feet of ascent are accomplished via rocky switchbacks up the west wall of a barren cirque. From McGee Pass (11,900') views to the west are good of the peaks above Fish Creek.

An interesting turn-of-the-century legend has it that two Indian sheepherders running sheep around the headwaters of McGee Creek were returning from the high country. En route, a pack on one of their mules shifted, and they jury-rigged a large rock to balance the shifting action. Upon reaching their destination, they unloaded the jury-rigged balance and discovered that the rock felt abnormally heavy. As in all good gold legends, the rock assayed rich, and, ostensibly, neither the two Indians nor subsequent treasure-seekers have found the lode from which the rock was taken.

From the pass much of the descent to timberline is on new trail that has too many switchbacks for most people's taste. We reach timberline above a large meadow, and from here our trail follows a route north of that shown on the topo map. The trail descends through sparse timber and meets the creek at the foot of a meadow. Just below, the creek and the trail drop steeply and turn right. Ford the creek here and head south up a grassy swale to the good campsite in the trees above Tully Lake. Good campsites may also be found on the meadowed fringes along the northeast side of the lake. Tully Lake (10,400') is a small (about 10 acres) high-country lake that sustains fair-to-good fishing for golden and brook (to 13"). Anglers will want to try the nearby waters of Red and White Lake, about 1 mile over the ridge to the east. Fishing here is also fair-to-good for rainbow that often run to 16". Those wishing stream fishing can find smaller rainbow, brook and some golden along meandering Fish Creek.

3rd Hiking Day (**Tully Lake** to **Tully Hole**, 3 miles): This short trail day allows the traveler who admires wild backcountry scenery to absorb the primitive beauty of this area. Anglers, particularly fly fisherman, will find the leisurely pace along Fish Creek satisfying. From Tully Lake retrace the route to the main Fish Creek Trail, where you turn left (west). The trail now follows the south bank of Fish Creek as it descends below treeline ¼ mile to a ford of Fish Creek (wet in early season), where it meets the trail that follows the outlet from Tully Lake. Our trail soon fords the creek again and enters timber. Here we pass a signed junction with the trail to Cecil and Lee lakes.

Then the descent steepens and the trail switchbacks down to lush Horse Heaven. Through the meadow, the trail is muddy into late season, and the ford at the west end of the meadow is difficult in early season. Beyond this ford the trail passes a drift fence and descends through lodgepole and hemlock on the south side of the creek to Tully Hole (9500'). Like the meadows at Horse Heaven, the grasslands of Tully Hole (9500') are rife with wildflower color. The stream is sometimes bowered with willows, but the long, swirling, curved line of Fish Creek is for the most part an open, pleasant stretch of water with grassy, overhung banks and several deep holes. Good campsites at the northwest edge of the meadow near the John Muir Trail junction take advantage of the fine views up the meadow.

4th Hiking Day (**Tully Hole** to **Lake of the Lone Indian**, 5 miles): The route at this point joins the John Muir Trail, and leaves Tully Hole by a gentle descent. From the trail, the traveler has splendid views and access to the numerous small falls and holes that characterize nearby Fish Creek. The trail then passes a junction with the Cascade Valley Trail and climbs steeply over a densely forested slope east of the outlet stream from Squaw Lake. Midway up this stretch the trail levels off, fords the stream twice in quick succession, and passes several campsites situated in picturesque meadows. Then it begins the final, long, steep climb to Squaw Lake. This section of trail is rocky, eroded and exposed.

Meadow-fringed Squaw Lake is a good place to stop and ponder the effects of glacial erosion—the clean granite cliffs, the large erratics here and there, and the lake basin itself. Anglers will wish to fish Squaw Lake—and Warrior Lake above it—which offer good-to-excellent fishing for brook (to 9").

From Squaw Lake our route winds up the rocky slope to the southwest, and in ½ mile meets the Goodale Pass Trail at a small pool. Here we leave the John Muir Trail, turn right, top a ridge, and descend through rocky meadows to the foot of turquoise Papoose Lake. This small lake (under 5 acres) affords good fishing for brook, as does Chief Lake, up the granite slope to the east. At the junction by the outlet of Papoose Lake our route branches north, and then descends over a long dusty traverse to the good campsites in the grassy pockets at the southwest end of Lake of the Lone Indian (10,200'). Angling is good for brook and rainbow (8–14").

5th Hiking Day (**Lake of the Lone Indian** to **Lower Graveyard Lake**, 5.2 miles): First retrace the steps of the previous day to the Goodale Pass Trail at the foot of Papoose Lake. Our route then turns right (southwest), and 100 yards beyond the ford of Papoose Lake's outlet is a signed junction with the trail to Minnow Creek. Here our trail begins a steep, rocky ascent to a long, grass-bottomed swale below Goodale Pass. Where the trail levels off momentarily, an unsigned trail goes right, down the hill to Lake of the Lone Indian. The exfoliating, rocky slopes of the Silver Divide show the usual signs of glaciation—polish, rounding and striation. The whistling of marmots that inhabit the jumbled slopes accompanies the traveler as he climbs the last leg to Goodale Pass (11,000'). From the pass views extend as far north as the Ritter Range and Yosemite, and south over the San Joaquin River watershed to the peaks beyond the Mono Divide. The first part of the descent down the south side of Goodale Pass is rocky and steep, but as the switchbacking trail progresses, it offers fine views of the nearby cirque that feeds Cold Creek.

Soon the trail levels out somewhat and stepladders down through a series of charming green pocket meadows. As the trail descends in and out of lodgepole-pine stands, it crosses many small streams that pour out of the canyon's north wall. Unfortunately, some of these may be fouled by the summer cattle population. Soon after the ford of Cold Creek (difficult in early season) the trail arrives at a junction with the Graveyard Lakes Trail. Here our route branches right (west) onto it and follows the last part of the 2nd hiking day, Trip 88.

6th Hiking day: Reverse the steps of the 2nd hiking day, Trip 88, 3.2 miles.

7th Hiking Day: Reverse the steps of the 1st hiking day, Trip 87, 5.2 miles.

Rock Creek to Lake Edison

94

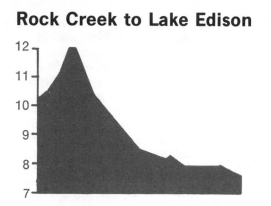

Distance	21.4 miles
Type	Shuttle trip
Best season	Late
Topo maps	Mt. Tom, Mt. Abbot, Kaiser Peak

Grade (hiking days/recommended layover days)
Leisurely 4/1
Moderate 3/1
Strenuous 2/1

Trailhead 42, 41

HIGHLIGHTS Taking this trans-Sierra crossing in late season gives the traveler three distinct pluses: First, the luxuriant aspen groves along Mono Creek take on their golden hue about this time. Second, the mid-season fishing slump usually ends as the weather cools off. Last, this popular route sees heavy foot and animal traffic during early and mid season, but this activity tapers off when the leaves begin to turn.

DESCRIPTION (Leisurely trip)

1st Hiking Day: Follow Trip 90 to **Ruby Lake**, 2.5 miles.

2nd Hiking Day (**Ruby Lake** to **Fish Camp**, 7.8 miles): First, retrace your steps back to the Mono Pass Trail. From the junction, the trail ascends steeply over the rocky switchbacks on the south slope of Mt. Starr to Mono Pass (12,000'), a notch in the cirque wall just west of Mt. Starr. On this climb, views constantly improve, and views from the pass are excellent, but those wishing a panoramic outlook on the spectacular Sierra crest should ascend the granite shoulder of Mt. Starr, an easy climb to the east. From this vantage point one has a complete perspective of Pioneer Basin and Mts. Stanford, Huntington, Crocker and Hopkins, and Red and White Mountain to the north. to the south one has an "end-on" view of Mts. Abbot and Dade, Bear Creek Spire, and Mt. Humphreys.

From Mono Pass the trail descends over granite slopes past barren Summit Lake, and then drops more severely as it veers west above Trail Lakes (poor-to-fair fishing for brook). Our route then turns northward and fords Golden Creek. Following the north side of the stream in a moderately dense forest cover, the trail passes the lateral to Pioneer Basin (north) and the lateral to Fourth Recess Lake (south). Anglers may elect to try their luck at the good fishing for brook (8–14″) at Fourth Recess Lake, ½ mile south over a gentle climb.

Our route continues to descend, fording the outlet streams from Pioneer Basin and paralleling the westward course of Mono Creek. As the Mono Creek valley opens up beyond Mono Rock, the trail passes the steep lateral to Third Recess Lake (south), and, about a mile farther, descends past the turnoff to Lower Hopkins Lake and the Hopkins Lake basin (north). Anglers will find the many fine holes that interrupt dashing Mono Creek good fishing for brook, rainbow and occasional golden (to 12″). In late season the groves of quaking aspen that line the stream's banks are an incomparably colorful back drop to an otherwise steady conifer green. Owing to heavy traffic, this segment of trail becomes somewhat dusty where it passes the Grinnell Lake lateral and descends to Fish Camp (8500′). This traditional camping place marks the junction of the Mono Creek Trail with the Second Recess lateral. Due to heavy use here, the Forest Service encourages you to camp downstream.

3rd Hiking Day (**Fish Camp** to **Quail Meadows**, 5 miles): As this day's route descends along the north side of Mono Creek, the rich yellows of the aspen groves accompany the stream. Occasionally the traveler has views of the stern northern face of Volcanic Knob to the south, and from several spots along the trail one looks up the long, chutelike valley of the First Recess to the granite-topped heights of Recess Peak. Fishing for brook, rainbow and occasional golden is much like that of the previous day, but the stream is somewhat less accessible from the trail.

About 2½ miles below Fish Camp the trail turns right, away

from the narrowing canyon, and climbs by rocky switchbacks to the crown of a ridge, where it joins the John Muir Trail. Thence it descends a short distance on the east side of North Fork Mono Creek, and fords the North Fork (difficult in early season) just above its confluence with Mono Creek. From the ford to the edge of Quail Meadows is a gentle downhill walk through dense forest cover. Fair-to-good campsites can be found on the forested fringe of Quail Meadows (7760'), downstream from the point where the John Muir Trail branches left (south) and crosses Mono Creek.

4th Hiking Day: (**Quail Meadows** to **Vermilion Campground**, 6.1 miles): Our route from Quail Meadows proceeds west on a level stretch. Mono Creek now cascades over a series of granite-bedrocked holes (fine swimming in late season) before flowing into the northeast tip of Lake Edison. This man-made, granite-edged lake dominates the views to the south for the remainder of this trip. A boat-taxi service operates the length of the lake, based at a resort adjoining Vermilion Campground, but advance inquiry should be made about length of operating season and ferry schedule. (Write to Vermilion Valley Resort/Mono Hot Springs/California 93642.) The ferry lands at the northeast tip of the lake, and the marked footpath giving access to this point can be seen from the trail.

The trail along the upper reaches of the north side of Lake Edison undulates severely over alternately rocky and dusty stretches. At some points the trail crosses granite ridges 600 feet above the lake surface, and from these ridges the traveler has fine views of heavily timbered Bear Ridge across the lake. The forest cover reflects the lower altitude, as Jeffrey pine and red fir mix with ever-present lodgepole. This forest becomes quite dense as our route passes the trail going right (north) to Graveyard Meadows and Goodale Pass. Our route continues west, crosses the bridge over Cold Creek, and passes the trail to Devils Bathtub. Beyond this junction the hiker leaves the worst of the dust behind as the trail winds through Jeffrey pine to an abandoned Forest Service road. This sandy road descends gently to the east edge of Vermilion Campground (7650').

95   McGee Creek to Rock Creek

Distance   29.3 miles
Type   Shuttle trip; part cross-country
Best season   Late
Topo maps   Mt. Morrison, Mt. Abbot, Mt. Tom
Grade (hiking days/recommended layover days)
  Leisurely 6/2
  Moderate 4/2
  Strenuous 3/1
Trailhead   43, 42

HIGHLIGHTS For *experienced knapsackers only*, this rugged route offers excitement and challenge sufficient to satisfy the most jaded appetite. High-country lakes surrounded by rampartlike peaks characterize this colorful route, and the fishing is good-to-excellent.

DESCRIPTION (Leisurely trip)

1st and 2nd Hiking Days: Follow Trip 93 to **Tully Lake**, 11 miles.

3rd Hiking Day (**Tully Lake** to **Grinnell Lake**, 3.5 miles cross country): From the east shore of Tully Lake our route ascends the grassy swale that lies due east of the lake. At the outlet stream from Red and White Lake our route turns right (south-east) and follows this stream to the lake itself. Fishermen will wish to try these icy, clear, blue waters for large rainbow (to 18″). Although there's no good camping, Red and White Lake offers an excellent vantage point from which to take in the spectacular and aptly named heights of Red and White Mountain. The saddle (11,600′) that this day's route traverses is clearly discernible at the lowest point of the right shoulder of Red and White Mountain, and the easiest route to the saddle takes the traveler around the rocky east shore of the lake. The steepest part of the ascent is over treacherous shale— or snow in early and mid season—and the climber is well-advised to take it slow and easy. Rope should be carried and used, especially if ascending the west side of the pass.

From the top one obtains a well-deserved and exciting view of the surrounding terrain. To the north the immediate, dazzling blue of Red and White Lake sets off the buff browns and ochre reds of the surrounding rock. Beyond this basin the meadowy cirque forming the headwaters of Fish Creek is a large greensward that contrasts sharply with the austere, red-stained eminence of Red Slate Mountain, and the distant skyline offers sawtooth profiles of the Ritter Range, with its readily identifiable Minarets, and the Mammoth Crest. To the south, the barren, rocky shores of the Grinnell chain of lakes occupy the foreground, and, just beyond, the green-sheathed slopes of the Mono Creek watershed drop away, rising in the distance to the Mono Divide.

Like the ascent of this saddle, the descent should be taken with some care. The sudden, shaley drop terminates in a large "rock garden," a jumble of large boulders, just above Little Grinnell Lake. Our rock-hopping route takes us along the east shore of this tiny lake to the long, grassy descent leading to the west side of Grinnell Lake (10,800'). Midway along this side, where the most prominent peninsula infringes on the long lake, our route strikes the marked fisherman's trail that veers south-west down a long swale to tiny Laurel Lake. There are several fair campsites at this junction which offer excellent views due to their situation on a plateau above the lake. Fishermen will find Grinnell Lake fair-to-good fishing for brook and rainbow (8–14"). Alternative good campsites can be found along the meadowy fringes of Laurel Lake (10,300'), about 1 mile south-west. Fishing on this lake is excellent for brook (to 10").

4th Hiking Day (**Grinnell Lake** to **Fish Camp**, 4.5 miles): The fisherman's trail from Grinnell Lake to Laurel Lake descends via a long, scooplike swale to the grassy meadows forming the headwaters of Laurel Creek. The trail, though very faint from Grinnell to Laurel Lake, becomes clearer as it descends gently along Laurel Creek. At this point the creek is still a "jump-across" stream, but a careful approach along the banks will reveal an abundance of brook trout (to 9"), and fly fishermen who favor stream angling will find this tiny watercourse a delight.

The gradual descent along the creek becomes somewhat steeper just above the larger meadows. The pleasant, timber-fringed grassland is divided by the serpentine curves of Laurel Creek. The trail across the meadow is difficult to follow, and the traveler who loses it should cross to the west side of Laurel Creek and look for the trail in the vicinity of the campsites at the south end of the meadow. The dense lodgepole cover at the end of the meadow soon gives way to manzanita thickets and occasional clumps of quaking aspen as the trail reaches the steep, switchbacking descent above Mono Creek. These switchbacks are unmaintained, and are subject to heavy erosion. However, the difficult going is more than compensated for by the excellent views across the Mono Creek watershed into the Second Recess. Particularly impressive are the heights of Mt. Gabb and Mt. Hilgard, which guard the upper end of this side canyon. When our route strikes the Mono Creek Trail, it turns right (west) for a gently descending ½ mile to the campsites at Fish Camp (8500'). Due to heavy use here, the Forest Service encourages you to camp downstream. Fishing is good for brook and rainbow (to 12") on Mono Creek.

5th Hiking Day: Reverse the steps of the 2nd hiking day, Trip 93, 7.8 miles.

6th hiking day: Reverse the steps of the 1st hiking day, Trip 90, 2.5 miles.

Mammoth Lakes to Purple Lake 96

Distance	16 miles
Type	Round trip
Best season	Late
Topo maps	Mt. Morrison

Grade (hiking days/recommended layover days)
> *Leisurely* 3/1
> *Moderate* 2/1
> *Strenuous* 2/0

Trailhead   40

HIGHLIGHTS The rewards for crossing a mountain pass amount to more than the views that are presented. Most experienced knapsackers know that passes have a way of separating the day hikers from the overnighters. So it is with this trip across the Mammoth Crest. Those seeking the satisfaction of seeing what lies beyond the top of the hill, will find this hike a worthwhile choice.

DESCRIPTION (Moderate trip)

1st Hiking Day (**Coldwater Campground** to **Purple Lake**, 8 miles): From Coldwater Campground (8960') the Duck Pass Trail ascends on an alternately sandy and rocky section along a moderately forested slope, soon entering John Muir Wilderness. The first four miles of this trail, from the trailhead to Barney Lake, receives a good deal of day hiker and fisherman use, so by midseason the trail is fairly dusty.

As the going levels off after the first rise, Arrowhead Lake is visible off to the left (east). Then the trail ascends again to Skelton Lake. The lake was named for the brothers Skelton, who, during this mining area's heyday, established and maintained a stamp mill at the lower end of the lake. Owing to heavy fishing pressure on these lakes, the angling is only fair. As our route crosses the rolling terrain south of Skelton Lake, the barren canyon walls along the Mammoth Crest show the scouring action of the ancient glaciers that once covered the land. From the rocky shores of emerald-green Barney Lake (no fires within 300 feet of lake), the steep ascent to Duck Pass is easily seen. The switchbacks ascending this steep slope leave hemlock and lodgepole pine behind and except for an occasional whitebark pine this climb is barren and exposed.

Just before Duck Pass (10,790′) there are views of the Mammoth Creek watershed and the Mammoth Crest to the northwest. Beyond, the skyline is dominated by the distinctive spires of the Ritter Range. Just beyond the pass we see Pika and Duck lakes, which occupy the basin immediately below; and these blue, still waters are flanked by somber, dark metamorphic peaks. Across yawning Cascade Valley the Silver Divide's granite peaks occupy the horizon. The descent to the outlet of large Duck Lake begins by passing a trail to Pika Lake. This lake offers perhaps the best camping in the basin. About 330 yards beyond the junction, marked only by an inadequate cairn on the right side of the trail, is the start of the route to Deer Lakes. The main trail, which stays high at first, eventually drops to the outlet of Duck Lake. Except for a few gnarled whitebark pines, the jumbled slopes and rocky crags surrounding the lake are barren and austere. (No fires allowed in Duck Lake watershed; no camping within 300 feet of outlet of Duck or Purple Lake.)

From Duck Lake our route crosses the outlet and descends to join the scenic John Muir Trail. It then turns left (south), and for several miles on level trail rounds a rocky, granite shoulder, then veers east to the several good campsites at large, well-used Purple Lake (9860′). Fishing is fair-to-good for rainbow and some golden and brook (8–13″). Purple Lake's partly timbered, rocky shoreline gives way to meadow at the northeast end of the lake. The rocks above the meadow give this lake its name; they have a rosy tint during the day, but around sunset they turn purple and violet.

2nd Hiking Day: Retrace you steps, 8 miles.

Mammoth Lakes to Lake Edison **97**

Distance	29.9 miles
Type	Shuttle trip
Best season	Late
Topo maps	Mt. Morrison, Mt. Abbot, Kaiser Peak

Grade (hiking days/recommended layover days)
  Leisurely 6/1
  Moderate 5/1
  Strenuous 4/1

Trailhead 40, 41

HIGHLIGHTS This trans-Sierra route explores two watersheds, ascends two passes, and offers a world of fine fishing along the way. About one fourth of the route follows the famous John Muir Trail, and high, alpine scenery alternates with intimate, friendly meadows, fast-running streams, and lonely, placid lakes. Long mileage and stiff climbs make this a trip for the hiker who has prepared himself with a couple of early- or mid-season warm-ups, but the rewards, in views and fishing, repay the required effort.

DESCRIPTION (Moderate trip)

1st Hiking Day: Follow Trip 96 to **Purple Lake**, 8 miles.

2nd Hiking Day (**Purple Lake** to **Cascade Valley/Fish Creek ford**, 3.5 miles): Immediately west of the outlet of Purple Lake is a signed junction. Our indicated route to Cascade Valley branches right (southwest) from the John Muir Trail and descends gently at first, parallel to Purple Creek. The forest cover along this switchbacking descent is primarily lodgepole pine, giving way to Jeffrey pine and juniper near the valley floor. On this descent the hiker has fine views of the Silver Divide across the valley. The long switchbacks of this steep descent terminate in a large meadow on the floor of Cascade Valley. Here our route strikes the Cascade Valley Trail and turns left (east) along Fish Creek.

The fairly level going along the valley floor gives the angler ample opportunity to test the good fishing for brook and rainbow (to 9"). California's DF&G *Anglers' Guide* says about Cascade Valley: "One of the finest trout streams left in the High Sierra; meandering and scenic with splendid campsites and forest cover." As the hiker works his way up the valley, Fish Creek rushes and then meanders on his right, and open meadow fringes beckon. Where this trail crosses Fish Creek via a wading ford, this hiking day ends at one of many campsites (8560'). Fishing is good, as noted above.

3rd Hiking Day (**Cascade Valley/Fish Creek ford** to **Lake of the Lone Indian**, 4.8 miles): Beyond the ford of Fish Creek the trail ascends somewhat more steeply over rocky stretches. Fish Creek, now on the left, changes as the canyon narrows. The water flows faster and the creek becomes a riotous tumble of waterfalls and tiny holes. Just below the point where our route rejoins the John Muir Trail, the canyon wall on the north side of the valley becomes a sheer, dramatically polished granite surface. Our trail crosses the outlet stream from Helen Lake and meets the John Muir Trail, onto which we turn right (south). From this junction to Helen Lake the ascent is steep. The first part of the climb is densely forested as we climb up the east side of the outlet stream from Helen Lake, and midway up the trail passes several alternative meadowed campsites on the right. Beyond these campsites the trail becomes rocky, exposed and eroded as it makes the last steep climb to Helen Lake. One has excellent views back down the U-shaped valley with which to fill the breather stops, and as the trail crests at the granite lip of the Helen Lake cirque, one can see whence the glacier emanated that carved the valley below. Anglers will want to fish Helen Lake—and Bobs Lake about ½ mile southeast. Both offer good-to-excellent angling for brook (to 9").

The trail then rock-hops the outlet of Helen Lake, passes two small alpine tarns, and branches right, leaving the John

Muir Trail, which continues south to Silver Pass. Our route passes below rocky Papoose Lake, which offers good fishing for brook trout, as does Warrior Lake, a short distance over the granite to the east. At the outlet stream of Papoose Lake our route branches north, away from the Goodale Pass Trail, and descends over a dusty traverse to the good, grassy-pocketed campsites at the southwest end of Lake of the Lone Indian (10,200′). Fishing is good for brook and rainbow (8–14″).

4th Hiking Day: Follow the 5th hiking day, Trip 93, 5.2 miles.

5th Hiking Day: Follow the 2nd hiking day, Trip 88, and the 1st hiking day, Trip 87, 8.4 miles.

98   Mammoth Lakes to Lake Edison

Distance   35.9 miles
Type   Shuttle trip; part cross-country
Best season   Late
Topo maps   Mt. Morrison, Mt. Abbot, Kaiser Peak
Grade (hiking days/recommended layover days)
   Leisurely 8/2
   Moderate 5/2
   Strenuous 4/2
Trailhead   40, 41

HIGHLIGHTS This is a trip for *experienced backpackers only.*
Employing a short but strenuous cross-country route over the Silver Divide, this unusual and remote trip should appeal to fisherman, hiker and naturalist—or any combination thereof. Travelers looking for a trip of lonely alpine grandeur will find it in the Silver Divide country.

DESCRIPTION (Leisurely trip)

1st and 2nd Hiking Days: Follow Trip 97 to **Cascade Valley/Fish Creek ford**, 11.5 miles.

3rd Hiking Day (**Cascade Valley/Fish Creek ford** to **Tully Hole**, 2.8 miles): From the Fish Creek ford the trail ascends the sometimes-rocky valley floor on the south side of Fish Creek. This section offers splendid access to nice deep holes and gurgling riffles, but as the canyon narrows, the trail becomes steeper and the creek becomes faster, small waterfalls alternating with noisy cascades. Looking up at the sheer canyon walls, the hiker cannot help but be impressed with the glacial forces that polished their granite faces. Just below the junction with the John Muir Trail, the trail fords the outlet stream from Helen Lake. Here our route turns left (north) onto the John Muir Trail and crosses to the north side of plunging Fish Creek via a steel bridge. The trail then climbs steeply by switchbacks, offering fine views back to the falls above the bridge. The climb is short, and the trail levels out somewhat as it rejoins Fish Creek. The reunion with the creek is startling, for its waters are now almost placid as they flow through deep green holes. The earlier roar and thunder of the falls are but an echo, and beside the now-mellow Fish Creek the trail ascends to the lovely, open meadows of Tully Hole (9500'). Fish Creek is a pleasant, meandering background to the good campsites at the northwest edge of the meadow. Here the angler should break out his rod for the good-to-excellent fishing for brook, rainbow, and some golden (to 12").

4th Hiking Day: Reverse the steps of the 3rd hiking day, Trip 93, 2.5 miles.

5th and 6th Hiking Days: Follow the steps of the 3rd and 4th hiking days, Trip 95, 8 miles.

7th and 8th Hiking Days: Follow the steps of the 3rd and 4th hiking days, Trip 94, 11.1 miles.

Deer Lakes

99   Mammoth Lakes to Deer Lakes

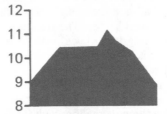

Distance   13 miles
Type   Shuttle trip; part cross-country
Best season   Mid
Topo maps   **Devils Postpile**, Mt. Morrison
Grade (hiking days/recommended layover days)
  Leisurely ---
  Moderate 2/0
  Strenuous Day
Trailhead   39, 40

HIGHLIGHTS This fine weekend trip crosses both stark alpine
                and dense forest terrains. The lightly traveled
route to Deer Lakes follows the Mammoth Crest, with expansive views to either side, to these lakes of exceptional beauty.

DESCRIPTION (Moderate trip)

1st Hiking Day (**Lake George** to **Deer Lakes**, 7 miles):
The trail leaves the Lake George parking lot (9008') at its north
end. Climbing above the resort cabins there, it switchbacks
fairly steeply up through tall mountain hemlocks and lodgepole pines. Recent trail improvements afford additional views
down to Lake George and eastward to Gold Mountain. At a
signed junction with the trail to Crystal Lake, your route continues toward Mammoth Crest. A long switchback leg ends at a
view of Horseshoe Lake almost directly below, and each
succeeding north switchback turn offers more open views.
From being granite, the rock underfoot abruptly changes to volcanic red cinders; stunted whitebark pines record the prevailing
wind direction.

Just past the John Muir Wilderness boundary (signed, but
mislocated) the trail descends briefly, and you pass an unsigned
trail to the right. Continuing leftward (south), you dip through

the remnant of a crater, pass another unsigned trail to the right, and reach the crest. From this point, you can see the Ritter Range to the west, and to the southwest, the Middle Fork San Joaquin River canyon, converging with Fish Creek's canyon. Your route continues south, and the crest broadens into a moonscape of red and white pumice, dotted with rounded clumps of wind-pruned whitebarks. By making brief excursions eastward, you'll get spectacular views of Crystal Crag, Crystal Lake, and the Owens Valley.

The often sandy trail climbs moderately, then steeply, just west of the crestline, with expanding views into Crater Meadow. The trail briefly touches the crest on an eastward-facing knife edge, normally the brink of a permanent snowfield. The terrain here is misleading: Deer Lakes are not in the bowl to the right. The crest curves eastward (left) and so does the trail, and then it descends fairly steeply into Deer Lakes basin. The trail terminates near the middle (northernmost) Deer Lake (10,700'). Choose one of the numerous excellent campsites near this lake or along the stream connecting it with the lowest Deer Lake. Wood is very scarce around here.

2nd Hiking Day (**Deer Lakes** to **Coldwater Campground**, 6 miles): The terrain is gentle and rocky, and several indistinct trails head toward the pass that overlooks Duck Lake, directly east of the highest (easternmost) Deer Lake. One trail of use leaves from the east end of the middle Deer Lake. Another, often-indistinct trail, your route, leaves just east of the outlet of the same lake. Take it, and if you lose it, continue in a straight line toward the very obvious low point just east of the highest Deer Lake. When you reach the edge of the talus, walk along its base, almost reaching a small tarn not shown on the topo map. From this point an obvious steep trail snakes 200 feet up on firm footing to a lovely, wide meadow. The trail crosses this meadow eastward past a lone, very large boulder in a low saddle. Ignore the ducks and the use trail that lead upward to the left (north) face from this boulder, and continue directly ahead toward Duck Lake. Soon the trail descends among whitebark pines. It is occasionally hard to see. If you lose the trail, head straight downhill (avoid contouring left-ward) and you will soon intersect the well-maintained Duck Lake Trail. Turn left (north) onto the trail, which leads levelly to Duck Pass, 350 yards ahead. The remainder of your route, all downhill, retraces the first part of the 1st hiking day, Trip 98.

Mammoth Lakes to Iva Bell Hot Springs

00

Distance	28 miles
Type	Shuttle trip
Best season	Mid or late
Topo maps	**Devil's Postpile**, Mt. Morrison

Grade (hiking days/recommended layover days)
>   *Leisurely* ---
>   *Moderate* 3/1
>   *Strenuous* 2/0

Trailhead   40, 38

HIGHLIGHTS This trip offers beautiful views along much of the route, good trails, and idyllic cold-water pools. But the high point is one of the handful of wilderness hot springs in the entire High Sierra.

DESCRIPTION (Moderate trip)

1st Hiking Day (**Coldwater Campground** to **Fish Creek**, 11 miles): Follow the 1st and part of the 2nd hiking day, Trip 97, to the signed trail junction in Cascade Valley. Your route turns west (right), and in ¼ mile you pass a signed trail to Minnow Creek. Then you descend on a dusty path through beautiful mixed forest, repeatedly approaching and veering away from Fish Creek, which cascades in smooth sheets over molded boulders into glorious pools. Choose one of the many idyllic campsites between here and Second Crossing. Wood is plentiful.

2nd Hiking Day (**Fish Creek** to **Fox Meadow**, 9 miles): The trail crosses Fish Creek at Second Crossing (very difficult in early season), then continues down-canyon. Polished granite walls rise steeply on both sides, and giant Jeffreys and cedars spring from the rock. Turning north, the route steeply ascends the south wall, then breaks out onto a granite saddle with vistas up Cascade Valley. To the south rise the slopes of Sharktooth Ridge, and directly below you can see the intense green foliage marking the outflow of the hot springs. The trail drops steeply through dry manzanita, then levels out abruptly in dense, wet forest, with a ground cover of ferns and wildflowers. Shortly, just beyond a stream crossing, your route meets the Fish Valley Trail (signed). Campsites here are fair.

Immediately before you cross this stream, an unsigned trail leads uphill (east) about ⅓ mile to Iva Bell Hot Springs. Each streamlet you pass on the way is increasingly warmer. The trail ends in a meadow, at the northwest end of which a hot spring flows directly out of a granite outcrop into a small pool, offering luxury bathing at 100°, with improbable views. A second pool is located a little higher in the meadow. Heavy camping and constant stock use are rapidly destroying this meadow, so we recommend that if you spend the night around here, you camp below it.

Return to the main trail, cross the stream and, at the signed junction, take the right fork to Fish Valley. The level trail follows the stream through large Jeffrey pines and firs to Fox Meadow. Many laterals lead to excellent camping here.

3rd Hiking Day (**Fox Meadow** to **Reds Meadow**, 8 miles): The outdated topo map shows Island Crossing east of Fox Meadows. Instead, just west of Fox Meadow at a signed junction, turn north (right) over a sturdy bridge at Island Crossing. Get water here: contrary to the topo, the trail does not touch water for some time. Now the trail switchbacks steeply up the hot, dusty, exposed south slope of Fish Creek canyon. There are expanding views up and down Fish Creek, and eventually into Middle Fork San Joaquin. Then the route levels off through a mixed forest, now including oak, alternating with open meadows. After a welcome pause at Cold Creek, you break out onto exposed ledges of continuously sloping granite. This dramatic section of trail alone is worth the trip. The extensive views include Crater Creek falls. Excellent camping sites are located near the Crater Creek crossing and beyond along the creek. The trail follows Crater Creek, mostly in forest, then ascends on dusty footing through tall trees, passing several sheer granite walls and waterfalls. Forest and water combine to host numerous wildlife: noisy Steller jays and busy chickadees record your progress, and you are likely to see several kinds of small ground animals. The last section of this dusty trail ascends under tall trees to join the heavily traveled route to Reds Meadow just east of beautiful Rainbow Falls. Rainbow Falls in only ¼ mile from this junction and well worth a detour before you trudge north to the resort and the nearby hot spring.

Soaking in Iva Bell Hot Springs

293

Recommended Reading

Bateman, Paul C. and Clyde Wahrhaftig. "Geology of the Sierra Nevada," in *California Division of Mines and Geology, Bulletin 190,* 1966, pp. 107–72.

Brewer, William H. *Up and Down California.* Berkeley: University of California Press, 1966.

Browning, Peter. *Place Names of the Sierra Nevada.* Berkeley: Wilderness Press, 1991.

Bunnelle, Hasse. *Food for Knapsackers.* San Francisco: Sierra Club, 1971.

Farquhar, Francis. *History of the Sierra Nevada.* Berkeley: University of California Press, 1965.

Darvill, Fred. *Mountaineering Medicine.* Berkeley: Wilderness Press, 1989.

Hill, Mary. *Geology of the Sierra Nevada.* Berkeley: University of California Press, 1975.

Ingles, Lloyd G. *Mammals of the Pacific States.* Stanford, CA: Stanford University Press, 1965.

King, Clarence. *Mountaineering in the Sierra Nevada.* New York: Penguin, 1989.

Latimer, Carole. *Wilderness Cuisine.* Berkeley: Wilderness Press, 1991.

Matthess, Francois. *The Incomparable Valley.* Berkeley: University of California Press, 1964.

Muir, John. *My First Summer in the Sierra.* Boston: Houghton Mifflin, 1979.

———. (ed. Fred Gunsky). *South of Yosemite.* Berkeley: Wilderness Press, 1987.

Niehaus, Theodore. *Sierra Wildflowers.* Berkeley: University of California Press, 1974.

Peters, Ed (ed.). *Mountaineering: The Freedom of the Hills.* Seattle: The Mountaineers, 1982.

Peterson, Victor P. and Victor P. Peterson, Jr. *Native Trees of the Sierra Nevada.* Berkeley: University of California Press, 1975.

Peterson, Roger Tory. *A Field Guide to Western Birds.* Boston: Houghton Mifflin, 1990.

Roper, Steve. *Climber's Guide to the High Sierra*. San Francisco: Sierra Club, 1976.

_____ . *Sierra High Route*. San Francisco: Sierra Club, 1982.

Russell, Carl P. *100 Years in Yosemite*. Yosemite: Yosemite Association, 1968.

Schaffer, Jeffrey P. *Yosemite National Park*. Berkeley: Wilderness Press, 1983.

_____ . *Carson-Iceberg Wilderness*. Berkeley: Wilderness Press, 1987.

Schifrin, Ben. *Emigrant Wilderness*. Berkeley: Wilderness Press, 1990.

Storer, Tracy I. and Robert L. Usinger. *Sierra Nevada Natural History*. Berkeley: University of California Press, 1964.

Watts, Tom. *Pacific Coast Tree Finder*. Berkeley: Nature Study Guild, 1973.

Weeden, Norman. *A Sierra Nevada Flora*. Berkeley: Wilderness Press, 1986.

Whitney, Stephen. *A Sierra Club Naturalist's Guide to the Sierra Nevada*. San Francisco: Sierra Club, 1979.

Winnett, Thomas. *The Tahoe-Yosemite Trail*. Berkeley: Wilderness Press, 1987.

Trip Cross-Reference Table

Trip No.	No. Hiking Days	Season			Pace			Trip Type			
		Early	Mid	Late	Leisurely	Moderate	Strenuous	Round	Shuttle	Loop	Semiloop
1	2		x		x			x			
2	4		x		x			x			
3	6		x		x			x			
4	2		x		x			x			
5	4		x			x		x			
6	5		x			x			x		
7	2		x		x			x			
8	2		x		x				x		
9	3		x		x				x		
10	2		x			x					x
11	2		x	x		x			x		
12	3		x				x		x		
13	4		x			x					x
14	2		x	x	x						x
15	4		x			x			x		
16	6		x	x		x			x		
17	2	x	x		x			x			
18	4		x	x	x			x			
19	4		x	x	x			x			
20	5		x	x	x						x
21	7		x	x	x					x	
22	7		x	x	x				x		
23	2		x	x	x			x			
24	4		x	x	x			x			
25	4		x	x	x			x			
26	5		x	x	x				x		
27	5		x	x	x				x		
28	7		x	x	x				x		
29	2		x	x	x			x			
30	3		x	x	x			x			
31	4		x	x		x					x
32	5		x	x		x					x

Trip No.	No. Hiking Days	Season			Pace			Trip Type			
		Early	Mid	Late	Leisurely	Moderate	Strenuous	Round	Shuttle	Loop	Semiloop
33	5	x	x			x			x		
34	2		x	x		x		x			
35	2	x	x	x		x		x			
36	4		x	x		x		x			
37	3		x	x		x			x		
38	3		x	x		x					x
39	6		x	x		x			x		
40	6		x	x		x		x			
41	8		x	x	x						x
42	2	x	x	x	x			x			
43	4		x	x		x			x		
44	2		x	x	x				x		
45	2	x			x			x			
46	4	x			x			x			
47	3		x	x	x			x			
48	3		x	x		x			x		
49	5		x	x		x			x		
50	2		x	x		x					x
51	2		x	x	x			x			
52	2		x	x	x			x			
53	2		x	x	x			x			
54	4		x	x	x			x			
55	5		x	x		x			x		
56	4		x	x	x				x		
57	4		x	x	x				x		
58	2		x	x	x				x		
59	2		x	x		x		x			
60	2	x	x	x	x			x			
61	2		x	x	x			x			
62	4		x	x		x					x
63	6		x	x		x					x
64	7		x	x		x					x
65	4		x	x		x			x		
66	4	x			x			x			

Trip No.	No. Hiking Days	Season			Pace			Trip Type			
		Early	Mid	Late	Leisurely	Moderate	Strenuous	Round	Shuttle	Loop	Semiloop
67	4	x	x		x			x			
68	4	x	x			x			x		
69	5	x	x		x				x		
70	5	x	x		x						x
71	4	x			x			x			
72	10		x	x		x				x	
73	7		x	x	x				x		
74	3	x				x				x	
75	2		x	x	x			x			
76	3		x	x	x					x	
77	3		x	x	x					x	
78	3		x	x	x					x	
79	2		x	x	x			x			
80	3		x	x		x			x		
81	2		x	x		x			x		
82	2		x			x		x			
83	3		x	x		x			x		
84	4		x	x	x				x		
85	3		x	x	x						x
86	5		x	x	x				x		
87	2		x		x			x			
88	4		x	x	x			x			
89	2		x	x	x			x			
90	2		x	x	x			x			
91	2		x	x	x			x			
92	2		x	x	x			x			
93	7		x	x	x				x		
94	4			x	x				x		
95	6			x	x				x		
96	2			x		x		x			
97	5			x		x			x		
98	8			x	x				x		
99	2		x			x			x		
100	3		x	x		x			x		

Index

Agnew Lake 228, 230
Agnew Meadows 22, 203, 204, 231,
    233, 234, 235, 236, 237, 238, 240,
    241, 244
Alger Creek 227
Allen's Ranch 32
Alpine, Lake 19, 72, 76
altitude sickness 8
Ansel Adams Wilderness 16, 170,
    171, 226, 242, 251, 254, 258
Arri mutillak 67
Arndt Lake 135, 136, 140
Arrowhead Lake 281
Asa Lake 56, 68, 70, 72

Babcock Lake 181, 198, 199
Badger Lakes 238
Banana Lake 96, 100, 102
Barney Lake 125, 281, 282
Basque shepherds 67
Bear Lake 97
Bear River 33
Bear Valley 44
Bear Valley Lake 136, 137
bears 10
beavers 125
Beehive 90, 91
Bell Creek 97
Benson Lake 140, 141, 142
Benson Pass 143
Benwood Meadow 42, 43
Bernice Lake 195
Black Rock Lake 33
Blackbird Lake 84, 86
Blue Lake 154
Bobs Lake 284
Bond Pass 88, 89
Bonnie Lake 114
Boothe Lake 181, 199
Box Lake 265
Breeze Lake 250, 252
Brewer, William H. 111
Bridalveil Creek 21, 123, 208, 211,
    214, 216, 252
Brown Bear Pass 81
Bryan Meadow 42
Buck Camp 253

Buck Lakes 85, 86, 103, 104, 105
Buck Meadow Creek 85, 103
Buckeye Campground 20
Buckeye Creek 119, 120, 121, 122,
    131, 132
Buckeye Creek, North Fork 120
Buckeye Forks 120, 131
Buckeye Hot Springs 132
Buckeye Pass 131
Buckeye Roadend 20
Buena Vista Creek 211, 212, 214
Buena Vista Lake 211, 217, 253
Bull Run Creek 74
Bull Run Lake 45, 46
Bull Run Lake Trailhead 19, 47
Burro Pass 144

Camp Lake 97
Caples Lake Resort 24
Carson Falls 58
Carson Pass 18, 24, 39, 41
Carson River 44
Carson River, East Fork 49, 50, 52,
    53, 54, 55, 57, 58, 59, 60
Carson-Iceberg Wilderness 15, 44
Cascade Creek 113, 114, 115
Cascade Lake 160
Cascade Valley 283, 284, 286, 290
Castle Lake 245
Cathedral Lake 174, 175, 178
Cecile Lake 241, 242
Chain Lakes 247, 248, 249, 252
Chain of Lakes 111
Cherry Creek 104
Cherry Creek, East Fork 86, 104
Cherry Creek, North Fork 84, 85, 87
Cherry Creek, West Fork 96, 98,
    101, 105
Chewing Gum Lake 94, 97
Chickenfoot Lake 265
Chief Lake 273
Chilnualna Creek 209, 216
Chilnualna Lakes 216, 217
Chiquito Creek 247, 249, 252
Chiquito Creek Trailhead 21
Chiquito Lake 247
Cinko Lake 110, 112, 113

Clark Lakes 229
Clark, Galen 1
Clouds Rest 185, 187
Cold Creek 260, 261, 262, 277
Coldwater Campground 23, 281,
    289, 290
Cole Creek Lakes 33
Conness Creek 151, 167
Conness, Mt. 167
Cooney Lake 154
Cora Lake, Middle 259
Corral Valley 65
Corral Valley Creek 67
Cow Meadow Lake 85, 86, 104
Coyote Valley 65
Crabtree Camp 19, 97, 100
Crater Creek 291
Crescent Lake 209, 252, 253
Crest Creek 228
Crown Lake 126, 127, 129, 133
Crystal Lake 288
Cutter, Dean 2

Davis Lakes 204, 229
Deer Lake 85, 97, 98, 99, 100, 102,
    103, 104, 105
Deer Lakes 282, 288. 289
Delaney Creek 151, 168, 169
Devils Postpile 22, 226, 241, 242,
    243, 244
Dingley Creek 151, 168, 169
Dixon Creek 56
Dog Lake 168, 169
Donohue Pass 204
Dorothy Lake 88, 89, 113, 114, 115,
    116
Dorothy Lake Pass 114
Duck Lake 282, 289
Duck Pass 282, 289

East Lake 146, 147, 148, 153
Ebbetts Pass 19, 44, 68, 70, 71
Echo Creek 179, 182, 189, 207
Echo Summit 15, 18, 41, 43
Echo Valley 179, 180, 207
Edison, Lake 260, 262, 271, 275,
    277, 283, 286
Ediza Lake 240, 241
Elizabeth Lake 188, 189

Emerald Lake 229, 235, 236
Emeric Lake 181, 194, 195, 196,
    202
Emigrant Lake 81, 82, 83, 84, 85,
    102, 103
Emigrant Lake, Middle 87
Emigrant Meadow 80, 104
Emigrant Meadow Lake 80, 81, 84,
    86, 87, 88, 104
Emigrant Wilderness 16, 77, 93, 95,
    97, 102, 104
Emily Lake 245

Falls Creek 88, 89, 90, 91, 113, 156
Fernandez Creek 223, 251, 255, 257
Fernandez Pass 249, 250
Fernandez Trailhead 22
Fish Camp 275, 276, 279, 280
Fish Creek 272, 273, 283, 284, 286,
    287, 290, 291
Fish Valley 291
Fish Valley, lower 64, 66, 68
Fish Valley, upper 65, 66
Fletcher Creek 181, 193, 194, 199
Florence Creek 194, 195, 197
Foerster Creek 201
Foerster Lake 201
Four Lakes 40
Fourth Recess Lake 276
Fox Meadow 290
Fremont Lake 106, 108, 110
Frog Lakes 154

Gallison Lake 195
Gardner Meadow, lower 69, 72
Gardner Meadow, upper 72
Garnet Lake 229, 233, 234, 235
Gem Lake 228, 264, 265
Gem Lakes (Emigrant Wilderness)
    98, 101
George, Lake 22, 288
Gianelli Cabin 93, 95, 100, 102, 104
giardia 8
Gibbs Canyon 171
Gibbs Lake 170, 171
Gibbs Lake Trailhead 21
Gilman Lake 146, 147, 148, 149
Givens Creek 253
Glacier Point 21, 211, 212, 213,

218, 220, 224
Gladys Lake 245
Glen Aulin 150, 151, 162, 163, 167, 168
Glen Aulin Trailhead 21
Golden Creek 276
Golden Lake 270
Goodale Pass 274
Grace Meadow 88, 89, 90
Grand Canyon of the Tuolumne 155
Granite Creek 224, 254, 257
Granite Creek Campground 22
Granite Creek, East Fork 259
Granite Creek, West Fork 223, 259
Graveyard Lakes 262, 263, 274
Graveyard Meadows 260, 261, 262, 263
Green Creek 146, 148, 153
Green Creek Roadend 20
Green Creek, West Fork 147
Green Lake 147
Greenstone Lake 160
Grinnell Lake 278, 279
Grouse Creek 79
Grouse Lake 209

Half Dome 185
Happy Isles 21
Harriet, Lake 114
Heart Lake 265
Heiser Lake 45, 46
Heiser Lake Trailhead 19
Helen, Lake 114, 284
Hetch Hetchy 155, 157
Hetch Hetchy Reservoir 20, 88, 91, 135
Highland Creek 73, 74, 75, 76
Highland Lake, lower 73
Highland Lake, upper 73
Hiram Meadow 72, 74
Hoover Lake 146, 147, 149
Hoover Wilderness 77, 121, 125
Horse Canyon 27, 28, 29
Horse Canyon Trailhead 18
Horse Meadow 170
Huckleberry Lake 86
hypothermia 8

Icerberg Lake 241

Illilouette Creek 212, 214, 215, 219
Illilouette Fall 219
Ireland Creek 191
Irene, Camp 35, 36, 37, 38
Isberg Lakes 225, 257, 258, 259
Isberg Pass 201, 202, 224, 225
Island Pass 204, 229
Iva Bell Hot Springs 290, 291

Jack Main Canyon 88, 89, 91
Jewelry Lake 98, 100, 101
John Muir Trail 183, 184, 185, 190, 191, 203, 205, 206, 214, 215, 219, 227, 229, 233, 234, 235, 236, 237, 240, 242, 245, 273, 277, 282, 283, 284, 285, 287
John Muir Wilderness 16, 246, 260, 261, 262, 264, 268, 281, 288
Johnson Lake 209, 252, 253

Kay's Silver Lake Resort 24
Kennedy Lake 79
Kennedy Meadow 19, 78, 80, 82, 84, 85, 88, 102, 104
Kerrick Canyon 137
Kerrick Meadow 131, 133, 134, 135
Kidney Lake 171
Kirkwood Creek 118, 120
Kit Carson Lodge 24

Lady Lake 255
Lake Alpine Lodge 44
Lake of the Lone Indian 273, 274, 284, 285
Lane Lake 107
Laurel Creek 280
Laurel Lake 91, 279
Leavitt Meadow 20, 106, 107, 110, 113, 116, 119
Lembert Dome 169
Lembert, John 167
Lertora Lake 86
Lewis Creek 180, 194, 195, 196, 198, 202, 220
lightning 9
Lillian Lake 251, 254, 255
Little Antelope Pack Station 64
Little Lakes Valley 264, 265, 266
Little Yosemite Valley 186, 205,

206, 207, 218, 219, 220, 224
Llewellyn Falls 65
Long Canyon Creek 115
Long Lake 265
Long Lake (Carson Pass area) 32,
    34, 35, 37
Long Lake, lower 111
Long Lake, upper 111
Lost Valley 207
Lyell Canyon 189, 191, 203

Maclure Creek 203
Madera Creek 251
Mammoth Lakes 226, 281, 283,
    286, 288, 290
Marie Lakes 204
Markleeville 44
marmots 10
Marsh Lake 264, 265
Matterhorn Canyon 143, 144, 164,
    166
Matthes, Francois 185, 189
Maxwell Lake 86
McCabe Creek 150, 163, 165
McCabe Lake 150, 159
McCabe Lake, lower 161, 162, 163,
    164
McCabe Lake, upper 161, 162
McClure, Lt. N.F. 114, 144
McGee Creek 268, 269, 270, 271,
    278
McGee Creek Roadend 23
McGee Lake, Big 270
McGee Lake, Little 271
McGee Pass 272
Meiss Lake 40
Merced Lake 178, 179, 180, 205,
    206, 207, 218, 219, 220, 224
Merced Lake Camp 180, 207
Merced River 179, 180, 205, 221,
    250
Merced River, Lyell Fork 197, 198,
    200, 220, 221
Merced River, Merced Peak Fork
    221
Merced River, Triple Peak Fork
    200, 221, 222, 224, 225
Mill Creek 160
Miller Lake 165

Minaret Creek 242
Minaret Lake 241, 242
Minaret Summit 226
Minarets Wilderness 226
Mist Trail 206, 219
Moat Lake 154
Mokelumne River 29, 30, 31, 36, 37
Mokelumne Wilderness 15, 24, 32,
    33
Mono Creek 275, 276, 277, 280
Mono Creek, North Fork 277
Mono Pass 275
Mono Village 124
Mosquito Flat 23, 264, 266
Mosquito Lake 45
mosquitoes 11
Munson Meadow 35, 36, 38
Murray Canyon 55, 57, 68

Nelson Lake 188, 189
Nevada Fall 206, 219
Nobel Canyon 71
Nobel Creek 70
Nobel Lake 70
Nutter Lake 146, 147, 148

O'Shaughnessy Dam 20, 91, 155
Olaine Lake 231

Pacific Crest Trail 39, 59, 60, 61,
    69, 70, 71, 90, 113, 137, 140, 144,
    149, 229, 231, 235, 238, 243, 245
Panorama Cliff 219
Papoose Lake 273, 285
Paradise Valley 90
Pardoe Lake 33
Peeler Lake 124, 126, 131, 133,
    134, 135
Pika Lake 282
Pioneer Basin 276
Piute Creek (Emigrant Wilderness)
    97, 98
Piute Creek (Yosemite) 129, 130,
    138, 140, 142, 144
Piute Lake 98, 100, 101
Piute Meadow (Emigrant Wilder-
    ness) 98
Piute Meadows, upper 119
piute trout 66

Plasse's Resort 18, 32
Plasse's Trading Post 33
Pleasant Valley 137, 138
Poison Creek 50, 52
Poison Lake 62, 63
Poore Lake 107
Porphyry Lake 222, 258
Post Corral Canyon 96
Post Creek 223, 258
Post Peak Pass 202, 258
Powell Lake 93
Purple Creek 283
Purple Lake 281, 282, 283

Quail Meadows 276, 277

Rafferty Creek 191, 192
Railroad Canyon 53
Rainbow Falls 292
Rainbow Lake 251, 255
Rancheria Creek 123, 126, 134, 135,
    136, 137, 138, 139, 155, 156, 157
Rancheria Falls 139, 156
rattlesnakes 10
Red and White Lake 272, 278
Reds Meadow 22, 291, 292
Reds Meadow Resort 226
Relief Reservoir 79
Relief Valley, lower 79
Return Creek 149, 150, 165
Robinson Creek 124, 125, 126, 127,
    128, 129
Robinson Lakes 127, 128
Rock Creek 264, 266, 275, 278
Rock Island Pass 134
Rock Lake 74, 76
Rodriguez Flat 19, 64, 66, 68, 72
Roosevelt Lake 107
Rosalie Lake 244, 245
Round Lake 40
Royal Arch Lake 208, 209, 210,
    211, 214, 216, 217, 252, 253
Ruby Lake 229, 235, 236, 266, 267,
    275
Rush Creek 22, 203, 227, 229
Ruth, Lake 114, 116
Rutherford Lake 220, 223, 249, 250,
    254, 255, 256

Saddlebag Lake 21, 159, 160, 162,
    164
Saddlebag Lake Resort 159
Sadler Lake 259
Salt Lick Meadow 96, 105
San Joaquin River 234, 235
San Joaquin River, Middle Fork
    232, 243, 291
Schneider Camp 40, 42
Scout Carson Lake 24, 25, 26, 27
Seavey Pass 140
Shadow Creek 204, 231, 232, 233,
    236, 240, 244
Shadow Lake 231, 232, 235, 244
Shirley Creek 255
Showers Lake 24, 39, 40, 41
Sierra Club 167, 168
Silver King Creek 63, 66, 67
Silver Lake (Carson Pass area) 25,
    27, 29, 32, 35, 37
Silver Lake (on June Lake loop)
    227, 229
Skelton Lake 281
Smedberg Lake 142, 143
Snodgrass Canyon 64
snow bridges 11
snow cornices 11
Snow Lake 129, 134
Snowslide Canyon 49
Soda Springs (Carson River area)
    48, 50, 51, 52, 54, 62, 63, 68
Soda Springs (Yosemite area) 151,
    167, 168
Sonora Pass 20, 60, 61, 77
Sorensen's 24
Spiller Creek 165
Spotted Lakes 248, 252
Spring Meadow 96, 105
Squaw Lake 273
Staniford Lakes 255
Stanislaus Meadow 46, 47
Stanislaus River, Middle Fork 78
Stanislaus River, North Fork 47, 76
Steelhead Lake 268, 269
Stella Lake 114
Stockton Municipal Camp 32
stream crossings 11
Stubblefield Canyon 123
Summit City Canyon 27, 28, 29

Summit City Creek 28, 29, 30, 31
Summit Creek 78, 79, 80, 82
Summit Lake 149
Sunrise Camp 172, 173, 176, 177, 184
Sunrise Creek 182, 183, 184, 185, 187
Sunrise Lakes 173

Tahoe-Yosemite Trail 28, 29, 36, 38, 74
Tamarack Creek 66
Tenaya Lake 21, 172, 182, 186
Third Recess Lake 276
Thompson Canyon 123
Thousand Island Lake 204, 227, 229, 235, 236, 237, 238
Tilden Lake 90
Tiltill Creek 156, 157, 158
Tiltill Valley 157
Tioga Road Trailhead 21
Toejam Lake 105
Tower Lake 116, 117, 118
Tragedy Springs 32
Trinity Lakes 245
Truckee River 40
Tully Hole 272, 273, 287
Tully Lake 271, 272, 278
Tuolumne Falls 151
Tuolumne Lodge 21, 190, 199, 202
Tuolumne Meadows 123, 148, 151, 152, 162, 167, 168, 169, 181, 188, 189, 192, 194, 197, 200, 203
Tuolumne Meadows Campground 21
Tuolumne Pass 181, 193, 194, 199
Tuolumne River 151, 162, 167
Turner Meadows 208, 209, 216
Turner, Bill 209
Twin Lakes 20, 124, 127, 129, 131, 133, 135, 140, 142, 164

U.S. Cavalry 136, 165, 209
U.S. Marines 61
Unicorn Creek 188

Vandeburg Lake 254, 255, 257
Vermilion Campground 23, 277
Vermilion Valley Resort 246, 277

Vernal Fall 206
Vernon, Lake 91
Virginia Canyon 148, 150, 163, 165
Virginia Lakes 153, 154
Virginia Lakes Trailhead 20
Vogelsang Camp 181, 192, 193, 194
Vogelsang Lake 195

Walker Meadows 111
Wapama Falls 156
Warrior Lake 273, 285
Washburn Lake 202, 221
Waugh Lake 227, 228
Weber Lakes 228
Weiser Creek 74
West Lake 147
West Walker River 77, 106, 107, 115, 118
West Walker River, West Fork 110, 111, 112, 113
White Cascade 151
whitefish 50
Whitesides Meadow 95, 105
Wilderness Creek 76
wilderness permits 15, 16, 17
Wilmer Lake 90
Wilson Canyon 143
Wilson Creek 143
Wire Lakes 95, 96, 100, 102
Wolf Creek 54, 56, 57, 69
Wolf Creek Lake 57, 60
Wolf Creek Meadows 18, 48, 52, 54, 57, 62
Wolf Creek Meadows, upper 18, 55
Wood, Abram Epperson 165

Y Meadow Lake 93, 94, 95, 105
Yosemite Valley 184, 185, 205, 214
Young Lakes 167, 168, 169